2/01

D1062185

WITHDRAWN

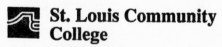

St. Louis Community College

Forest Park
Florissant Valley
Meramec

Instructional Resources
St. Louis, Missouri

CHILDHOOD ABUSED

To My Husband James Michael

Programme on International Rights of the Child
Series Editor: Geraldine Van Bueren

Titles in the Series:

Children's Rights and Traditional Values
Edited by Gillian Douglas and Leslie Sebba

Cultural Pluralism and the Rights of the Child
Michael Freeman

Of Innocence and Autonomy
Children, Sex and Human Rights
Eric Heinze

The Human Right to Education
Douglas Hodgson

The Child and the European Convention on Human Rights
Ursula Kilkelly

Legal Secrets, Cultural and Scientific Truths
Katherine O'Donovan

Childhood Abused
Protecting Children against Torture, Cruel, Inhuman and
Degrading Treatment and Punishment
Edited by Geraldine Van Bueren

Childhood Abused

Protecting Children against Torture, Cruel, Inhuman and
Degrading Treatment and Punishment

Edited by
Geraldine Van Bueren

St. Louis Community College
at Meramec
Library

DARTMOUTH

Aldershot • Brookfield USA • Singapore • Sydney

© Geraldine Van Bueren 1998

All rights reserved. No part of this publication may be reproduced, stored in a retrieval system, or transmitted in any form or by any means electronic, mechanical, photocopying, recording or otherwise without the prior permission of the publisher.

Published by
Dartmouth Publishing Company Limited
Ashgate Publishing Limited
Gower House
Croft Road
Aldershot
Hants GU11 3HR
England

Ashgate Publishing Company
Old Post Road
Brookfield
Vermont 05036
USA

British Library Cataloguing in Publication Data
Childhood abused : protecting children against torture,
    cruel, inhuman and degrading treatment and punishment. –
    (Programme on international rights of the child)
    1. Children (International law)   2. Children's rights   3. Child
    welfare – International cooperation   4. Children – Legal
    status, laws, etc.
    I. Van Bueren, Geraldine
    341.4'81'083

Library of Congress Cataloging-in-Publication Data
Childhood abused : protecting children against torture, cruel,
    inhuman, and degrading treatment and punishment / edited by
    Geraldine Van Bueren.
        p.   cm.
    ISBN 1-85521-918-2 (hb)
    1. Child abuse.   2. Children and violence.   3. Children's rights.
    I. Van Bueren, Geraldine.
    HV6626.5.C55   1998
    362.76'72–DC21   97-50013
                                                                              CIP

ISBN 1 85521 918 2

Typeset by Manton Typesetters, 5–7 Eastfield Road, Louth, Lincolnshire, LN11 7AJ, UK.

Printed and bound in Great Britain by MPG Books Ltd, Bodmin, Cornwall

Contents

List of Contributors

Dr Dora Black is now honorary consultant child and adolescent psychiatrist and honorary senior lecturer at the Traumatic Stress Clinic, London, as well as holding honorary consultant posts at Great Ormond Street Hospital, Tavistock Clinic and Royal Free Hospital. She founded the Children's Psychological Trauma Clinic first at the Royal Free Hospital and then at the Traumatic Stress Clinic. She is a Fellow of both the Royal College of Psychiatrists and the Royal College of Paediatrics and Child Health. She has been advisor to UNICEF in former Yugoslavia. She has made a special research and clinical study of bereavement in children and of the effects of trauma and is author of over 70 papers and four books, including *When Father Kills Mother: Guiding Children through Trauma and Grief* (with J. Harris-Nedriks and T. Kaplan, Routledge, London, 1993); *Psychological Trauma: A Developmental Approach* (with M. Newman, J. Harris-Hendriks and G. Mezey, Gaskell, London, 1997).

Christine Chinkin is Professor of International Law at the London School of Economics, University London. Her main teaching and research interests are in international law with a particular emphasis on the international guarantee of women's rights. She has published widely in this area, including *Violence Against Women: A Global Issue*, in J. Stubbs (ed), *Women, Male Violence and the Law* (Sydney, 1994) (with H. Charlesworth); *Women's Rights as Human Rights under International Law* in C. Gearty and A. Tomkins, *Understanding Human Rights* (1996); *Feminist Approaches to International Law, 85 American Journal of International Law* (1991) (with H. Charlesworth and S. Wright); *The Hunger Trap: Women, Food and Self-Determination, 14 Michigan Journal of International Law*.

Len Doyal has taught the philosophy of science and moral and political philosophy at Middlesex University for over 20 years. For the past six years he has worked at St Bartholomew's and the Royal London Hospital School of Medicine and Dentistry and is now Professor of Medical Ethics within the new clinical faculty of Queen Mary and Westfield College, University of

London. He provides advice on ethico-legal matters to the Royal London Hospitals Trust where he is an honorary consultant.

Judith Ennew is a Senior Research Associate in the Centre for Family Research at the University of Cambridge, where she is International Coordinator of the Childwatch International Monitoring Children's Rights Project. A social anthropologist by training she has been working since 1979 as a researcher in children's issues, particularly street and working children, in many different countries. She is also an activist for children's rights. Child-related publications include *The Sexual Exploitation of Children* (Polity, 1986), *The Next Generation: Lives of Third World Children* (with Brian Milne; Zed, 1989), *Street and Working Children: a Guide to Planning* (SCF UK, 1994) and *Children in Focus: a Manual for Participatory Research with Children* (with Jo Boyden, 1997).

Gisela Perren-Klingler has since 1978 been in private practice as a child psychiatrist. Since 1980 she has been a medical delegate of the International Committee of the Red Cross, Geneva and in this capacity has inspected prisons in Latin America, the Middle East and Africa. She is the co-author of the Guidelines for Traumatized Populations for the United Nations High Commissioner for Refugees. She is also a Member of the Commission for the Prevention of Torture and Inhuman Treatment in European Prisons, Strasbourg.

Jeremy McBride is a Senior Lecturer in Law at the University of Birmingham where he directs a Human Rights Law and Practice Programme for judges and lawyers from Central and Eastern Europe. He is a co-founder and currently treasurer of INTERIGHTS and acts as a consultant on human rights to governments, NGO'S and individuals.

Edith Montgomery is Chief Psychologist at the Rehabilitation and Research Centre for Torture Victims in Copenhagen, Denmark. She trained as a psychologist and is head of the 'family' team of the Rehabilitation and Research Centre for Torture Victims, a multidisciplinary treatment team for torture survivors with children and for children who have themselves been exposed to torture. Edith Montgomery has carried out research into the psychological effects of war and other organized violence for children and has published widely on this issue.

Martin Newman is a consultant child and adolescent psychiatrist to Pathfinder Mental Health Services NHS Trust and honorary senior lecturer in child and adolescent psychiatry at St. George's Hospital Medical School,

London SW17. Prior to training in psychiatry, he served for eight years in the Royal Navy and saw active service in the Falklands conflict. He has worked extensively with children who have witnessed violence, including those who have witnessed the murder of one parent by the other. He worked in Bosnia during the civil war. He has published articles on the effects of violence on children, and is second editor of *Psychological Trauma: A Developmental Approach*, published in 1997.

Pamela Reynolds, an anthropologist in Southern Africa, has worked with children in the Zambezi Valley and Mashonaland in Zimbabwe, among Xhosa children in the Crossroads squatter settlement, and among students at universities in South Africa who, as political activists, spent many years in prison. She is the author of *Childhood in Crossroads: Cognition and Society in South Africa* (David Philip, 1989); *Dance Civet Cat: Child Labor in the Zambezi Valley* (Ohio University Press, 1990) and with Lwaano Lwanyika: *The Tonga Book of the Earth* (1993). She is also author of *Traditional Healers and Childhood in Zimbabwe* (Ohio University Press, 1996) and, with Sandra Burman, editor of *Growing Up in a Divided Society: The context of Childhood in South Africa* (Northwestern University Press, 1986). She is Dean of the Department of Social Anthropology, University of Cape Town.

Martin Richards is Reader in Human Development, University of Cambridge. His publications include: *What About the Children? Some Reflections on the Divorce White Paper* (Child and Family Law) Morrow and Richards, *The Ethics of Social Research with Children: An Overview*, *Children and Society*, in press 1996, Marteau and Richards (eds), *The Troubled Helix: Social and Psychological Implications of the New Human Genetics* (Cambridge University Press, 1996), Richards, McWilliams, Batten, Cameron, and Cutler, *Foreign Nationals in United Kingdom Prisons*. In: *Family Ties and their Maintenance* in the *Howard Journal of Criminal Justice*, 34, 158–75 and 195–208, 1995.

Nigel Rodley is Professor of Law at the University of Essex and United Nations Special Rapporteur on Torture. He is the author of *The Treatment of Prisoners Under International Law*, has co-edited *International Law in the Western Hemisphere* (with C.N. Ronning; Nijhoff, 1974), co-authored *Enhancing Global Human Rights* (with J.I. Dominguez, B. Wood and R.A. Falk; McGraw Hill, 1979), edited *To Loose the Bands of Wickedness – International Intervention in Defence of Human Rights* (Brassey's, 1992) and co-edited *International Responses to Traumatic Stress* (with Y. Danieli and L. Weisaeth; Baywood/UN, 1995.)

Bent Sørensen is at the International Rehabilitation Council for Torture Victims, Copenhagen, Denmark. He holds a full professorship of surgery and was former Dean of the Medical Faculty at the University of Copenhagen. Clinically, he was Head of the Burns Unit and was President of the Medical Research Council, European Union. His activities include: Chairman of the Board of the Rehabilitation and Research Centre for Torture Victims (RCT) in Copenhagen, Denmark 1984–1990; Vice-chairman of the Board of the International Rehabilitation Council for Torture Victims (IRCT) in Copenhagen, Denmark 1988–1990; advisor on the prevention of torture for World Health Organisation since 1986; member of the United Nations Committee Against Torture (CAT) since its start in 1988; rapporteur since 1994; member of the Council of Europe Committee for the Prevention of Torture (CPT) since its start in 1989 and first Vice-president 1989–1995; and the representative of CAT and CPT at the UN World Conference on Human Rights in Vienna, 1993.

Eric Sottas is the Director of OMCT (World Organisation Against Torture), based in Geneva, the largest international coalition of non-governmental organizations against torture. He is a lawyer specializing in international and human rights law. He was awarded the French Prize for Human Rights in 1986. His publications include: *The Least Developed Countries* (UN, New York, 1984: Arabic, English, French, Spanish), *Democracy Development and Human Rights* (Manila, 1991: English, French), *Exactions et Enfants* (Geneve, 1993: French).

Geraldine Van Bueren is the Director of the Programme on International Rights of the Child, Queen Mary and Westfield College. She represented Amnesty International at the United Nations during the drafting of the Convention on the Rights of the Child and participated in the drafting of the UN Rules for the Protection of Juveniles Deprived of their Liberty. She has acted as a consultant on children's rights to Uganda and to the Commonwealth Secretariat in Dhaka. She is the author of *The International Law on the Rights of the Child* and General Editor of the *Programme on International Rights of the Child* series to be published by Dartmouth.

Lois Whitman is the Director of the Children's Rights Project of Human Rights Watch based in New York. She has also served as the Deputy Director of Helsinki Watch. She has written or co-authored reports on human rights including *Easy Prey: Child Soldiers in Liberia* (1994) and *Children in Northern Ireland: Abused by Security Forces and Paramilitaries* and presented evidence to the UN Committee on the Rights of the Child.

Louise Williamson qualified as a social worker in 1977, working in local authority social services departments from 1977–1986 in fieldwork, residential and training roles. From 1986–1990 she lived in Sweden, and worked as Deputy Manager in a children's home for unaccompanied refugee children. Returning to the United Kingdom in 1991, she began post-graduate research in Queen Mary and Westfield College, University of London into influences on policy-making for refugee children in the UK and is now writing up her PhD. From 1995–97 she worked as Director of the Children's Division of the British Refugee Council.

Acknowledgements

The chapters in this book are based upon papers presented to the International Symposium On Protecting Children Against Torture, Cruel, Inhuman And Degrading Treatment And Punishment. The symposium was multi-disciplinary and included anthropologists, doctors, international human rights lawyers, non-governmental organizations, psychiatrists, psychologists and members of the Council of Europe and United Nations Committees on Torture.

I am particularly grateful to Nigel Rodley, the United Nations Special Rapporteur on Torture, who took time from a very heavy schedule both to attend and speak and to write the foreword. I am also grateful to Piera Barzano of the United Nations Crime Prevention and Criminal Justice Division who was also able to make an oral presentation.

The aim of the symposium was to share ideas and learn from the different approaches. At the end of the symposium the records of the discussions, recorded by the rapporteurs, were made available to the contributors so that they could be incorporated in their chapters. The rapporteurs during the symposium were past and present postgraduate students in the Programme on the International Rights of the Child. The principal rapporteur was Melanie Roberts, ably assisted by Mitchell Woolf, Abbie Barber and Paul White.

This book could not have been written without the generous support and funding of Queen Mary and Westfield College. I am also grateful to my secretary Sharon Braybrook for her assistance both during the international symposium and in the preparation of this book; to all my colleagues in the Department of Law for their support; and to Mick Brennan, Christine Lennie and Jacqueline Dufaur for their help with the symposium.

Finally I wish to thank John Irwin and Ashgate for their enthusiasm and assistance.

Programme on International Rights of the Child
Faculty of Laws
Queen Mary and Westfield College
University of London.

Foreword

Nigel S. Rodley

According to Article 5 of the Universal Declaration of Human Rights, whose fiftieth anniversary the world will be commemorating next year, '[n]o one shall be subjected to torture or to cruel, inhuman or degrading treatment or punishment'. This language has been reproduced in numerous treaties and other international instruments, by one or other of which most of the world's countries are bound. One might think that it would then have been superfluous to include similar language in the 1989 United Nations' Convention on the Rights of the Child.[1] Unfortunately, persistent practices in all too many countries made it of continuing relevance. And, despite the fact that the Convention is already the most widely adhered to human rights treaty, the organizers of the conference, at which the papers in this volume were presented, and which I was grateful to have been able to attend, correctly identified the need for attention to the problem of children being tortured.

If one feels anger, as I find most people do, at the fact that even in this day and age adults are still being tortured around the world, it is hard to find words to express the revulsion that all but the most hardened experience at the notion that even children can be the victims of torture. In my annual report to the 1996 session of the UN Commission of Human Rights, I had occasion as the Commission's Special Rapporteur on Torture to draw international attention to the problem.[2] The communications media took particular notice of the matter. Yet I still find myself having to intervene in cases where there is serious evidence of children subjected to torture or held in circumstances where they are at risk of being tortured.

So far I am speaking of torture as commonly understood: the deliberate infliction of extreme suffering by official personnel on persons held for the purpose of extracting information, securing confessions or punishing them or intimidating others. In fact, children by virtue of their special vulnerability may well be the victims of similar suffering by practices that would not be expected to be as grave if inflicted on adults, such as inadequate conditions of detention.

And, just as my report to the 1995 session of the Commission drew attention to the torture of women, including rape, inflicted because of their status as women,[3] so the torture of children is often aimed at them because of their status as children, for example, to bring pressure on their parents or to 'clean' the streets. As Professor Chinkin points out in Chapter 6, girl children may find themselves targeted by virtue of both their age and their sex.

It is also necessary not to overlook certain practices that take place in the private sphere, such as female circumcision, when the organized community legislates or otherwise acts (or omits to act) in a manner that can be taken as complicity in the behaviour. (I do not share the opinions of those who see no difference in the public and private spheres: the term 'human rights' is grounded in the relationship between the individual and organized power; to undermine that notion is, I believe to deprive the term of its meaning and, worse, its potency.)

The essays in this book address many aspects of the problem: legal, philosophical, political, sociological, medical, psychological. They also consider how to combat it. They are written with commitment to the values of human dignity but with the dispassion that is necessary for professional and scholarly understanding. I hope they will contribute to efforts to shame those who torture children into abandoning their activities.

Notes

1   Article 37.
2   UN doc E/CN.4/1996/35, paragraphs 9–17.
3   UN doc E/CN.4/1995/34, paragraphs 15–24.

Series Preface

The concept of international children's rights has come of age, and the Programme on International Rights of the Child Series is the first series of volumes dedicated to exploring specific aspects of international children's rights. The series comprises both sole authored and edited volumes, and single disciplinary and multi-disciplinary monographs, all considering issues which are at the rapidly expanding boundaries of international children's rights.

Geraldine Van Bueren
Series Editor
Programme on International Rights of the Child
Queen Mary and Westfield College
University of London

Introduction

Geraldine Van Bueren

This is not an easy book to read. Nor ought it to be. The subject is harrowing and many understandably shy away in disbelief that children can be tortured. Nevertheless *Childhood Abused* is a subject which needs to be studied in order to be able better to prevent and protect children against such abhorrent and prohibited forms of ill-treatment.

A multi-disciplinary study of children and torture has not been undertaken before and *Childhood Abused* seeks to consider the application of international human rights standards to situations where children are at risk of torture and other forms of ill-treatment. In exploring the issues it is hoped that this book also helps to raise their profile because invisibility, ignorance and secrecy may contribute to the continuation of such practices.

Each of the contributors has examined torture and cruel, inhuman and degrading treatment from the perspectives of their own discipline and experience. Whitman observes that some cases are straightforward. There are no conceptual difficulties where children are beaten on the palms and soles of their feet.[1] Other cases may be more problematic as, in general, definitions of and protection from torture have been drafted and interpreted with reference to adults rather than from the perspective of children.

Cultural traditions and the physical and psychological development of children also have to be considered. As Richards observes, 'at first glance one might imagine a straightforward model for understanding the reactions of children to ill-treatment – the younger the more vulnerable' but as he argues the situation is more complex and what is needed is a model of the 'processes of physical and social development of children as social actors in a social world'.[2]

Ennew includes within her consideration of culture not only cultures which are different in time and space but also 'different generational cultures'.[3] Although many international human rights lawyers are perfectly familiar with the concepts of torture, and cruel, inhuman and degrading treatment and punishment and their distinguishing features, not all languages reflect this distinction. As Ennew observes, 'there is no single concept of torture in Wolof.' Ennew also highlights the use of informal punishments on children who for one reason or another fall outside of the family or institutional domains. The punishments street children receive may also bear the full force of state power 'simply because they are not occupying the proper spaces of childhood'.

From her research in Southern Africa and particularly as an observer of the Truth and Reconciliation Commission in South Africa Reynolds observes that society's concept of a child in part determines the type of punishment sanctioned by society.[4] Her chapter examines the political roles that children undertook in South Africa during apartheid and their consequential torture and ill-treatment and how they are dealing with such suffering.

Sørensen, a member of both the United Nations and Council of Europe Committees against Torture describes the duties of the former Committee and its overlap with the Committee on the Rights of the Child and regards the definition of torture incorporated in the United Nations Convention Against Torture and Other Cruel, Inhuman and Degrading Treatment or Punishment 1984 as satisfactory in relation to children.[5] Chinkin is one of a number of contributors who disagree. In particular many forms of violence deliberately perpetrated against girls 'are by definition excluded and consequently do not attract the opprobrium aroused by torture'.[6] This in part, according to Chinkin, is because the United Nations Convention on the Rights of the Child 1989 does not address the 'double susceptibility of the girl-child to violence'. If this is addressed the result would not be a dilution of the concept of torture but would help release victims from their sense of helplessness and shame and would enable public condemnation of their suffering.

Williamson asks why it is that the denial of food to children in detention may be torture but that, in general, deliberate or unintended interference with food supplies and health services for children in times of armed conflict or structural adjustment is not.[7] Sottas observes that the multi-disciplinary approach never relates to social and economic factors.[8] McBride faces up to this challenge and examines whether a violation of an economic, social or cultural right can be conceptualized as torture or as cruel, inhuman or degrading treatment. McBride finds that it is first necessary to establish the effects on children who are deprived of their economic, social and cultural rights and compare their mental and physical suffering to that experienced by children suffering torture in situations such as police stations and prisons. He comments that although some of the deprivations may be beyond the capacity of some states to remedy, 'there is a danger of accepting this sort of defence too readily' as non-availability of resources is 'not generally as clear-cut a matter as is sometimes presented'.[9]

Williamson focuses on one specific group of marginalized children, child refugees and raises the difficulties that those outside of international human rights law have in both knowing about the international human rights instruments on torture and in understanding how to use such instruments effectively. If the protection of children against torture is to be effective it cannot be, nor was it ever intended to be, left to international human rights lawyers alone. She questions how child refugees can receive as much protection through the instruments as any other person and inquires whether the structures are adequate to ensure 'a good flow of information between refugee children, their carers, practioners who support them ... so that the instruments can be made a reality for refugee children'. In light of her and others' comments the relevant instruments have been included as appendices.

Sottas examines the torture, cruel, inhuman and degrading treatment and punishment of children particularly within child justice systems focusing both on the child's perspective and the consequences for the perpetrators. Sottas also takes up Van Bueren's recommendation of an individual right of petition to the United Nations Committee on the Rights of the Child[10] which as well as being a preventative mechanism would have the advantage of producing a much needed case law, particularly on what constitutes cruel treatment and punishment in relation to children.[11]

Doyal asks whether medicine can ever amount to torture or to cruel treatment and considers the moral boundaries of the rights of children to give their informed consent to medical care. He argues that it is vital that all adults 'including clinicians, parents and judges – recognize that sometimes children will be competent enough to decide to reject treatment which can save their lives'. To force treatment, he argues, may be cruel.[12]

Whitman analyses the methods used by children's rights organizations to effect change. Human Rights Watch/Children's Rights Project uses a number of tools, including documentation, work with local non-governmental organizations, use of the media, embarrassing offending governments, enlisting the assistance of other states, pressing international organizations to take action and working jointly with international children's and human rights organizations.[13]

As well as seeking to prevent children being subject to torture or to other forms of ill-treatment, 193 states are now under a duty to provide recovery and reintegration services to child victims, although the ambit of that duty has never been clearly defined.[14] Perren-Klingler examines how the psychosocial destruction of children who have suffered torture may be avoided.[15] As Montgomery observes, traumatic experiences can influence children's emotional, cognitive and moral development because it influences their self image and their expectations of self and environment.[16] Her work has been with both children who have suffered torture and with the children of adult torture survivors and she concludes that when parents are able to talk with children about their experiences the children had fewer symptoms. Black and Newman highlight four principal coping strategies for children: 'withdrawal, mental flight, eagerness to acclimatise and fighting'. From studies of political refugees they also find that there is close relationship between the mental health of the children and of their parents, particularly the mother.[17] They argue that early intervention post-trauma may prevent or limit psychological distress, and attention to the provision of substitute parenting, medical care, housing, education and nutrition may help minimize the secondary effects of traumatic events.

From the late Middle Ages until the latter half of the eighteenth century torture was a judicially approved practice in Europe. Similarly specific forms of treatment and punishment, such as flogging, which were widely accepted have now become prohibited. A certain caution, however, has to be exercised, as most human rights violations are inherently degrading and could therefore fall within the prohibition on torture, cruel, inhuman and degrading treatment and punishment. This would have the counter productive effect of weakening the potency of the prohibition. However, in the end a balance has to be struck between humanity's move towards more humane standards of treatment of children and in maintaining a meaningful legal, internationally accepted, framework.

Just as once-acceptable treatment and punishment is now prohibited by the international community, so the time has come to re-evaluate the ill-treatment of children from a multi-disciplinary perspective, and to question, in the best interests of the child, certain received wisdoms. Children are more resilient than many realise but it is for the benefit of all that this resilience ought not to be abused, but ought to lead to greater participation by children in their society.

Notes

1   In Turkey children who have been interrogated have been subject to such beatings called falaka: see below Whitman, *The Torture of Children: Assessing Torture and Devising Methods to Prevent It.*

2   See below Richards, *The Ill-Treatment of Children – Some Developmental Considerations.*

3   See below Ennew, *Shame and Physical Pain: Cultural Relativity, Children, Torture and Punishment.*

4   Reynolds, *Activism, Politics and the Punishment of Children.*

5   See below Sørensen, *International Conventions Against Torture and on the Rights of the Child – The Work of Two United Nations Committees.*

6   See below Chinkin, *Torture of the Girl-Child.*

7   See below Williamson, *Are the Rights of Refugee Children Protected Adequately Against Torture?*

8   See below Sottas, *A Non-Governmental Organization Perspective of the United Nations' Approach to Children and Torture.*

9   See below McBride, *The Violation of Economic, Social and Cultural Rights as Torture or Cruel, Inhuman or Degrading Treatment.*

10 Van Bueren (1995), *The International Law on the Rights of the Child*, Kluwer, at 410.

11 See further below Van Bueren, *Opening Pandora's Box – Protecting Children Against Torture, Cruel, Inhuman and Degrading Treatment or Punishment.*

12 Doyal, *Can Medicine be Torture? The Case of Children.*

13 Whitman *op. cit.*

14 193 states are party to the UN Convention on the Rights of the Child 1989, which in Article 39 provides for recovery and reintegration services.

15 See below Perren-Klingler, *Children and Reintegration.*

16 See below Montgomery, *Children Exposed to War, Torture and Other Organized Violence – Developmental Consequences.*

17 Black and Newman, *The Effects on Children of Witnessing Violence Perpetrated against their Parents or Siblings.*

1   Shame and Physical Pain: Cultural Relativity, Children, Torture and Punishment

Judith Ennew

'The refined punishments of the spiritual mode are usually much more indecent than a good smack.'[1]

Introduction: Cultural Relativity

In inter-disciplinary forums, the expected role of a social anthropologist often seems to be to provide anecdotal challenges to the dominance of Western rationality.[2] The increasing literature on comparative jurisprudence shows that Western-oriented, international human rights lawyers recognize the need to do this and often welcome the challenge of well-articulated alternative viewpoints, such as Islamic law.[3] Nevertheless, when social anthropologists consider law they are usually discussing systems that are uncodified, in addition to being based on systems of moral philosophy and logic that are far removed from the relatively similar, codified systems of Islam and Christianity.

It is quite clear that one notion of rationality dominates in international work, whether in law, economics or science. Western thought and action are, as one sociologist has put it, 'oriented to formal, empirical rationality in a controlled environment'.[4] But this does not mean that they are necessarily superior. Indeed, social anthropology insists that other structures of thought and behaviour are no less logical, rational and moral than those that currently hold sway. With respect to the practical (as well as legal) implementation of international human rights instruments such as the Convention on the Rights of the Child (CRC), I would suggest that it is important to respect

7

these other world views. And by 'respect' I do not just mean accepting that these forms of understanding exist, but rather trying to enter into and learn from them.

Current discourses on the CRC tend to be dominated by legal standard-setting. When it comes to setting policy goals and interventions for implementing these standards, it is appropriate to explore the meanings they have in different cultural contexts. One danger of accepting that other systems of concepts and beliefs can be equally rational in their own terms is that this can lead to the argument that it is impossible to make cross-cultural comparisons, in which case it would be impossible to establish universal human rights law except through cultural imperialism. I would argue, however, that international standards can be set, not through establishing which system is 'best', nor by negotiating some kind of lowest possible denominator, but rather by moving the debate to another level in which, as another sociologist has put it, 'different institutions, embodying different conceptual schemes, may illuminatingly be seen as serving the same social necessities'.[5] This can be easiest to demonstrate at a practical level. As Pamela Reynolds has shown with respect to children traumatized by the Zimbabwean War of Liberation, traditional methods of healing may be more effective than psychological counselling imported by foreign aid workers.[6] They are certainly cheaper, and probably restore children more effectively into the lives of their communities in which such healing methods are integral to the way the world is conceptualized.

The importance of respecting other forms of rationality within the arena of international human rights law is currently being demonstrated to me in the form of certain practical difficulties I experience coordinating a project that explores the possibility of developing systems for monitoring the implementation of the CRC in eight very different countries (The Childwatch International Indicators for Children's Rights Project).[7] In this context I am working with national teams of researchers, examining the potential of current data about children for developing monitoring systems. Part of the process requires a critical reading of the Convention on the Rights of the Child in local languages, exploring the relevance of the articles and the concepts they imply in each cultural setting, by examining the resonance of words and phrases.

As has been widely recognized, the CRC contains many linguistic and cultural traps and has been criticized at times for being at best inapplicable outside Western countries or at worst as an instrument of cultural imperialism.[8] The most notable example is probably that of Article 3(1) on the best interests of the child. Although this Article is usually taken to be fundamental in both Western and non-Western settings, in the former it is associated with legal and social work practice, while in the latter it often means something akin to 'children first'.[9] Not for nothing is Alston's book *The Best Interests of The Child* subtitled '*Reconciling Culture and Human Rights*'. As he points out, the CRC, perhaps more than any other international human rights instrument, has revealed a need to seek 'approaches which involve neither the embrace of an artificial and sterile universalism nor the acceptance of an ultimately self-defeating cultural relativism.'[10]

Resistance to the very idea of cultural relativism, as Abdullahi An-Na'im points out, is often based on the suspicion that it 'denies to individuals the moral right to make comparisons and to insist on universal standards of right and wrong'.[11] Yet individuals, however outraged they may be by certain customs and practices, especially in the fields of child abuse and exploitation, cannot set either local or international standards by themselves and moreover respect for culture can be used, as Alston citing Dawkins argues, as a 'trump card'.[12] All customs and standards are social, the product of interactions within groups, whether these are small-scale or what is sometimes called the 'human' or 'international' community. Moreover, as An-Na'im further reminds us, cultures do not simply differ from group to group, they are also dynamic, flexible and often internally inconsistent or ambivalent.[13] Reality is socially constructed and values constantly negotiated. The ideational structure of international human rights law is itself a new cultural product.

The CRC presents some fairly obvious difficulties. One example is Article 16(1) on privacy, which has little relevance in countries where individual, physical privacy does not have high cultural value. Another is the use of the phrase 'periodic review of placement' in Article 25, which is hard to envisage in the context of traditional fostering systems as in West Africa.[14] More deep-rooted difficulties can be experienced with respect to Article 1, the definition of the child, not simply in legal terms, with respect to the ages at which certain activities can be permitted or expected, but also in terms of the cultural definitions of the ages and stages of childhood. Even in the English-speaking world there is no single word that can meaningfully be applied to infants, toddlers, primary school children, early teenagers and youths under the age of 18 years. Indeed, some terms may be exclusively applied to either girls or boys. In addition, there are wide cultural variations in expectations of the level of maturity expected at different ages or stages, which also has implications for the interpretation of Article 12.

My aim here is to explore some of the meanings that might be attached to some of the terms used in a single article of the CRC, Article 37. I will use anthropological anecdotes as well as some textual comparisons. Although the first anecdote is taken from the ethnographic record of Papua New Guinea, the majority of examples are limited to Africa, most particularly Senegambia, the area in which the first of the monitoring country case studies took place. This focuses the argument on debates about culture that arise through comparison between the 1989 United Nations CRC and the African Charter on the Rights and Welfare of the Child (African Charter), adopted by the Organisation of African Unity (OAU) in 1990.[15]

The First Anecdote

In keeping with their acceptance of other kinds of thought and rationality, anthropologists are not supposed to intervene in, or argue against, the customs of people they live with and study. Ethnographic texts are intended to be objective rather than normative. This can result in personal dilemmas. These are not always discussed in the literature, although there are exceptions. Kenneth Read lived in a village called Susuroka among the Gahuku people of Highland New Guinea for two years and wrote one of the most honest ethnographic accounts ever published. A central chapter in his book, *High Valley*, concerns the initiation of a member of his house staff, for whom Read had developed considerable affection:

> Asemo was fourteen or fifteen, a little younger than the age of initiation for most Gahuku boys. He was slight and serious, never playing the buffoon like Piripiri, his age mate, who stirred up gales of laughter in the street by hopping around with his head between his knees, flapping his elbows and crowing like a cock. Though Asemo joined in the laughter and shook his head with pleasure, he was a more dignified and thoughtful boy... .
>
> He had a quality of contained but relaxed participation – his hands held loosely in his lap, shoulders slightly to the fore, his back a supple curve from the base of his neck to the crossed legs that carried the weight of his body. Asemo's head and eyes showed that he was taking stock of everything around him, yet he also seemed to be aloof, watching from some inner vantage point where his mind made its own judgements and decisions.[16]

Asemo's father had asked Read if, as the boy's employer, he had any objection to Asemo going through Gahuku initiation rituals. As the time of the ceremonies approached, Read's feelings about this assumed responsibility turned to dread:

> I followed the preparations from a distance, questioning my house boys. The frank accounts of their terror when they had stood in his place joined me more closely in sympathy to Asemo and added to my burden of doubt and responsibility. It was not enough consolation to know that the dangers he faced were exaggerated by the boys: initiates seldom died from the rites.[17]

The main public rites, conducted at the river's edge, lasted a day. Although Read states he could appreciate their drama and symbolism he also wrote that 'what I saw that day revolted me'.[18] The initiates were conducted by their sponsors through two trials, which were first demonstrated by male leaders. In the first a powerful man in his early thirties:

> moved out into the river and faced the crowded bank where the water swirled round his calves. He was holding two cigar-shaped objects fashioned from the razor-sharp leaves of green pit-pit. Flourishing them like a conjurer in a spotlight, raising them above the level of his shoulders, he tilted his head back and thrust the rolls of leaf into his nostrils. My flesh recoiled in shock, nerves contracting as though they were seared by the pain that must have swept through his own body as his fingers sawed at the protruding ends of the wadded leaves, thrusting them rapidly up and down inside his nose. I felt sick with distaste, wanting to turn from the exhibition of self-mutilation that provoked a chorus of approving shouts from the crowd, a sound climaxed by the familiar ululating cry of accomplishment as he withdrew the bloody leaves and lowered his head toward the water. Blood gushed from his nose. His fingers, holding the instruments of purification, dripped it onto the surface of the river, where its cloudy stain divided around his legs. His knees trembled, seemed almost to buckle under him as he bled, and when he raised his head to stagger out toward the beach his lips, his chin, and his throat ran with bright red.[19]

One by one, the boys were subjected to this purifying ritual, which they would then have to practice regularly throughout life in order to protect them from what Gahuku believed was the essentially contaminating influence of women. When it was Asemo's turn, he was hidden from Read's view by the figure of his sponsor but, when the older man moved aside, 'his violent mission done', Read could see 'the bright blood flowing from Asemo's lowered head'.[20]

In the second demonstration Read learned for the first time the function of the long cane that most Gahuku men wore wound around their waists:

> I experienced a sudden apprehension as he shaped it into a long, narrow U. Leaning forward from the waist, he placed the rounded section in his mouth, straightened, tilted his head, extending the line of his neck, and fed it into his stomach. My throat contracted and my stomach heaved, compelling me to look away. When I turned to him again most of the cane had disappeared, only two small sections, the open ends of the U, protruding from the corners of his mouth.
>
> I have no idea how long he held this grotesque stance, his straining abdomen and chest racked with involuntary shudders. Already sickened by the display, I stiffened with shock as he raised his hands, grasped the ends of the cane and sawed it rapidly up and down, drawing it almost free of his mouth at the peak of every upward stroke. The fervour of the crowd mounted to a clamorous pitch, breaking in wave upon wave of pulsing cries, the final surge matching my own relief when he dropped the cane, bent from the waist, and vomited into the river.

A new, sour smell threaded through the overheated odours of the beach. The palms of my hands were wet, and my mouth filled with the taste of nausea. I had to force myself to look when the men repeated the performance on the boys, my distaste and the urge to turn away checked by apprehension of their danger. Though it was surely less painful than the first ordeal, there was a serious risk of internal injury if the initiates struggled when they were forced to swallow the canes. Fortunately, or perhaps it had been deliberately planned, they were already too exhausted, too shocked and weak to resist, but I watched anxiously for signs of blood as their sponsors held the boys' heads between their knees. When it was over, I was giddy from the light, the noise, the acid smells, a revulsion so strong that I had to turn my back to the river.[21]

Making Cross-cultural Comparisons

I have given this example at length, and largely in Read's own words, to demonstrate that even when anthropologists are trying to be objective and respect other cultures, they too can be shocked, revolted and disturbed by customs that are different. According to most current Western norms, this Guhuku initiation ceremony would probably be interpreted as cruel and degrading treatment. It might also be regarded as violating Article 24(3) of the CRC, which calls for the abolition of 'traditional practices prejudicial to the health of children'. Read worried about the health effects on boys and, although 'initiates seldom died from the rites', any who did perish were being denied the right to life, enshrined in Article 6 of the Convention.

According to anthropological convention, there can be two interpretations of social events:

(i)   'Etic': external or analytical – Often a sociological or anthropological interpretation, but equally the interpretation of anyone who experiences or reads about another culture;

(ii) 'Emic': internal – What the legal anthropologist Paul Bohannan described as a folk system: 'the subjective interpretation of the events made by the participant actors creating a 'meaningful system out of the social relationships in which they are involved.'[22]

The implicit meanings of an emic interpretation are not 'right' or 'wrong' or even (to be less normative) 'correct' or 'incorrect'. They simply exist, and the key to them is the language in which they are expressed.

The notion of a folk system does not just refer to a tribal society, such as the Tiv whom Bohannan studied, but also to Western, or any other systems. Bohannan claimed that the anthropologist's greatest challenge is to avoid turning his/her own folk system into an analytical system, which interprets other systems inappropriately. This does not preclude cross-cultural comparison, which takes place at another epistemological level.[23] The cultural relativity problem, from an anthropological perspective, is not simply that outlined by Alston (how to make universal standards universal in a culturally diverse world) but rather how to avoid superimposing one set of concepts on another when transcribing ethnographic data from one culture to another. This is not just a question of separating the ethnographer's interpretation of the folk (emic) system from the ethnographer's analytical (etic) model and his/her own folk system, but of acknowledging the presence of the actual 'concrete' folk system even though this is 'unknowable except in terms of somebody or other's perception of it'.[24] This means that the possibility of comparative jurisprudence is not in doubt. The critical questions concern the precautions that should be taken when making comparisons between one jural system and another, as well as those that should be taken when collecting and interpreting data.

Read makes it clear that his reaction to Asemo's initiation was more culturally conditioned than analytical; at times he was not interpreting, only feeling. He frequently refers in the course of *High Valley* to the impossibility of understanding the Guhuku. Some time after the ceremony at the river's edge, when initiates returned to the village following a period of seclusion, he writes 'There was no way of knowing what Asemo saw that afternoon as he trod the street carefully under the heavy ornaments of manhood'.[25] And, writing of the way the two of them customarily sat in silence at the end of the day in the shade of a dense clump of bamboo, looking at the dramatic view over the mountain ridge, he says:

At least from our outward appearance Asemo and I could have been engrossed by an identical purpose, but he could not be expected to bring a similar perspective to bear on the visible features of the valley any more than I could share, except vicariously, his range of experience. It was not that I was unable to relate what I saw to the pattern of life in which I was partially involved. Out of the events I had seen and the past that had been recalled for me, everything became informed by a distinctive quality, so that the high ground beyond the river was not simply an expanse of grass barred by the contrasting alternations of sun and shadow but also a no man's land separating traditional enemies. Each point of reference carried a specific implication, was coloured by knowledge that was certainly shared by Asemo or any other man who sat beside me; yet there was no way of telling if there was any common ground in our perception of the same object.[26]

On Defining Cruel and Inhuman Treatment

One field worth exploring to aid the attempt to find the elements required for a universal definition of cruel and inhuman treatment is child abuse. The anthropologist Jill Korbin has made a cross-cultural study of child abuse and suggests that there are three levels at which the maltreatment of children can be defined:

(i)   Cultural practices that are viewed as abusive or neglectful by other cultures, but not by the culture in question;
(ii)   Idiosyncratic departure from one's cultural continuum of acceptable behaviour; and
(iii) Societally induced harm to children beyond the control of individual parents and caretakers.[27]

She adds that 'Literature from developing nations supports distinguishing traditional practices that involve pain and suffering from idiosyncratic forms of maltreatment that more recently have been identified in urban centres'.[28]

Korbin points out that there may be wide variations in what is taken to be either beneficial or harmful treatment and that nothing should be taken for granted as intrinsically either good or bad. Thus she suggests that:

> It is instructive to view Euro-American child-care practices through the eyes of other cultures. Many Euro-American child-care practices, even those as seemingly benign as sleeping arrangements in which infants have separate beds and rooms, are seen as ill-informed at best and uncaring and abusive at worst by many of the world's societies.[29]

In another study, carried out with child psychologist David Finkelhor, Korbin suggests that an operational definition of child maltreatment might be 'the portion of harm to children that is proscribed, proximate, and preventable'.[30] Although this is a useful definition it does not take two important aspects into account. In the first place, it begs the question of the cultural definition of harm, which throws the issue back into the arena of relativity. In the case of initiands, such as Asemo, the physical harm consequent on the rites performed at the riverside is less important than the social harm of not becoming a man. In adult life, the performance of these painful acts is necessary for all men, if they are to protect themselves against the dangers of female pollution, not only during sexual intercourse but also in the course of everyday life. Nevertheless, it is clear that Asemo's father had perceived that there were other value systems and that Asemo did not necessarily have to undergo the rites, otherwise his father would not have asked Read's permission.

Knowing about different possibilities and their consequences is the first step towards making choices, with respect to any social customs. The question then becomes whether inside or outside (emic or etic) perceptions of punishment should be taken into consideration when setting universal standards. And this is complicated, as An-Na'im points out in an essay on the meaning of cruel, inhuman or degrading treatment, by the fact that few societies now display cultural hegemony. Dominant group values probably prevail but there also tends to be 'an internal struggle for control over the cultural sources and symbols of power'.[31] He argues that 'universal cultural legitimacy is necessary' and that it is possible to develop it with respect to human rights through what he calls 'enlightened ethnocentricity'[32] by which he appears to mean respect for all cultures and 'enlightened interpretation' of the cultural norms of others from the 'ethnocentric' (Western) perspective of international human rights culture.

Although An-Na'im's suggestion may be philosophically sound, it is difficult to see how 'enlightened ethnocentricity' might be worked out in practice with respect to human rights, anymore than Korbin and Finkelhor's definition of child abuse. Indeed, the idea of 'cruel and inhuman treatment' is more difficult in some ways than the ideas of abuse or maltreatment, which do not bring into play the idea of what it is to be human. At one level, it would be difficult to reach a consensus on any aspect of human rights because few current (or historical) cultures possess a concept of rights.[33] But at another, more fundamental, level it is worth remembering that few societies in history have ever possessed an idea of what it is like to be human in a universal, or species, sense. Ethnographic accounts are full of examples of societies that have no word for 'human' other than the name they give themselves. In their conceptual worlds, other societies, other cultures – even those they know through trade or warfare – are not human societies, from which it follows that the members are not human beings. One of the defining characteristics of the 'Other', thus defined, is precisely that of engaging in 'inhuman practices'.

It is worth remembering here that it is not uncommon for adults to define children as the 'Other'; as unsocialised and barbaric human becomings, rather than as human beings.[34] This brings me to the second problem posed by the definition proposed by Finkelhor and Korbin. Although they consider the perspectives of cultures that are different in time and space, they do not consider the perspectives of different generational cultures. Korbin and Finkelhor do not discuss children's views, nor mention in the context of this definition the way children's low social status makes them particularly vulnerable to abuse and unable to protest at what they perceive to be adult mistreatment. Read's account of the Gahuku makes it clear that there was already some difference in approach to initiation between the generations of

Asemo and his father. What Read cannot tell us is whether or not Asemo considered the treatment he received during his initiation to be cruel, inhuman or degrading. We have no means of judging the pain he suffered other than through Read's emotive account. Yet, as Eric Sottas, Director of the World Organisation against Torture (OMCT), has said:

> the degree of suffering or pain should be established taking into account the age of the child and the effect experienced rather than on the basis of an examination, which claims to be objective, of the gravity of the suffering inflicted.[35]

Children's Perspectives on Initiation

Although, like Read, we have no way of knowing what Asemo felt, we can find a few first person descriptions of initiation in the literary genre of remembered childhoods. In recent decades, initiation rites in Africa have begun to take place at longer intervals and to take less time. Children are busy learning 'rational' knowledge in school and this leaves less time available for lengthy periods of seclusion during which they would be learning the 'illogical' knowledge of their communities. Nevertheless, one personal account occurs in Camera Laye's well-known memoires of his Malinké childhood in Guinea. Laye makes it clear that before the ceremony he thought of circumcision as a menacing test, but one that he appreciated was necessary if he was to become a man.[36] About the moment before circumcision, while he was waiting in line with the members of his age set, he writes:

> I was afraid, frightfully afraid, but I brought all my concentration to not revealing it: all those men in front of us, who were watching us must not catch sight of my fear ... this was not a moment to lose face.[37]

The actual moment of circumcision was swift, with little time for this foreboding to develop during a prolonged experience of pain. The man performing his operation, who had been chosen by Laye's family because he had a reputation for speed and the relative lack of pain he inflicted, 'transformed me from one state to the other with a speed that I can't express'.[38]

Nevertheless the blood flowed copiously, and seemingly endlessly, from his wound. The boy's fear returned. He wondered if his body would be entirely drained of blood. With some of the watching men in tears the initiates stood awkwardly in line, dizzy, nauseated, feverish and shivering: 'We had lost too much blood, seen too much blood'.[39] Added to the pain and weakness was despair that they had to spend the days of convalescence in seclusion with men, rather than return to their mothers'care.[40]

Tests of endurance are common but not obligatory in initiation rites, for girls as well as boys. Physical pain is frequently regarded as a vital component of the transition from child to adult, 'transforming from one state to the other'. Adults can sympathise, as the tears in the adult, male Malinkés' eyes show, but this does not stop them from performing rites that are regarded as essential for the proper continuation of society. Both adults and children in Malinké culture acknowledge that circumcision is painful, but consider it beneficial because it brings long term societal good – boys become men and society continues. This means that pain inflicted as punishment is not the same as pain suffered in a 'good' cause, such as initiation. In fact, the distinction between the two may be made about the same experience of pain. Thus, in another ethnographic account of Papua New Guinea, Langness tells us that 'Children who have been disobedient and poorly behaved may be subject to harsher treatment than their peers during initiation rituals ... when there is a collective context for remonstration that cannot be exhibited by individual parents'.[41]

On Defining Torture

The CRC provides no definition for any of the terms 'torture ... cruel, inhuman or degrading punishment' in Article 37(a). Likewise the definitions given in the 1975 Declaration on Torture of the UN General Assembly and the Convention on Torture adopted by the UN General Assembly in 1984 are not identical. In any case, as Sottas points out, they set out only minimal rules for States Parties. In domestic legislations, 'many States either fail to adopt any definition on the subject or define torture in terms which differ from those used in the Convention'. At times, domestic legislation may broaden the scope of the term, at others the result is 'more restrictive definitions' that 'reduce the protection of potential victims and frequently prevent the prosecution of those presumed responsible'.[42] The Convention against Torture also 'makes clear that pain or suffering must be inflicted intentionally', (in the Declaration the word was 'deliberately'). Yet, The World Organisation Against Torture considers that intention is not 'a relevant element': with respect to children 'to the extent to which torture is applied to children it is necessary to take into account not only intention but also grave negligence'.

The inability of Western emic systems to define torture, even in precise legal documents, does not make it easy to use international human rights documents in the context of other cultures. Part of the process of the Childwatch Indicators for Children's Rights project entails a critical reading of the CRC to explore the ways in which each Article is interpreted in local cultural and linguistic terms. In Senegal, where the first country case study took place, there was initially no apparent difficulty in interpreting Article 37. The translation from English to French (which is the official language in Senegal) is unproblematic because the words are drawn from the same Latin root, although this did not solve the problem of the lack of definition in the Convention itself. Moreover, the most common language used for everyday communication in Senegal is not French but Wolof, the language of the dominant ethnic group. My Wolof-speaking colleagues had trouble finding a single word for torture, but reported that several are used, each having its own nuance. All end with the suffix 'al', which bears the sense of 'doing something to someone else':

Lottal: Means reducing the force or strength of a person, especially in the sense of forcing someone to speak or confess;
Toroxal: Combines physical and psychological humiliation, whether private or (worse) public;
Metital: 'Metit' means pain, specifically referring to inflicting pain on someone else;
Faagaagal: A term that was often used in Wolof-language press to report police treatment of protesters against apartheid in South Africa. The translation of *faagaagal* into French is 'mater' – to bring to heel, bring under control, suppress or subdue by striking or inflicting pain on someone until they no longer have the will to resist.

There is thus no single concept of torture in Wolof. These words have the common element of reducing an enemy's force, by 'the powers that be' (in other words torture is not a private matter). But the gratuitous infliction of pain is not conceptualized – in agreement with UN Convention on Torture, torture is defined by an intention on the part of the torturer.[43]

Intentions, however, differ considerably and also require definition. In European history, torture was formerly part of punishment, a public spectacle that consisted, as Foucault points out, of ritual as a technology of representation.[44] In this the body is a symbol of the 'entire natural and moral universe'.[45] Just as in public initiation rites, circumcision marks a boy's body in order to make him a man, so the spectacle of torture had a symbolic function 'the being who violates the moral universe is corrected by having his or her physical universe violated in turn'.[46] Public torture differs from the technology of representation of initiation simply by virtue of the fact that initiation is not intended to punish individuals.

Systems of punishment now do not generally depend primarily on inflicting pain, but rather on removing freedoms – 'an economy of suspended rights'.[47] The essence of modern torture is that it takes place in private so that systems of justice are divorced from, and refuse to take responsibility for, the violence that is consequent on the power they wield. Foucault would also have it that the exercise of such power is now more general, not focusing on correcting individual miscreants but rather encompassing all who are supervised, trained or corrected – the insane, workers, the colonized and children both at home and at school.[48] This reference to the normality of punishment and the general exercise of power to correct and supervise children is something I will return to later. Here I wish to expand on the Wolof example and examine differing cultural approaches to defining torture by comparing two international instruments for children's rights – the Convention on the Rights of the Child and the African Charter on the Rights and Welfare of the Child.

The African Contexts of Children's Rights

As of December 1996, all African nations that are member states of the United Nations, with the exception of Somalia, are states party to the CRC, while the African Charter, adopted by the OAU in 1990, still lacks sufficient ratifications to come into force. It can be, and is, argued by some that the Charter is unnecessary. Yet the OAU considers that a complementary instrument is important in order to ensure the implementation of the CRC in African countries, in the face of 'certain local conditions' such as:

> severely depressed economic situations, shortage of basic social amenities, widespread occurrence of armed conflict, and resultant displacement of populations.[49]

The African Charter. drafted by the OAU and the African Network on Prevention and Protection Against Child Abuse and Neglect (ANPPCAN) with the assistance of UNICEF, is designed to 'retain the spirit as well as the substance of [the] letter' of the CRC while making 'special provisions guided by the ground situation in Africa'.[50]

A further regional aspect that permeates the entire Charter is the specificity of African cultures. In many ways, the African Charter is a fuller and more satisfying document than the CRC, the vague wording of which often makes it appear to have been drawn up in a cultural vacuum, although this was largely a result of 'delicately-negotiated consensus and compromise'.[51] The African Charter is based on reflections on African civilization and culture[52] recognising the place of children in society,[53] making reference to the importance of children with respect to inter-generational transmission of culture[54] and also recognizing their responsibilities in society.[55] The idea of striking a balance between rights and responsibilities is in keeping with the

African Charter on Human and Peoples Rights, although many claim that this 'creates the risk of abuse by authorities'[56] or, more specifically with respect to children, of diluting the provisions of the CRC.[57] It has been claimed that for human rights to have meaning in Africa they should relate to group rather than individual rights, because identity relates to groups, rather than individuals. According to Howard, 'The African concept of human rights is actually a concept of human dignity ...' which is derived from preserving inner worth and proper, or harmonious, social relations: 'African communalism ... stresses the dignity of membership in, and fulfilment of one's prescribed roles in, a group'.[58] This less individualistic view of the relationship between people and social groups has also been noted by ethnographers. Of one Nigerian society, for example, it has been stated that 'The concept of "I" only exists in relation to the extent that "I" can accept and encourage the existence of others'. With respect to children, this bears the implication that 'Parents and the family group are the child's immediate society'.[59]

With respect to culture, it has been claimed that there is a 'fundamental inconsistency' in the Charter, which bases its principles on cultural heritage but discourages inconsistent traditions.[60] Even though the African Charter is 'a radical departure from African cultural traditionalism'[61] it still takes cultural context into consideration. In the case of the CRC some reference to cultural practices such as initiation is made in the article on health in which States Parties are enjoined to take 'all effective and appropriate measures with a view to abolishing practices prejudicial to the health of children'.[62] In keeping with this, the African Charter enjoins States Parties to discourage 'Any custom, tradition, cultural or religious practice that is inconsistent with the rights, duties and obligations' specifically naming child marriage and betrothal.[63] Yet elsewhere it states that positive African 'morals, traditional values and cultures' should be preserved and strengthened through education, without giving any guidance on what might be considered to be positive examples. It is interesting to note that the 1979 Declaration on the Rights of the African Child did mention female circumcision as a negative cultural practice.[64]

With respect to torture, Article 16(1) of the African Charter, on 'Protection against child abuse and torture' seeks to protect children against 'torture, inhuman or degrading treatment and especially physical or mental injury or abuse, neglect or maltreatment including sexual abuse, while in the care of a parent, legal guardian or school authority or any other person who has the care of the child', while Article 17(2)(a) on the 'Administration of juvenile justice' ensures that 'no child who is detained or imprisoned or otherwise deprived of his/her liberty is subjected to torture, inhuman or degrading treatment or punishment'. Thus the African Charter appears to separate torture as a part of child abuse from torture as a matter of judicial process;[65] in contrast, the CRC references to 'torture or other cruel, inhuman or degrading treatment or punishment'[66] and rehabilitationa,[67] do not make any connection to families or schools. Neither document attempts a definition of torture.

Children and Punishment

The CRC does not mention either torture or other forms of cruel and inhuman treatment with respect to punishment for infringements of the law, although this is implicit in Article 37, which concentrates on deprivation of liberty. Punishment is not mentioned at all in Article 40 on juvenile justice. The African Charter, on the other hand, mentions both punishment and torture in the same article.[68] For adults, particularly adult males, punishment is most likely to take place within the context of a judicial system, or at the hands of the community. For children, on the other hand, the most important locations of punishment are the family and schools. Juvenile justice systems affect relatively few children and are poorly developed in many countries. Nevertheless, the African Charter and the CRC have special articles that deal with juvenile justice, both stating that this should be administered in a manner consistent with the child's 'sense of dignity and worth', a notion to which I shall return later.[69]

State punishment of children can be formal or informal, depending to a large extent on a child's location. Punishment in a family setting is largely informal, being unregulated by States except for attempts to define the level of 'punishment' that can be permitted before it becomes 'abuse'. Policing and surveillance of this dividing line is, however, difficult to ensure within the private domain of family life. On the other hand, children in socially legitimated (and state regulated) places, such as schools, orphanages or correctional homes tend, as Foucault pointed out, to be subjected to:

> a whole micro-penalty of time (lateness, absences, interruptions of tasks), of activity (inattention, negligence, lack of zeal), of behaviour (impoliteness, disobedience), of speech (idle chatter, insolence), of the body ('incorrect' attitudes, irregular gestures, lack of cleanliness), of sexuality (impurity, indecency).[70]

Children who for one reason or another fall outside family or institutional domains may also be subjected to informal punishment that still bears the full force of state power, simply because they are not occupying the proper spaces of childhood. Street children, for example, are frequently targeted for arbitrary punishment and brutality by the police, on the street and in police stations. Although Latin America has provided the best-known examples of adult violence against street children, this is a worldwide phenomenon of which many African examples can be found. In Ethiopia, street children have reported broken bones, bruises and stabbings by police, not only as punishment (for stealing, or gambling) but also for being street children, or in order to steal money from the child, or because the child was a 'known thief'.[71]

Even formal punishment of children for criminal offences does not always follow the provisions of the CRC. The reports to the Committee on the Rights of the Child by African countries show a range of alternative treatments. To take two examples:

(i)   The Senegal report does not mention corporal punishment and Senegal does have a range of alternative treatments available, although these are probably inadequate to the need.[72]
(ii)   In the Sudan report it is stated that 'the Sudanese family never uses ill-treatment or violence, in accordance with the teachings and precepts of religion and custom'.[73] Nevertheless in the case of child criminal offenders, the punishments a court may implement include: 'he may be punished by whipping, with not more than 20 lashes, if he has reached the age of 10'.[74]

Overall, the general attitude towards corporal punishment in African countries has probably not changed a great deal since the author of a report on the justice systems in East Africa of the 1930s stated that 'Especially in the case of juvenile offenders a whipping is often considered a most desirable remedy'.[75] Then as now, resources did not permit the establishment of the alternative regimes of rehabilitation and reintegration that are mentioned in both the CRC and the African Charter. Nevertheless, the report from Namibia mentions that corporal punishment for both juvenile and adult offenders is precluded by the 'constitutional guarantee of human dignity' of a 1991 Supreme Court ruling, since when there has been an emphasis on 'discipline from within' as an alternative to corporal punishment in schools.[76] As corporal punishment is unconstitutional, the new Namibian Educational Code of Conduct states that 'while students are expected to comply with legitimate disciplinary measures, they have a right to protection from corporal punishment, verbal abuse and unjust or excessive punishment'.[77]

Corporal Punishment in School and at Home

School punishment is perhaps the most universal form of child discipline in a state-regulated setting. In the West, attitudes at least have changed since

Charles Dickens described in *Nicholas Nickelby*, the type of school in which a sadistic headteacher was able to create a regime of terror unregulated by the state although practices have not always changed, as revelations about the 'pin-down' system of restraint and discipline in institutional settings in England and Wales showed in the 1980s.[78] In various parts of the world, including some former United Kingdom colonies, corporal punishment is a persistent manifestation of authoritarian child rearing practices, in which 'children are supposed to know' that physical punishment 'reflects parental care and concern'.[79] Children do indeed seem to feel that this is the case but are also able to make quite clear distinctions between legitimate and illegitimate contexts of punishment. A survey of 1,000 secondary school pupils in Barbados in 1989/90 showed 60 per cent approval of formally administered corporal punishment for defined offenses, even though this punishment consisted of 'flogging' or 'lashing'. But they did not approve of random punishment.[80] Children in elementary schools, also showed a somewhat similar attitude, although this could be modified. According to one Grade 5 girl in the study (aged between 10 and 11 years): 'There are many different ways to punish us. You and all people must remember kids have rights too. We are human beings like anybody else'.[81]

This consciousness of rights is echoed in an essay on punishment collected from a 17-year-old boy by an Ethiopian researcher in a secondary school in Addis Ababa, where corporal punishment was observed being administered regularly, and often both arbitrarily and harshly. Teachers, wrote this boy:

> are unfamiliar with the ethics of teaching and discipline. They do not respect the rights of students. They do not attend to our interests. They tell us their rights of earning money even without working. Don't we have the right to learn? ... Children commit mistakes knowingly or unknowingly ... . When such offences are committed, the culprits should be advised and made to learn. It is not right to beat like a donkey (in other countries donkeys have rights). Causing injuries in the different parts of the body is unacceptable. In our country beating has become part of our culture ... . I do not support the use of force. Advise them! Teach them! Do not take any other measures.[82]

Punishment in schools is explicitly mentioned in both the CRC and the African Charter, once again with specific reference to dignity; the phrases used being 'human dignity' in the CRC and 'inherent dignity' in the African Charter.[83] The Charter also mentions punishment under parental responsibilities.[84] Parents and guardians, it says, have the duty 'to ensure that domestic discipline is administered with humanity and in a manner consistent with the inherent dignity of the child'. The nearest the CRC comes to consider entering the family arena with respect to punishment is in Article

19, which could be interpreted as referring to punishment in paragraph 1, in which States Parties are enjoined to protect children in parental care from 'all forms of physical or mental violence, injury or abuse, neglect or negligent treatment, maltreatment or exploitation'.

In all parts of the world, schools are now the major locus of socialisation outside the family. Each form of rationality produces a specific normative structure, which is maintained on the one hand by reference to ideas and on the other by the application of punishments, which typically consist of inflicting pain, fines, confinements, shame and social rejection. Discipline, as Foucault points out, 'makes' individuals: it is the specific technique of a power that regards individuals both as objects and as instruments of its essence'.[85] Socialisation into the appropriate rationality and norms, whether by families, elders or education systems, is the essence of childhood, and socialisation proceeds as much by sanctions as by rewards. Thus punishment and childhood are usually (although not inevitably) inseparable. School punishment, specifically mentioned in both the CRC and the African Charter, can result not only in immediate pain, but also long term harm, and is often emotional as well as physical.

This economy of discipline is explicit for both adults and children. Paula Heinonen, studying urban marginalised children in Addis Ababa, writes that:

> I often ask both children and parents to tell me what they consider to be a child's bad act or behaviour. The automatic answer I get from parents is that a child needs to be controlled, disciplined and punished. A well brought up child is one that has been socially controlled and severely disciplined, meaning physically beaten.[86]

Some other recent Ethiopian ethnography has explored the ideas of misdemeanour and punishment held by children, showing that they have clear appreciation of the exact relationship between misdemeanour and sanction. A study of school-children in the Eastern town of Dire Dewa, explored the content of the Amharic word for punishment, '*Q'tat*', and found that it included a clearly delimited set of activities, some of which, such as 'pepper burning',[87] can result in long-term physical harm, others including additional elements of humiliation such as being tied up and left alone, as well as public beatings.[88] Children in other studies in Addis Ababa and in Nazareth, Ethiopia, were able to articulate what punishments fit which crimes, as well as the extent to which adults use their power over children appropriately.[89]

Despite knowing this economy of punishment, and not infrequently stating that it is appropriate, children do not always exercise power appropriately themselves when given the opportunity. Prolonged observation in school classrooms in Peru, which is a highly authoritarian society, showed me how brutal school monitors could be, once they were provided with epaulettes and a stick. Other children were regularly chastised by being beaten over the head, in view of the teachers, not always for infringements of rules but, like police with street children, apparently simply for being there. Even without the legitimate authority to exercise power over other children, informal, illegitimate power may be exercised in bullying behaviour, which has recently been the subject of increased research by Western social scientists.[90] Bullying, typical of the years of middle childhood, is often associated with school activities and may take the form of both physical and verbal aggression. Like torture it is difficult to define, because it is essentially experiential and there is no way in which the phenomenological experience of bullying can be used as a measure of its severity.[91] One important aspect that emerges from the research is the way in which adult attitudes to bullying frame children's experience of it. Reviewing a number of studies, Italian researchers found that both boys and girls were more likely to tell adults about direct (physical) bullying than about indirect (verbal) aggression.[92] Results of research with British Asian and caucasian children in the United Kingdom, show that many children regard teasing as bullying and lead the author to conclude that, although British adults may repeat the adage that 'Sticks and stones may hurt my bones but hard words never hurt me', children may not agree.[93]

Non-corporal Punishment

Teacher-directed punishment in schools can take advantage of sensitivity to verbal or symbolic aggression. What has been called the 'dark sarcasm' of classrooms[94] is part of the informal punishment teachers are able to inflict, often targeting a particular child. In the novel *Jeremy at Crale*, Hugh Walpole describes the arbitrary process by which the teacher Mr Parlow (who is presented as one of Jeremy's role models in the novel) selects a victim from among the new boys at the beginning of the school year.
'You're a bright-looking boy.' He fixed his large, round, child-like eyes upon Cumberledge. 'What's your name?'
'Please, sir, Cumberledge, sir.'
'Yes. I hope you're smarter than you look!'
A relieved laugh from the form at this. The fool for the term had been appointed.[95]
  Symbolic punishments can also enter the domain of explicit, even legitimate, teacher-directed discipline, particularly in the reinforcement of domi-

nant cultural forms in language usage. It is only recently that Celtic languages have been encouraged in schools in Scotland and Wales. Adults who are now middle-aged recall being mocked and even beaten if they used their mother tongue in schools, even in playgrounds. The confidence to use Scots Gaelic in public settings, for example, had to be recovered in the 1970s, when Gaelic/English bilingual education and media were introduced.[96] Similarly, in Wolof-speaking areas of Gambia, the language of education is English. Until recently, it was common to punish children who slipped into Wolof in the classroom by hanging a necklace of rubbish round their necks and encouraging other children to mock them. In the worst cases they would be forced to return home wearing the necklace, exposed both to shame in the streets and potential parental anger.[97] The sanction of shame can be powerful. In this case, offenders were taught the lifelong lesson that the language of their home, community and culture was, quite literally, rubbish.

This brings us to the consideration that it may be better to hurt physically than with words or through emotional means. Korbin writes that:

> Hawaiian parents prefer physical discipline to other measures because it is thought to be swift, quickly forgotten, and therefore less disruptive to the parent-child relationship than scolding or harsh words … . Hawaiian parents more frequently express concern that hitting a child too often or too hard will cause resentment rather than concern that the parent will physically harm the child. … Among rural Hawaiians, relatives do not hesitate to yell from one house to the next that a spanking has gone on long enough or is too severe for the child's misbehaviour. Children are quite open about calling for help more quickly and loudly than a spanking warrants as an effective strategy for disarming an angry parent.[98]

On Shame and Dignity

Shaming is perhaps the most typical non-physical punishment. Although it is common in most cultures it is not easy to define. Nor are the causes of shame universal. This is what I call the 'bare bum problem'. To hit the naked buttocks of a child who normally does not wear clothes, may hurt but not shame. To expose to an audience buttocks that are normally covered by trousers may be very shaming, or at least that may be the intention. On the other hand, having one's stripes exposed to peer review may also increase one's dignity in their sight, provided one bears the pain in silence.

Although shame seems to be a universal human emotion, it is not universally experienced in the same way or in response to the same factors. In one of the few psychological explorations of shame, Lewis claims that it is 'related to guilt, pride, and hubris, all of which require self-awareness'.[99] It follows that it will have different textures and mechanisms depending on whether self-awareness is oriented towards group membership or individual development[100] – in other words, paralleling the distinction made with respect to rights between 'universal' and African contexts.

The importance of group membership in the development of identity is not exclusive to Africa. One study of bullying among schoolchildren in Japan reports that a particularly potent form consists of individual children being shunned by their peers. The author comments that such isolation is not only shaming but also experienced by the victim as 'dehumanizing'; 'the isolated individual feels as if the central core of his or her being were degraded or lost'. Like excommunication in Roman Catholicism, or 'outlawing' in ancient Anglo-Saxon law, this is 'equivalent to a death sentence'. In Japan this is not only social death but also separation from humanity and has been reported to result in child suicides.[101]

Another discourse on shame exists within ethnographic accounts of Iberian and Latin American societies, in which it is explicitly related to, and contrasted with, the honour of adult males. In particular, male honour is secured by successfully and publicly protecting the sexual purity of females in his immediate family; mothers, wives, sisters and daughters. Being a man of honour entails maintaining the honour of the women in your own family, while asserting your own virility by threatening the purity of women under the protection of other men.[102] Most anthropological writings on purity seem to concur that cultural notions of honour and shame are implicated in constructions of sexuality and sexual morality. Yet, with respect to children, who are widely supposed (*pace* Freud) to be sexually innocent this brings into play a particular ambiguity and, perhaps, the implication that the honour, or dignity, of men, women and children have different social constructions.[103] For example, Fernand-Laurent, a former special rapporteur to the United Nations on sexual trafficking, suggests with respect to definitions of pornography that images published should not 'degrade women and shock children'. Codes of Practice should take 'account of all aspects of the fundamental principle of respect for human dignity and which safeguards in particular the dignity of women and the innocence of children'.[104] Perhaps, therefore, what is defined as 'dignity' in women (which might be equated with sexual purity defended by male honour) is paralleled by 'innocence' in children.

As already mentioned, both the CRC and the African Charter refer to the dignity of children in various places, without any form of definition. Fernand-Laurent points out that, 'in the first article of the Universal Declaration of Human Rights, the word 'dignity' comes before 'rights'. This means that human dignity is the foundation and justification for all the rights defined later in the same Declaration'.[105] As far as I understand it, there is no developed debate in law about what constitutes human dignity, let alone the dignity of a child. In other words, dignity is a touchstone the specific content of which is human rights, yet it is not specifically defined. International children's rights commentator Melton claims that, besides being mentioned seven times in the CRC, the idea that children have dignity as members of the human community 'permeates the document'.[106] However, he seems to imply that this is an indication that the CRC is a means by which children can be accorded full respect in the same way as adults, by being regarded as human beings rather than human becomings, and does not amount to a distinctive construction of child dignity.[107]

Legal constructions of dignity, however, may not be the same as social or cultural constructions. In his description of Asemo as a person, for example, Read specifically used the word 'dignified'.[108] Moreover, in the final episode of the initiation in Susuroka, the final ceremonies in which their manhood is accepted by the community, the initiates, weighed down by enormous headdresses, enter the village in procession behind older men. After being welcomed into the village with great clamour, the street turns quiet as they begin to dance:

> 'They moved unsteadily under ungainly decorations, and I failed to see the splendid stirring change that had been apparent to their elders' eyes. But dignity touched them when they began to dance, a slow measure based on the assertive stepping of the men but held to a restrained, promenading pace by the weight they carried on their heads'.[109]

Nevertheless, it could be argued that this is the dignity of adult males, which is regarded as being worth experiencing the pain of initiation.

There is no developed discourse on dignity, child or adult, male or female. One is forced to examine isolated discussions in the literature. In the case of Senegambia according to Sylla, a Wolof (man) can sacrifice anything except his dignity. Although Sylla makes no reference to the Latin complex of honour and shame, there appear to be many parallels. Dignity seems to be encompassed by two words: *full* meaning '*dignite apparante*' – outward dignity, which is better to have than beauty (*full gënup taar*) – and *fayda*, which is superior to full and means something akin to honour, being concerned with dignified action.[110] Sylla adds that 'For the Wolof a man's dignity has no price, to safeguard his honour without which life would not be worth living, he is always ready to fight'.[111]

This dignity, having to do with conduct, is thus dignity in the sight of others (and thus susceptible to loss through dishonour and shame). It has nothing to do with social position, but according to Sylla is an innate quality – some people have it others not – which is interesting in view of the intricately stratified nature of Wolof society.[112] Thus, when I asked Wolof-speaking informants how they would translate the idea of the instrinsic dignity of a human being, in the sense in which it is used in human rights documents such as the CRC and African Charter, which is a quality of all people including children, they told me that exact translation would be impossible. Wolof dignity is more contextual than inherent.

Wolof children, on the other hand, are instructed about the nature of *full* and *fayda*, through the medium of stories and proverbs, in many of which the main protagonists are Bouki the hyena and Leuck the hare.[113] In one of these, recounted by Sylla, the animals were in the process of forming a club. In order to develop solidarity among members of the club, each animal had to tell the others of one thing that they could not tolerate. The panther said that he could not stand anyone looking into his eyes, the lion that he hated to see the strong abuse the weak, the elephant that he could not bear to be disturbed when he was resting, the serpent that he was most annoyed when his tail was tweaked, and so on. When it came to Bouki the hyena, however, he said that nothing annoyed him and everything could be permitted. Thus saying, he looked the panther in the eyes. Desperately affronted the panther leapt on the hyena. This enraged the lion, who attacked the panther. The noise woke the elephant. He rushed about in a rage, accidentally treading on the tail of the serpent, who immediately bit him. Thus the animals' club fell apart, thanks to the hyena, who could not be vexed because, unlike the other animals, he had no dignity to defend. The moral is very clear. This kind of dignity (honour) is the very fabric of society.

Nevertheless, for the symbolic punishment of having to wear a necklace of rubbish to be effective, children must have some kind of honour or dignity, which can be breached in the sight of both children and adults. The success of this kind of social mechanism of cultural aggression could be lifelong shame and a false sense of the lack of worth/inauthenticity of one's own culture. It is worth emphasising that other children are encouraged to join in the mockery, meaning that the lesson is learned by more than the unfortunate who slipped out a word of Wolof. Not only does the culprit suffer from being unable to turn for support to his own kind (becoming temporarily an outlaw from the peer group) but also the other children are forced into turning against and betraying both their companion and their cultural selves.

In Lieu of Conclusion

I have argued that anthropological perspectives on conceptualizations of social values that are different from dominant Western systems of thought can broaden the scope of discussions about cultural relativity in the field of international human rights. Ethnographic anecdotes should not be used as simple descriptions of different customs, but employed to understand and respect the moral systems of which these customs are manifestations. An examination of the cultural meanings of the terms used in international human rights documents with respect to torture and punishment seems to indicate that discussions on the universal implementation of Article 37 of the CRC may not be able to proceed without first developing discourses on some underlying basic terms, such as shame and dignity. With respect to children's rights, there appears to be a distinction to be made between respecting children's dignity as human beings and understanding the interpretations children have of what constitutes, cruel, inhuman, or degrading treatment, torture and punishment. Whatever adults may feel about the idea of physical pain inflicted on children, this may not be the prime definitional factor for children themselves. Children's dignity is fragile, their self-awareness (whether based in group or individual identity) is in the process of development. Thus punishments and maltreatments that infringe that dignity may be worse than physical pain, not only at the time they are inflicted but also with respect to their long-term effects.

Acknowledgements

Thanks are due to Vu Ngoc Binh, Jo Boyden, Tsegaye Chernet, Victoria Ebin, Gary Englebert, David Good, Richard Fentiman, Shashu Araya Nacid, Susan Marks, Brian Milne, Ebrima Sall and Belay Zeleke for additional materials and shared thoughts while I was working on this article.

Notes

1   D.H. Lawrence, *Fantasia of the Unconscious*, Chapter 4.
2   The perspective from which this paper is written is social anthropology, which can be distinguished from North American 'cultural anthropology', by having no recourse to either archeological or biological arguments. This is important with respect to the way in which the term 'culture' is used. Here, the term is used to indicate those activities of specific groups of humans that are not expressions of the biological species homo sapiens, including ideas, practices, material and symbolic artefacts, and, of course, laws.
3   Two interesting examples are An-Na'im, A.A. (1992) (ed.), *Human Rights in Cross-Cultural Perspectives*, Philadelphia, University of Pennsylvania Press, and An-Na'im and Deng (1990) (eds), *Human Rights in Africa*, Washington: The Brookings Institute.
4   Wilson (1970), 'A sociologist's introduction', in Wilson (ed.), *Rationality*, London, Blackwell, xiii.
5   MacIntyre (1970), 'The idea of a social science' in Wilson (ed.), *op. cit.*

6 Reynolds (1989), 'Children of tribulation: the need to heal and the means to heal war trauma', paper presented at the Fourth International Workshop on the Ethnography of Childhood, 23–26 July, Victoria Falls, Zimbabwe. This point has also been made by Maurice Eisenbruch (1991), From post-traumatic stress to cultural bereavement: diagnoses of the South Asian refugees, unpublished paper, University of Melbourne Medical School, in his work with Vietnamese refugee children in Australia.

7 The Childwatch International Indicators for Children's Rights Project is described in Ennew and Miljeteig (1996), 'Indicators for Children's Rights: Progress Report on a Project', *International Journal of Children's Rights*, **4**, 213.

8 See for example, Boyden, 'Childhood and the policy-makers: a comparative perspective on the globalization of childhood', in James and Prout, (eds), *Constructing and Reconstructing Childhood*, Brighton, Falmer Press, 184.

9 Even the translation into European languages other than English can result in this change of meaning. For example, the official Spanish translation 'el interes superior del niño' cannot be understood in the same way as 'the best interests of the child', and likewise turns the issue from legal to moral discourse. See Ennew, 1998 forthcoming, 'Manual para la recopilación y analisis de la información sobre los derechos de la infancia, San José de Costa Rica', Instituto Interamericano de Derechos Humanos.

10 Alston (1994), 'The Best Interests of the Child: Reconciling Culture and Human Rights', Clarendon Press.

11 An-Na'im (1992), 'Taking a cross-cultural approach to defining international standards of human rights: the meaning of cruel, inhuman or degrading treatment or punishment', in An-Na'im (ed.), *Human Rights in Cross-Cultural Perspective: A Quest for Consensus*, Philadelphia, University of Pennsylvania Press, 19–43, 24.

12 Alston *op. cit.*, 20.

13 Ibid., 27.

14 See for example Goody (1970), 'Kinship fostering in Gonja: deprivation or advantage?' in, Mayer, (ed.), 'Socialization: the Approach from Social Anthropology', London, Tavistock, 51.

15 Reproduced in Van Bueren, *International Documents*, 2nd edition, Kluwer, 1997.

16 Read (1966), *High Valley*, 95, 102.

17 Ibid., 124.

18 Ibid., 127.

19 Ibid., 131.

20 Ibid., 133.

21 Ibid., 133–4.

22 Bohannan (1957), *Justice and Judgement among the Tiv*, Oxford, Oxford University Press.

23 An example would be Max Gluckman's question as to why some cultures have an overall concept of debt, whereas others distinguish between tort and contract. Gluckman (1971), *Politics. Law and Ritual in Tribal Society*, Basil Blackwell.

24 Bohannan (1969), 'Ethnography and comparison', in Nader, (ed.), *Law in Culture and Society*, Aldine, 407.

25 Ibid., 141.

26 Ibid., 104.

27 Korbin (1987), 'Child Maltreatment in cross-cultural perspective: Vulnerable children and circumstances', in Gelles, R.J and Lancaster, (eds), *Child Abuse and Neglect: Biosocial Dimensions*, New York, Aldine de Gruyter, 31–56, 34.

28 Ibid.

29 Ibid., 35.

30 Ibid.
31 An-Na'im (1992), Toward a cross-cultural approach to defining international stand-ards of human rights: the meaning of inhuman or degrading treatment or punishment, in An-Na'im, A.A. (ed.), *Human Rights in Cross-cultural Perspective: A Quest for Consensus*, Philadelphia, University of Pennsylvania Press, 19–43, 20.
32 Ibid., 21.
33 Howard, 'Dignity, Community and Human Rights', in An-Na'im (1990) (ed.), *Human Rights in Cross-cultural Perspective*, Philadelphia, University of Pennsylvania Press, 81–102.
34 This observation, originally made by Emile Durkheim, has been elaborated in the past decade in the work of Jens Qvortrup, see for example, Qvortrup, *Childhood Matters: an Introduction*, in Qvortrup, Bardy, Sgritta, and Wintersberger (1994) (eds.), Alder-shot, Brookfield, USA, Hong Kong, Singapore and Sydney, Avebury, 1–24, 4.
35 Statement made to the Committee on the Rights of the Child, 13.11.95, Geneva.
36 Laye (1966), *L'enfant noir*, Cambridge, Cambridge University Press, 106.
37 Ibid., 116–7. 'J'avais peur, affreusement peur, mais je portais toute mon attention a n'en rien témoigner: tous ces hommes devant nous, qui observaient ne devaient pas s'apercevoir de ma peur ... ce n'était pas l'heure de perdre la face!'
38 Ibid., 117 'l'opérateur m'a fait passer d'un état a l'autre à une rapidité que je ne puis pas exprimer'.
39 Ibid., 118 & 119 'nous avions perdu trop de sang, vu trop de sang'.
40 Ibid., 119.
41 Langness (1981), 'Child abuse and cultural values: The case of New Guinea', in Korbin (ed.), *Child Abuse and Neglect Cross-Cultural Perspectives*, Berkley, Univer-sity of California Press, 13–14.
42 Statement made to CRC, 13.11.95, Geneva.
43 For these insights I am indebted to Gary Engleberg and his Wolof language teachers at Africa Consultants International, Dakar.
44 Foucault (1979), *Discipline and Punish*, 104.
45 Howard (1882), 29. See also Mary Douglas, *Natural Symbols*.
46 Ibid.
47 Foucault, *op. cit.*, 11.
48 Ibid., 29.
49 OAU, Report on the Inter-Governmental Expert Group Meeting on the Draft African Charter on the Rights and Welfare of the Child, 17-21 April, 1990, Addis Ababa.
50 Ibid.
51 Derrick, 27.
52 Preamble, Article 46.
53 Preamble, Article 46.
54 Articles 11 & 31.
55 Article 31.
56 Arts 1993 The international protection of children's rights in Africa: the 1990 OAU Charter on the Rights and Welfare of the Child in, *African Journal of International and Comparative* Law, **5**, pp. 139–161, 148.
57 OAU *op. cit.*
58 Ibid., 166
59 An-Na'im 1986, *op. cit.* at 43.
60 Thompson (1992), 433.
61 Ibid.
62 Article 24(3).

63 Article 21.
64 Reproduced in Van Bueren, *International Documents*, ibid.
65 For a further discussion of this point see Ennew (1996), *Africa Insight*, November/December.
66 Article 37.
67 Article 39.
68 Article 17a.
69 Article 17(1) 'right to special treatment in a manner consistent with the child's sense of dignity and worth and which reinforces the child's respect for human rights and fundamental freedoms of others'.
    Article 40(1) 'right of every child alleged as, accused of, or recognised as having infringed the penal law to be treated in a manner consistent with the promotion of the child's sense of dignity and worth, which reinforces the child's respect for human rights and fundamental freedoms of others and takes into account the child's age ...'
70 Foucault, *op. cit.*, 178.
71 Veale and Adefrisew (1993), *Study on Street Children in Four Selected Towns of Ethiopia*, Addis Ababa, Ministry of Labour and Social Affairs, UNICEF Ethiopia, University College Cork Ireland, 78–9.
72 See OMCT (1996), *Rights of the Child in Senegal*, Geneva.
73 CRC/C/3/Add.3. 16 December 1992, 21.
74 Ibid., 46.
75 Clifton (1937), *Tangled Justice: Some Reasons for a Change of Policy in Africa*, London: Macmillan & Co. Ltd., 53.
76 CRC/C/3/Add.12, 22 January, 1993, 24.
77 Ibid., 69–70.
78 This document is unpaginated.
79 Anderson and Payne (1994), 378.
80 Ibid.
81 Ibid., 382.
82 Essay by Abas Bargicho, collected and translated from the Amharic original by Belay Zeleke of the Ethiopian chapter of ANPPCAN.
83 Article 28(2) 'States Parties shall take all appropriate measures to ensure that school discipline is administered in a manner consistent with the child's human dignity and in conformity with the present Convention.'
    Article 11(5) 'States Parties to the present Charter shall take all appropriate measures to ensure that a child who is subjected to school or parental discipline shall be treated with humanity and with respect for the inherent dignity of the child and in conformity with the present Charter.' (AC 11 (5)).
84 Article 20(1c).
85 Foucault, *op. cit.*, 170.
86 Heinonen (1996), Some Aspects of Child Rearing Practices in the Urban Setting of Addis Ababa, Unpublished Background document for Radda Barnen Ethiopia, 28.
87 Pepper burning, which I have heard mentioned in African and some Asian countries, consists of holding a child upside-down with his face close to the fumes from burning chili peppers (it is mentioned as being more common for boys than girls). Children report not only choking and fear from the fumes but also vomiting and subsequent respiratory problems.
88 Chernet (1995).
89 Zeleke (1995); Nacid (1995).
90 Olwen's *Aggression in the Schools: Bullies and Whipping Boys*, Washington, DC,

Hemisphere, Wiley, seminal study in Scandinavia (1978), defined a field that now includes research in most industrialized countries.

91   Boulton (1995), 'Patterns of Bully/Victim Problems in Mixed Race Groups of Children', *Social Development*, **4**(3), 277–293, 291.

92   Genta, Menesini, Fonzi, Costabile, and Smith, 'Bullies and Victims in Schools in Central and Southern Italy', *European Journal of Psychology of Education*, **IX** (1), 97–110, 97 et seq.

93   Boulton, *op. cit.*, 290.

94   This phrase appears in the rock group Pink Floyd's album *The Wall*, which deals with the brutality of socialisation.

95   Walpole (1941), *The Jeremy Stories,* London, Macmillan & Co. Ltd., 588.

96   Ennew (1980), *The Western Isles Today,* Cambridge, Cambridge University Press, 75.

97   Personal Communication, Ebrima Sall.

98   Korbin, *op. cit.* 36.

99   Lewis (1992), *Shame: The Exposed Self,* New York, Toronto, The Free Press; Oxford Singapore, Sydney, Maxwell Macmillan International, 2.

100   Ibid., 198–204.

101   Crystal (1994), 251.

102   See for example Peristiany (1966), *Honour and Shame: The Values of Mediterranean Society*, London, Peristiany, and Pitt-Rivers (1992), *Honour and Grace in Anthropology,* Cambridge, Cambridge University Press, as well as the papers in Pescatello (1978).

103   For a fuller discussion of this point see Ennew, Gopal, Heeran and Montgomery (1996), *Children and Prostitution: How Can We Measure and Monitor the Commercial Sexual Exploitation of Children?*, Cambridge, Centre for Family Research and Oslo, Childwatch International, 47–52.

104   Fernand-Laurent, the mass media and sexual exploitation, in *Children Worldwide,* **19** (2), 35–6, 36.

105   Ibid.

106   Melton (1991), 344.

107   Ibid., 345, 348.

108   Read, *op. cit.*, 95.

109   Ibid., 140.

110   Ibid., 90.

111   'Pour le wolof, la dignité de l'homme n'a pas de prix, pour sauvegarder l'honourabilité sans laquelle la vie ne vaut pas la peine d'être vétre, il est toujours prêt á se battre'.

112   Diop, 1981, *La societé wolof: tradition et changement: les systémes d'inegalité et de domination*, Paris, Éditions Karthala.

113   See for example, Gamble (1980) (ed.), *Wolof Stories from Senegambia*, with 1983 supplement, San Francisco (MSS). In this edition of some 149 stories, Bouki and Leuck are by far the most frequently occurring characters, the nearest competitor being Lion (161–2). The Hyena's stupidity and Hare's cleverness serve as constant motifs in fables that reiterate basic social values and proper conduct. Sylla (*op. cit.*, 111) claims that safeguarding dignity is one of the more common themes. Nevertheless, the collection made by Gamble consists entirely of versions of the stories written down in French or English, thus it is not possible to tell to what extent the terms *full* and *fayda* appear in oral versions.

2 The Ill-treatment of Children – Some Developmental Considerations

Martin Richards

Introduction

At first glance one might imagine a straightforward model for understanding the reactions of children to ill-treatment – the younger the more vulnerable. Such an approach would see children as weak, diminutive, immature and powerless and relate these characteristics to age or at least a developmental stage. However, things are rather more complex than this and, in order to understand how children react to ill-treatment, we need an adequate model of the processes of physical and social development and of children as social actors in a social world. To begin to sketch this, it is perhaps useful to start with a glance at our evolutionary history.

Compared with our primate ancestors, human development is a very long drawn out process. Our evolution has been marked by an extension of infancy and childhood and a delay in the achievement of physical and sexual maturity. The generally accepted explanation of this evolutionary trend is that it is associated with the development of language, culture and a more complex social life. Increasing the period of time when our bodies and brains are both immature and plastic promotes learning and, as psychologists have suggested, allows the reinvention of culture in each generation. The physical immaturity of childhood leads to continuing close social relationships with parents and other family members which provide highly effective social contexts within which to learn the human attributes of language, thought, self consciousness and the fundamentals of social understanding, conduct and relationships.[1] As social and physical skills advance, the delay of sexual maturity keeps the child within the family group where

35

the complexities of their social world, kinship and social organisation as well as the technical skills of everyday living are learnt through a continuing apprenticeship. Most human generations have been spent as hunter-gatherers. Hunter-gatherer social groups are, and probably always were, small, with widely spaced births so that children have a great deal of contact with adults as they go about their daily life. The slow coming of agriculture a mere 10,000 years ago brought the possibility of the accumulation of resources and so their unequal division within society. Working the land needed more hands and larger families, and populations grew. The final step to our industrialised world came with growth of urbanization and transport creating a much more complex social and technical world requiring even more time for learning. Education became more formalized and much of it moved from the family to the community and into specialized institutions. The achievement of independent adulthood has been further delayed by these developments, so that today we have a long drawn out process, with many different milestones along the way, which marks the transition from childhood to adulthood.[2]

The process by which babies become adults is not one of passive socialization. Infants are not simply shaped and moulded by the world they are born into but take an active role in their own development. They perceive their world through their processes of conceptualization and understanding and actively reach out to it to explore and gain what they want, or, conversely, to try and avoid what they find unpleasant. They are actors, not simply reactors. Consider two incidents involving children and break-ins at their homes.

As reported recently in the English newspapers, two intruders intent on burglary, entered a house and found a four-year-old boy. They engaged the boy in conversation and asked him where his parents kept money and other items of value. Apparently pleased to be helpful, the boy showed them. The thieves departed with the valuables leaving a rather proud child keen to tell his parents of the service he had given to the two strangers.

Another break-in. A 13-year-old girl has a day off school because she is unwell. All the other members of the household have gone out to work and school leaving her dozing in bed. A young man breaks into the house, believing it to be empty. He moves quietly from room to room collecting items to take. He enters the girl's bedroom, she wakes and sees him standing over her bed. She is terrified, he is surprised. He tells her to keep quiet, turns and leaves the house. She perceives the incident as a violation and a traumatic sexual threat. For months afterwards she has nightmares and other severe psychological symptoms.

In short, expectations, perceptions and the social context are everything in assessing the consequences of experiences in childhood.

In considering the abuse of children, Morrow[3] provides a valuable categorization of varieties of abuse which helps us to place it in a cultural context and relate it to developmental processes of children. She proposes three categories and I will discuss each in turn.

Cultural Practices that are Viewed as Abusive or Neglectful by Other Cultures, But Not by the Culture in Question

In many cultures children are subjected to body mutilation and other stressful and/or painful rituals. Sometimes these take place in infancy or may mark changes in status later in childhood or at the transition to adulthood. These have been much studied by anthropologists who see them in symbolic terms marking changes in status and maintaining social boundaries.[4] Clitoridectomy and circumcision are examples of such rituals. Children may find these frightening and painful but are likely to regard them as part of taken for granted daily life. Because they are taken for granted and part of social life such procedures may be experienced as much less traumatic than a cultural outsider might suppose. In the context of the societies which perform these rituals, they are not simply accepted, but are seen as an essential part of growing up and becoming an adult person. Outsiders who are critical of such rituals are likely to be seen by those from within as not understanding their importance and significance, or more generally as attacking the culture itself. Acknowledging the cultural or religious significance of such rituals leads to a situation in many societies where the same act of surgery in one context is seen as an acceptable, if not desirable, social ceremony and in others as an incomprehensible act of criminal abuse.

One can also find examples where such rituals 'escape' from their cultural or religious context. In Britain, in the early decades of this century male circumcision in the first days after birth became common practice among middle-class families outside the Jewish community. The practice was justified on a number of health grounds. However, this view was challenged in the 1940s by a prominent paediatrician.[5] He argued that the practice was painful and stressful (it was carried out without anaesthetics) and except in unusual cases of deformity, it was without health benefits. In rare cases of complication it could have very serious or even fatal consequences for babies. In the light of these arguments the practice disappeared rather quickly and now only persists in religious contexts in Britain.

In the United States the situation is rather different. Despite the medical evidence and pressure groups who campaign against it for instance No Circ, it persists in the medical context.[6] The reason for this is probably a combination of a much larger (than in Britain) religious group who continue the practice and so give it validity and a system of payment for medical care based on items of service.

Idiosyncratic Departure from What is Considered Acceptable Behaviour Within a Culture

By definition, actions that within a particular culture or society are seen as ill treatment or abusive, fall into this category. They are punishable by law and are usually attributed to the individual action of a bad, mad or an insufficiently socialized perpetrator. But societies vary widely in the actions that are defined in this way, as might be illustrated by the physical punishment of children.

Because we are dealing with social actions whose meaning and consequences will vary between contexts, it is often very difficult to provide clear legal (or other) definitions of such actions. Sexual abuse of children is a good example. Notions of what is sexual differs between adults and children, as well as on a more individual and context basis. While at the two ends of a spectrum we may fairly confidently distinguish childhood games and sexual abuse, there is a wide area for dispute in the middle. Difficulties of definition and social meaning, together with age, gender, and individual difference all work together to produce a very unclear pattern linking childhood events and later difficulties.[7]

Societally Induced Harm to Children Beyond the Control of Individual Parents and Caretakers

This very broad category ranges from ill-advised economic policies that lead to poverty, through changes in climate or international trade that may cause famine, to civil unrest, war and major forced movements of populations.

In recent years increasing attention has been paid to the effects of warfare on children. In 1995 the main focus of UNICEF's report, *The State of the World's Children*, was warfare. UNICEF estimate that in the last decade two million children have been killed in wars, four to five million disabled, 12 million left homeless and one million left without parents.[8] After a long period of neglect there are an increasing number of psychological studies of effects of warfare and conflict on children.[9] Studies in this area, once again, emphasize the importance of social context. For example, a study of Palestinian children in the West Bank in the Intifada demonstrated that the degree of exposure to physical risk and arrest was related to the children's level of psychological difficulties.[10] Boys were more vulnerable than girls.

This seems in part to be the result of changes in family and social structures during the Intifada which have provided new roles and increased status for women and girls. Many women's groups have emerged which are affiliated to the nationalist organizations. In contrast boys, in general, have had only very irregular schooling and have moved beyond parental control finding powerful leadership roles outside the traditional lines of adult authority which may make their reintegration into families and adult roles very difficult. This process is made more difficult as more men have been killed, jailed, tortured or gone into hiding.

Discussion and Conclusions

In situations of abuse of individual children or even more strikingly, when children are caught up in warfare, analysis by psychologists, anthropologists and other social scientists may be seen at best a distraction, and at worst, a gross misuse of resources. However, we need to understand the world, including that of neglect, ill-treatment and torture, from the perspective of children. As I have tried to discuss, children are social actors, not simply reactors to events that may befall them. Without such an understanding we will not fully comprehend which situations are most damaging to children nor how we may best offer support, healing and comfort.

But as Van Bueren outlines in her introduction, legislation and intervention are greatly complicated by the twin and connected issues of cultural relativism and developmental changes in children as they grow up.[11] Consider once again, the issues of circumcision and genital mutilation. From a Western Europe perspective, and in the face of the evidence of pain, medical complications and disability, the various procedures that are collectively known as female circumcision are more or less universally condemned and have been made illegal in many countries.[12] However, this does not prevent some parents in communities in Britain where the practice is traditional believing that it is in the best interests of their daughters and they go to considerable lengths and expense in defying the law. We know little about how the daughters may feel about it, but in so far as they accept the perspective and norms of their own culture, it is likely that they will see it in much the same way as their parents. That will not abolish the pain or reduce the incidence of medical complications, but it may help to normalize the experience of the operation and its later consequences. The ritual aspects of the procedures and their changed bodies are part of the process of creating their identity in their own community. But for most of us we do not stretch our cultural relativism to include these practices and we strive through education (indoctrination?) and regulation to change the cultural beliefs and practices.

Male circumcision is viewed rather differently and I do not wish to claim that its physical and medical consequences are on a par with the female procedures. Nevertheless it is a mutilation carried out for ritual or cosmetic reasons which can lead in rare cases to very serious complications and does not have well-founded medical benefits.[13] Taking a moderate cultural relativist's position one could offer a justification for the procedure in the religious context by saying it is a relatively minor procedure. When it is done in the neonatal period the evidence of stress only persists for a matter of days[14] and, provided there are no complications, serious blood loss or infection, there is no evidence of long-term difficulties – which is not to say that some men deeply resent having had the procedure done and believe themselves to be sexually disadvantaged by it, as can be seen in the accounts published in the literature produced by the groups who campaign against it.[15] It is generally carried out without anaesthetic but, so it may be said, are other minor surgical procedures carried out on young infants. In cultures where the procedure is carried out later in childhood or adolescence it is a part of public rituals and celebrations which give it a context and meaning for the child or young person. I am sure it still hurts, but the pain is part of a culturally sanctioned and supported social process.

Where newborn circumcision is common outside any religious context, as is the case in the USA, the issues would seem to be rather different. Parents consent to it, but not children. Medical staff often will tell parents they believe it is medically desirable and in some communities it has become a kind of cosmetic norm. But we may contrast this with the response in other countries, for instance Britain, where clinicians would refuse to carry out the procedure except in cases where, in their view, an abnormality makes it medically necessary. We might also point out that in Britain consenting adults who have chosen to indulge in mutual genital mutilation have been prosecuted.[16]

Beside the many cruel, inhumane and degrading practices children suffer, male circumcision, even when it is carried out for no better reason than cosmetic or medical tradition, is, at most, a relatively minor violation, and I would not wish attention paid to it to distract from very much more serious abuses. However, I would suggest that a careful and dispassionate analysis of this common practice in the many contexts and situations where it occurs may help to clarify issues and so aid our attempt to protect children from all abuses.

Notes

1 See Durkin (1995), *Developmental Social Psychology. From Infancy to Old Age*, Cambridge, Mass, Blackwell Publishers Inc.
2 Morrow and Richards (1996), *Transitions to Adulthood: A Family Matter?*, York, Joseph Rowntree Trust.
3 Morrow (1992), *Are there any universals in child abuse? An anthropological approach.* Symposium on Societies and Child Protection. Association for Child Psychology and Psychiatry, European Conference, York, September 1992.
4 La Fontaine (1985), *Initiation, Ritual Drama and Secret Knowledge Across the World*, Harmondsworth, Penguin.
5 Gairdner (1949), 'The fate of the foreskin', *Brit.Med.J.* **2**, 1433–7.
6 Richards, Bernal, and Brackbill (1976), 'Early behavioural differences: gender or circumcision?', *Developmental Psychobiology*, **9**, 89–95.
7 Kendall-Tackett, Meyer Williams and Finkelhor (1993), 'Impact of sexual abuse on children: a review and synthesis of recent empirical studies', *Psychol.Bull.*, **113**, 164–80.
8 'Children and Conflict' (1996), *Children First*, Issue 31.
9 Ladd, and Cairns (1996) 'Children: ethnic and political violence', *Child Development*, **67**, 14–18.
10 Garbarino and Kostelny (1996) 'The effects of political violence on Palestinian children's behaviour problems: a risk accumulation model', *Child Development*, **67**, 33–45.
11 See above Van Bueren, Introduction.
12 The Prohibition of Female Circumcision Act 1985 in Britain. There have been no prosecutions under this Act as yet but a doctor was brought before the General Medical Council in 1993 charged with performing female circumcision and he was struck off. It is now illegal for 191 States Parties to the Convention on the Rights of the Child to allow female circumcisions. See Van Bueren (1995), *The International Law on the Rights of the Child*, Kluwer, 307.
13 Here I am excluding the relatively rare cases where abnormality may justify the procedure on medical grounds.
14 Gunnar, Malone, Vance and Firsch (1985), 'Coping with aversive stimulation in the neonatal period: quiet sleep and plasma contisol levels during recovery from circumcision', *Child Development*, **56**, 824–34.
15 In the literature produced by groups such as No Circ who campaign against it.
16 *R* v *Brown*; *R* v *Lucas*; *R* v *Jaggard*; *R* v *Laskey*; *R* v *Carter* [1994] 1 AC 212.

3   Activism, Politics and the Punishment of Children

Pamela Reynolds

'Every period in history has its own punishments, and ours has multiple'[1]

Political Activism Among the Young

In addressing the matter of children's entitlements and vulnerabilities I shall draw on the experiences over the last 20 years of political activism among the young in South Africa. The question of agency and the range of subjectivities are of particular concern to me in this chapter.

One indication of the numbers of young people who were drawn into political engagement in standing against the apartheid regime can be found in figures on detentions. No detailed investigation of actual numbers of children held in police custody has yet been done. There is, as yet, no record of the full extent of state oppression as experienced by the young. Not knowing makes it easier to revise history. At the height of the oppression between 1985 and 1986, punishment of the young in police cells, in prisons and in a variety of other places such as Security Branch headquarters, both authorized and unauthorized, was not different from the punishment meted out to adults. Indeed, some atrocities like rape were probably experienced more frequently by the young.

All sorts of tortures, including false executions, were experienced.

All sorts of degradations were imposed – like being denied the right to change clothes for three months.

All sorts of deprivations – of food, exercise, visits, medical care, access to lawyers, contact with families, contact with anyone – were enforced

All sorts of threats to self, kin, loved ones, colleagues were delivered.

All sorts of efforts were made to turn the detainees into informers.

Age softened nothing.

There was widespread suffering among the young yet among those formally committed to political activism there was a widespread subscription to a particular stance with regard to pain. It was held that one suffered for the cause; that pain and suffering were to be anticipated along with political engagement; that those who had undergone any form of political induction would prepare to handle extreme pain; that it was assumed that others suffered more than oneself; and that pain was not a topic for discussion except where actual attention, physical or psychological, was required. For example, I recently asked a student of mine why she was not going to testify to the Truth and Reconciliation Commission about her experiences during the years of apartheid. She had been active politically for many years in a very dangerous area and had suffered imprisonment, rape, police harassment, threats, and had been forced into exile, yet she said, 'I have not been through much.' The assumption of stoicism in the face of suffering was widely ascribed to.

The consequences may have been deleterious. A closure of access to sharing such experiences could exacerbate difficulties in handling terror, fear and traumatic after-effects. For some, there were other means of handling pain. But not for all. Secrecy was essential as political movements were banned and they had to use clandestine and revolutionary tactics. Secrecy was also vital because the State Security Forces used informers or spies at all levels. Violence and disinformation were used to turn people against members of their own groups. In the statement to the Truth and Reconciliation Commission made in August 1996, the African National Congress (ANC) details some of the actions of state agents who were infiltrated into the liberation movement. In attempting to contain the damage and trace the networks among agents, the ANC admits that 'excesses did occur' and, to the extent that some detainees were maltreated, they apologise for the violation of human rights 'without qualification'.[2]

In September 1996, Eugene de Kock, former hit squad commander, gave testimony in mitigation of sentence for 89 crimes, including six counts of murder. Philip van Niekerk reports in *The Sunday Independent*,[3]

Many security policemen such as De Kock and Jac Buchner had their first lessons in warfare when South African police were seconded to fight alongside the Rhodesians, lessons they never forgot.

'Why keep to the Queensbury rules and fight one boxer when you can kick them in the balls and kill three?' was De Kock's pithy summation of the wit and wisdom that he carried with him from Zimbabwe.

He was a specialist. His troops were black: the use of askaris [informers], turned guerrillas, to perform the most brutal atrocities was a technique borrowed from the Rhodesian war.

It was done with Koevoet in Namibia, where De Kock commanded black troops, many of them former Angolans from the disbanded FNLA, against the movements fighting to liberate black people. The footsoldiers of Vlakplaas's C-10 units were former guerrillas – men who, De Kock pointed out with extreme clarity, 'had fought their hearts out but had no right to vote'. Renamo and Inkatha's Caprivi trainees were contras cut from the same mould.

There was reason to keep secrets, to trust few, to anticipate horrific treatment. In the words of the poet, Sandile Dikeni,[4]

they feared death
but waved it welcome
when it taunted
demanded
induced betrayals
in the terror of the jails

A major consequence both of the received attitudes toward pain and of the need for secrecy was that children and youth took it upon themselves to keep from their families as much information as they possibly could. In not allowing family members, especially parents, to know what was happening, they intended to protect them. There seems to be confirmation of this in the testimonies before the Truth and Reconciliation Commission from mothers who recount the disappearance or death of their children and who often seem to know very little about their activities. Many of the young were, of course, caught in the cross-fire of conflict or detained and tortured despite having played little or no part in political confrontations.

The parents, especially the mothers, of the people whom I interviewed about their activism,[5] tried to watch their children closely and learn as much as they could: they traced their children when they were abducted or arrested and they fought for the rights to see them in prison, take them food, do their washing and inspect their clothes for signs of torture or ill-health, and they tried to smuggle messages to them. Hylton White has documented mothers' actions and how they were drawn into politics by their actions.[6]

In not sharing, children closed avenues of relief in giving expression to their experiences. Many stood against the wishes of their families in becoming embroiled in politics. They knew that their activities would bring the invasive forces of the state into the privacy of their homes and with it, in all likelihood, real danger and awful harassment.

I want to stress that political involvement for many of the young was not lightly undertaken, at least after early engagements in school boycotts and street battles. Profoundly serious political and moral decisions in relation to their own safety and ambitions, as well as the safety and interests of their families, were made. For many, there was subsequent suffering and long terms of imprisonment, and even these did not cause them to desist. Even after long terms in prison, many of the young again committed themselves to dangerous political activities.

State interference in family life often undermined the strength of relations among kin. One young woman tells of her sorrow when members of the Security Forces humiliated her father in front of his children and how he never resumed his former status in their eyes.[7]

We do not yet have a clear idea of how many young people died, were abducted, were detained, were harmed beyond healthy repair, or were shaken to the roots of their being by the forces of the state. There were many ruses used to obscure the truth, including disappearance, recording political detentions as criminal offences, failure to record arrests, use of farm prisons, refusal to acknowledge harm done, and so on. Nevertheless, there is a lot on record of both the extent and the nature of damage done to children. The records document death, disappearance, rape, torture, poisoning, solitary confinement (sometimes for years), humiliation and degradation in police cells and prisons. They also document the inadequacy of diets and ablution facilities and refusals to allow changes of clothes or exercise. They record the frequent failure of members of the medical and legal professions to care for the young. There is too, evidence of the sense of failure and shame some felt at being unable to withstand interrogation and/or torture and of their fear in the face of pressure to become sell-outs. And some did make revelations about colleagues under interrogation, and some did become informers for the state. There have been very sad testimonies before the Truth and Reconciliation Commission from some who seek to refute allegations that they betrayed others or had become askari (informers), and from some who admit to accusations but call for an understanding of the contexts in which they were placed and for a re-instatement of their dignity in the eyes of their communities. There are testimonies, too, that show the young as having been both victims and perpetrators of violence. Many of the young suffered bad experiences again and again and they and their families were often harassed over years even although the person originally targeted by the Security Forces had been killed or was in prison. State-sanctioned cruelty spread like poisonous gases across the land destroying young people's lives and undermining family solidity.

Effects

A continuum of horror was meted out to the young systematically under the auspices of the state on a large scale over at least 30 years. The continuum stretched from the purposeful separation of children from their families (under the guise of a battery of legislation concerned with land ownership, citizen rights, labour rules that forced parents to live apart from their children) to the intentional killing by state forces of children. A full range of effects can be documented that include the loss of life, mental disturbance and physical maiming of the most extreme sort. Consider the following testimony given at a public hearing of the Truth and Reconciliation Commission in the 24th June 1996, by Zandesile Ntsomi.

In 1985, Zandesile had been active in school protests against state oppression. He lived in the township set aside for blacks near the small town of Worcester in the Cape Province. October 1985 was a time of great tension in the area as police targeted scholars and members of other groups who were resisting the brutal forms of local police control. On 12th October 1985, Zandesile was shot by the police in the yard of a friend's house. He was shot in the leg, dragged, beaten and driven around for hours in a police van. Eventually he was taken to Tygerberg hospital in Cape Town and his leg was amputated. At 12.00 noon the next day he was removed by the police from the hospital and made to sit on a bench in the police station to wait for hours for the police from Worcester to fetch him. At five in the evening he was placed on a bench in the back of a police van and driven to Worcester for over a 100 kilometres at high speed. Zandesile told the Commissioners that the police drove as fast as they could. He said:

> At a very high speed. I cannot describe it – very high. I sat on the small benches at the back of the van with pain and a swollen leg from the amputation. I couldn't stand the pain. I sat on the left. I couldn't tolerate the driving. There was a wind in the van. I could not bear the pain. I waved a hand. They stopped the van just beyond Paarl. They said, 'What is the problem?' I pleaded: I told them of my situation and the pain. I asked for help. Could I not sit in front beside them? They looked at each other and nodded their heads. They had a little humanity. They took me to the front seat. I felt comfortable and thanked them a lot, time and again. We drove to Worcester. In the charge office they called those who were inexperienced to see me … . They said terrible things, unacceptable to a human being. One said, 'You mustn't worry, your leg will grow again'. He repeated it. It is in my consciousness.

Zandesile cried as he recalled his treatment. He was kept in prison. Charged with public violence and acquitted. He laid a case against the state and lost it. The appeal was dismissed. The state is claiming costs of R45,000 from Zandesile (about 6,500 pounds sterling at the current exchange rate).

His story is a sobering tale of ill-treatment by doctors and lawyers. While there were exceptions among medical and legal personnel at every level – persons who dealt fairly with those in prison, who gave the best treatment or advice possible under the circumstances, and who stood bravely on victims' behalves – the record was, overall, shameful. In a master's thesis recently completed at the University of Cape Town Medical School on the medical care of prisoners under apartheid, Dr van Heerden concluded that, 'The recent history of the Apartheid era demonstrates that South African doctors generally have a poor track record of defending human dignity and taking an ethical stand'.[8]

The protection of the young from state abuse may be as effectively secured by the implementation of international sanctions against medical and legal personnel who fail to act in accord with the premises, codes and rules of their disciplines as by international rules outlawing certain forms of punishment.

It is important to record effects of state oppression and atrocity and it is important to record that many of the young affirm that they have survived harsh experiences and enjoy sound physical, emotional and mental well-being. There are, it seems to me, five dangers attendant on considering the effects of terrible experiences. One lies in assuming that trauma is inevitable, especially that long term distressing effects will result. A second danger lies in a tendency to underestimate local healing processes and the power of particular sets of attitudes and foundations of experience. The third danger lies in imputing innocence to victims, that is in simplifying the experiences and actions of political activists and, in the process, failing to account for the complexity of commitment and motivation and the range of training and support drawn upon. A fourth follows from the latter. There is a danger in assuming certain sorts of effects and not paying attention to unexpected consequences. I think here of the power of imported notions, especially those identified with Western and/or Christian ideas, in a country like South Africa where they can hold sway and obscure other ideas, especially the nature of evil and its sources and of the impetus for revenge. From what some young, angry people tell me about their desire for revenge it may pay dividends to place ideas of evil and revenge on the table for public debate for there is always the possibility of re-directing them. The last danger lies in conflating pain and suffering into universal forms that overlay local meanings ignoring particular interpretations of trauma and of coping mechanisms. Anticipation of the effects of trauma can be hardened into expectations that may shape therapies and the rules about care.

Representations of the Roles of the Young in the South African Truth and Reconciliation Commission

The Truth and Reconciliation Commission has been established by an Act of Parliament: The Promotion of National Unity and Reconciliation Act, number 34. It was passed into law on 27th July 1995. The preamble of the Act states that:

... it is deemed necessary to establish the truth in relation to past events as well as the motives for and circumstances in which gross violations of human rights have occurred and to make the findings known in order to prevent a repetition of such events in the future.[9]

In addition, the Act states that the aim of the Commission will be reconciliation, based on:

a need for understanding but not for vengeance, a need for reparation but not retaliation, a need for *ubuntu*[10] but not for victimization.[11]

Finally, the Act makes provision for the granting of amnesty in respect of acts, omissions and offences associated with political objectives committed in the course of the conflicts of the past.[12]

The Act provides for three committees. They are: the Committee on Human Rights Violations (CHRV), the Committee on Amnesty and the Committee on Reparations and Rehabilitation. Commissioners are supported by additional committee members and administrative staff and an Investigative Unit which is headed by one of the Commissioners.

The CHRV aims to investigate gross violations of human rights; to find out who was responsible for them; and to determine how and why human rights violations happened.

The definition of Gross Violations of Human Rights that informs the work of the CHRV is laid down in the Act:

(a) killing, abduction, torture or severe ill-treatment of any person, or
(b) any attempt, conspiracy, incitement, instigation, command or procurement to commit an act referred to in paragraph (a), which emanated from conflicts of the past and which was committed during the period 1st March 1960 and the cut-offdate [presently 5 December 1993] within or outside the Republic, and the commission of which was advised, planned, directed, commanded or ordered, by any person acting with a political motive.

The CHRV has invited people to make submissions before it in the language of their choice. Written statements are taken from victims and from eyewitnesses. A sample of those making statements are selected for public hearings. The criteria on which the sample is selected have to do with presenting the public with as broad a range as possible of victims, violations and perpetrators. Victims, defined as either the person who suffered the violation or their family members or dependents, are referred to the Committee on Reparation and Rehabilitation. Victims are to be treated with respect and compassion and without discrimination. The Truth and Reconciliation Commission must protect their privacy and ensure the safety of both the witness and the family.

Public hearings are held throughout the country and are televised, broadcast and recorded in the print media. The hearings focus on individual experiences and on events that affected whole communities, such as the youth uprisings of Soweto in 1976. Provision is also made for political parties to present context papers which describe the context within which parties acted.

Within the first six months of operation, from April to September 1996, the CHRV has taken about 4,000 statements from those who have testified about gross human rights violations. Perhaps 10 per cent of these have been heard in public. Thus far, there have been few testimonies about the experiences of young people. Most of those documenting their trauma have been made by the parents of the young, especially mothers, and often about the death, disappearance or terrible physical and/or mental damage.

It would seem that up until now the testimonies have added little to our understanding of the complexity of children's engagement; or to the various facets of their identities; or their strategies of survival; or the patterns of healing upon which they have drawn; or the development of their political ideas and the range of their reflections on broad issues to do with morality, duty and the nature of society. On the evidence gathered by the CHRV it cannot yet be said that an approximation of the truth in relation to the experiences of young people in South Africa has been achieved.

The CHRV is paying attention to this deficit and is planning means to cancel it, including special hearings for the young. I raise the matter here because it seems indicative of how difficult it is to give the young a fair hearing; to create situations in which they are prepared to risk speaking openly about serious matters that expose vulnerabilities and fears; and to give due consideration to their contributions to change.

I offer an example of one woman's story of the death of her son. The testimony is moving as an account of a woman's courage in itemising the intimate details of her gaze as she attempted to identify the decomposing body of her child. Yet the narrative adds very little to our understanding of his extraordinary life. On 8th May 1996 Mrs Joyce Seipei spoke at a public hearing of the Truth and Reconciliation Commission in Durban about James Moketsi Seipei, known as Stompie.

Stompie was called the 'boy general' by ANC members. He became the leader of 1,500 children called 'The Fourteens' on 9th July 1986 when he was 11 years old, Stompie was arrested and kept in prison for nearly nine months. In 1988 he spent another three weeks in detention. In response to police harassment he left his home in the Orange Free State and went to Johannesburg. On 29th December 1988, he and some other boys were kidnapped from a church home and taken to Winnie Mandela's house. Stompie was assaulted and stabbed and his body was thrown into water, probably on 1st February 1989.

Mrs Seipei's testimony gives the bare outline of his activities and very little on his political leadership, his prison experiences or Winnie Mandela's alleged role in the abduction, assault or death. Mrs Seipei focused on establishing the fact that he had died and that she had buried him. She told how she had been taken on 13th February 1989 to the mortuary in Brixton to identify a body that was decomposing. She told the Commissioners that:

> A son is a son. After he had been killed he had been thrown in a river. I could not [at first] identify him. I looked at Stompie as I am his mother. I saw the first sign … . I said 'this is Stompie'. He had a scar on his eye and a birthmark on his nose. On his chest there was a scar from a fight with a boy. His left hand was identical to mine. His thighs were fit, just like his mother's. I looked at his private parts. I saw a birthmark on his left thigh. He was short but he had stretched in the water. I saw his clothes … . They were his.

The point of her narrative was to refute claims made by various people, including Winnie Mandela, that Stompie was not dead but alive in Botswana. In Mrs Seipei's testimony, the boy's death is central, not his activism, nor his leadership, nor even his suffering. To elicit stories of young activists and their experiences, the Commission will have to seek them out, not to the detriment of the stories that kin have to tell.

Zenzile May's testimony, given on 23rd April 1996 at a Cape Town hearing, is one of the few testimonies that details the experiences of a young person caught in political conflict while still at school. His account reveals the suffering that young activists endured and the dangers they faced. His is a remarkable account of a considered response of a young person to a smear campaign by the Security Forces. Since the 1970s Zenzile had been part of a school activist group in the Eastern Cape. On 11th September 1980 police chased young people in a schoolyard, whipping and beating them. Zenzile was hit and he fell and pretended to be dead. The police threw him into a van and he and others were driven to the police station. Once there, he was found to be alive and one of the policemen bemoaned his missed opportunity to have killed him. He was thrown into a dog cage in a van; the door was left open as he was driven to a police station in another town. He was put into a cell. He was interrogated about the Congress of South African Students (COSAS) and ANC connections. The police had the minute book from COSAS executive meetings. Interrogations and torture continued every day for three months. Torture included beatings while his head was covered with a plastic bag, and false executions in the bush. He was told that his mother had died and he only found out later that it was not true. He was kept in terrible conditions in solitary confinement for 11 months. He was released with threats of death.

Zenzile was re-arrested twice and powerful attempts were made to turn him into a state informer. He was forced to give samples of his writing and his signature by his interrogators. On being asked to become a spy he said, 'I am a student and a part of COSAS, to implicate them I would implicate myself.' He was threatened with the fate of Siphiwo Mthimkulu who had been poisoned and who later disappeared. Zenzile's response was, 'I am used to torture and detention.'

A friend of Zenzile's gave testimony in his support. He told what happened after Zenzile's release. Security police visited the house in which a number of COSAS students stayed. They asked questions of the students for about 20 minutes during which time one of them placed his cigarettes and some papers on the floor. When they left, a piece of paper was still lying on the floor. It was a receipt from the South African Police for about R500 and on it was Zenzile May's name. The executive of COSAS was split in its reaction to the receipt. Some called it a police plant and others feared that it might be real evidence that Zenzile had been turned.

Zenzile heard about the receipt. He said he was very humiliated and embarrassed as he was seen as a role model by younger people. It was part of police blackmail tactics. He decided that he had to stop being politically active as he did not have the money to hire a lawyer to fight the police in court, nor did he have the evidence in the form of the receipt. He was respected as an activist and for having survived brutal treatment in the prison and so, he said, it was difficult for people in the community to challenge him. Nevertheless he felt he could not continue as an activist. He secured a job in a brewery and helped to found a labour union. Fourteen years later he was asking the Commissioners to help him establish the truth, and clear his name and expose police tactics. The dignity and confidence of both young men was impressive. They had sustained their friendship despite the smear campaign. There was no trace of self-pity in the story of pain, loss of trust and of status within an organization and a community.

As a third example of the kinds of testimony being heard I shall mention the horrible account of a 13-year-old boy who was stoned and publicly hanged because his father was an alleged informer – people were invited to see the death of 'an informer's child'. The child's father, brother and two cousins were killed by the crowd in Uitenhage in 1985.

There are many hidden accounts, especially of the punishment of girls. It is yet early in the unfolding of the Truth and Reconciliation Commission's process. A revision of history has begun with the young being dubbed 'the lost generation': their individual contributions and the trajectory of their growth could be subsumed under others' versions of the past.

Conclusion

In May 1994 I attended a Conference on the Rights of Children in Armed Conflict held in Amsterdam. A Draft Declaration on the Rights of Children in Armed Conflict was placed before the delegates for discussion and amendment. The Preamble began as follows:

> The Conference on the Rights of Children in Armed Conflict,
> *Deeply concerned* by the sufferings of children in situations of war and armed conflict,
> *Aware* of the fact that we cannot expect children who have grown up in a climate of hate, death and destruction to be, once the fighting is over, responsible citizens and parents themselves.

I put before the assembly my objection to the passage beginning 'Aware of the fact ...' on the ground that no-one has the right to assume that because a child grows up in a climate of hate, death and destruction he or she cannot become a responsible citizen and parent. It is an absurd assumption and there is no evidence to support it as a blanket generalization. If it were true then the aftermath of war would be as bad or worse than war. An alternative explanation was not considered: what kind of childhood experiences did those who initiate and conduct wars, including many current world leaders, have that they should have grown up to unleash climates of hate, death and destruction? Inherent in the assumption are notions of damage or trauma from which a child cannot possibly recover.

It took three interventions on my part to ensure that the assembly paid attention to the unacceptable nature of the clause and to change it. My objection was founded in work with children and young people who had been politically active during the resistance against white minority rule in Rhodesia (now Zimbabwe) and South Africa. Many of those who fought are persons of admirable stature, sound moral standing and astute political judgement. Which is not to say that they did not suffer nor that they are unburdened by the consequences of trauma. Many children and youth suffered irreparable damage during the times of conflict. To object to the phraseology used is not to excuse hurt to children of any sort at all.

I caution against the adoption of too narrow a definition of childhood. Conceptions of childhood vary across societies. Every society recognizes the difference between a child and an adult; every society acknowledges the need to protect children and to attend to their particular potential and vulnerabilities; every society uses childhood (and use often becomes abuse) but beyond these generalities societies differ in their ideas about childhood. They differ, for example, in their notions of the origin of children, that is, their connections to the supernatural; the role of fate or chance in their development; the origin of gifts or flaws in individuals; the inheritance of talents or evil potentials; the parental role in shaping the child; dangers that may be inherent in relationships like jealousy and envy or the power of an adult to initiate a child into evil; the culpability of the young wrong-doer; growth patterns, identity and obligations, and so on.

A conception of the child that has been current at certain periods among middle-class Westerners is of the child as an individual shorn of most obligations, economically dependent, politically uninvolved, emotionally and morally immature, and secure within and represented by a family. It is one that fits very few children's experiences in the world. It may be an ideal that is worth enshrining in international legislation. It should not, in the process, undermine children's strategies for survival, especially their economic strategies, nor obscure their actual contributions to society, nor prune their potential by constraining their options.

It matters what conception of a child is held, for it, in part, determines the punishment meted out and sanctioned by society. For example, certain types of behaviour among the young within powerful controlling patriarchal groups call down strict forms of punishment seen as legitimate by many in the group. For example, in 1980 in the Crossroads informal settlement in Cape Town, young girls who fell pregnant outside marriage were publicly whipped. It happened not infrequently. The nature of punishment is affected by ideas of pain, guilt, shame and blame and these, in turn, may influence how a child feels and interprets punitive actions. Some of the ways in which we are cruel to children emerge from the ways in which we define them as passive beings, as possessions, as dependants, and as persons in debt to their elders.

It makes sense to draw on understandings of child development to campaign against the ill-treatment of children. However, descriptions of child development may be particular yet applied universally. Marilyn Strathern observes that, 'Indeed it is a truism that theories or models, and especially models that purport to speak to universal conditions, are produced out of specific circumstances. How the universal is apprehended may even be taken as a veritable index of the parochial.'[13]

In an article on child development and international child rights legislation Burman says that the discourse of rights necessarily invokes general claims and she asks how well general statements about children map on to the conditions and positions of children in particular contexts.[14] In her view, 'global concepts such as "rights", by their very nature, cannot absolutely specify the conditions and precise interventions called for in each domain of application ... . Rather, it is a matter of interpreting what these general precepts mean in particular contexts'.[15] She urges us to question whose experiences are taken as the basis of the normative model used in defining rights and alerts us to the cultural and gender chauvinisms that can inform the process of defining what is best for children.

Burman's article explores how the universalized discourse of rights, including its undoubted moral component, allows for the naturalization of normative evaluations about what children are, and should be, like. She expresses her concern about normalized definitions of psychological development that invoke and maintain child rights. Burman even suggests that the enthusiasm with which the Convention of the Rights of the Child was embraced '… can be understood as indicating conceptual and political investments in maintaining particular conceptions of children as representative icons of western "civilized" subjectivity, with more or less explicit contrasts to its "others".[16] Children can function as cultural representations of freedom and idealized selves and the practical implications may "include the conflation of an adult-defined and retrospective developmental model with a set of social indicators that measure social rather than individual change".[17] Burman says that we need to maintain a critical vigilance on the adequacy of the conceptual resources that inform the discourse of child rights. To do so, we should explore, first, what childhood means and the roles children play within particular moral and political economies, and second, what these assumptions about children that are structured into theories and practices pass over and fail to address.[18] This paper has looked at the political roles that some children have filled in South Africa.

Some of the possible consequences of attempts to protect children could include denials of their agency; a narrowing of the bounds of identities; and failure to acknowledge their economic, social and political decision-making and activities. Children in many parts of the world will continue to labour, to fall foul of the law, to participate in wars and revolutions. They need protection from abuse. The exposure of adult duplicity in breaking rules to do with work, crime prevention and conflict could be effective in helping to protect children. History tells us little about children as history-makers. We might do well to avoid straightjacketing childhood. It might help children if we recognize their agency. It might protect them best if we acknowledge their participation in society.

Notes

1   Nooteboom, C. (1994), *The Following Story*. Translated from the Dutch by Ina Rilke, London, Harvill Press. (First published in Dutch in 1991).
2   African National Congress, 1996. Statement to the Truth and Reconciliation Commission, Marshalltown, ANC.

3   *The Sunday Independent*, 22 September 1996 at 4. *Legacy of Dirty War May Be Lurking in Your Drive Tonight*, van Niekerk.
4   Dikeni, S. (1992) at 66–7, *Guava Juice*, Cape Town, Mayibuye Books.
5   Reynolds, P. (1995), "'Not Known Because Not looked For': Ethnographers Listening to the Young in Southern Africa", *Ethnos*, **60**, 3–4, 193–221.
6   White, H. (1994), *In the Shadow of the Island: Women's Experience of their Kinsmen's Political Imprisonment, 1987-91*. Pretoria: Human Sciences Research Council.
7   Reynolds, P., 'Youth and the Politics of Culture in South Africa', in Stevens (1995) (ed.), *Children and the Politics of Culture*, Princeton, 218.
8   Van Heerden, J. (1996), *Prison Health Care in South Africa: A Study of Prison Conditions, Health Care and Medical Accountability for the Care of Prisoners*. Unpublished manuscript, Department of Medicine, University of Cape Town.
9   Promotion of National Unity and Reconciliation Act, number 34 of 1995:2.
10 *Ubuntu* in Nguni means 'humanity'.
11 Ibid.
12 Ibid.
13 Strathern, M. (1995), *Shifting Contexts: Transformations in Anthropological Knowledge*, London, Routledge.
14 Burman, E. (1996), 'Local, Global or Globalized? Child Development and International Child Rights Legislation', 3 *Childhood: A Global Journal of Child Research*, 46.
15 Ibid.
16 Ibid.
17 Ibid.
18 Ibid.

4 Opening Pandora's Box – Protecting Children Against Torture, Cruel, Inhuman and Degrading Treatment and Punishment

Geraldine Van Bueren

Introduction[1]

There is an understandable disbelief that torture can be perpetrated against children. This has led to an unfortunate slowness in reaction and even, on occasions, denial by the international community of such grave violations. Children are rarely perceived as victims of torture, although, ironically, they may be easier targets, not only because of their vulnerability, but also because of the effect on the local community. Children are regarded as a symbol of a community's future, and if they are targeted and seized in order to subjugate their families and neighbours it creates a general unease. Everyone realizes that no one is safe in a state capable of torturing children.

The inertia of the international community has been compounded by the fact that the international prohibition is not solely against torture, but also against 'other cruel, inhuman or degrading treatment or punishment'[2] and some of these prohibited treatments and punishments occur in what traditionally has been regarded as the private sphere, which traditionalists erroneously assume to be beyond the province of international human rights law.[3]

Children may also fall through the net of international legal protection because they may suffer the effects of traumatic events in ways which are different from adults.[4] The jurisprudence of regional and international human rights fora appears to be based principally on adult victims, and, despite some judicial dicta to the contrary, there is a real risk that international and regional standards may mechanically be applied to cases involving child victims. Such an approach is inappropriate because it promotes an analysis which fails to address both the particular vulnerabilities of children and the role of children as social actors.

Finally, as unpalatable as it may appear, to protect children effectively against torture the international community must consider not only the protection of children against adults but also the protection of children against other children.[5]

Four Dilemmas

The majority of international and regional human rights treaties prohibit not only torture but also cruel, inhuman and degrading treatment and punishment.[6] Cruel, inhuman and degrading treatment and punishment are conceptualised as being forms of torture.[7] In reality, however, it is torture and inhuman treatment and punishment which are regarded as being the ultimate forms of barbarity attracting society's disapprobation. Few would quarrel with the contents of the European Commission's list in *Denmark et al.* v. *Greece*;[8] the argument is with the omissions. Hence the first dilemma is: if the concept of torture were to be expanded, how would it still retain a moral dimension which puts it on a par with evil, and which acts as a potent deterrence.

The second related dilemma raises fundamental issues of implementation. In very general terms, international human rights law, despite being universal and indivisible,[9] adopts different approaches to the implementation of civil and political rights to that of economic, social and cultural rights. Civil and political rights are regarded as capable of immediate implementation, placing a duty on a state to implement immediately or desist from a course of action. Economic, social and cultural rights are regarded only as placing a duty on a state to implement these rights progressively to the maximum of its available resources. The prohibition of torture falls into the civil and political category. The issue therefore is whether specific treatments, such as particular forms of sexual and economic exploitation[10] or traditional practices prejudicial to the health of children, which have up to now been regarded as facets of economic, social or cultural rights can be reconceptualised and transformed into the immediate implementation category, thus providing an additional and more effective means of implementation.[11]

The argument that poverty is inherently degrading is a compelling one. As Cassese observes in relation to Article 3 of the European Convention on

Human Rights, this would constitute an appropriate means to make economic and social rights 'more incisive'.[12] It is, however, arguable that the majority of human rights violations are inherently degrading and so could be included within the ban on torture, cruel, inhuman and degrading treatment and punishment. This raises the dilemma of how to offer effective protection through immediate implementation whilst not falling into the dangerous strategy of arriving at an all-encompassing definition so broad that it robs the prohibition of its emotional potency.

A third dilemma is the extent to which international human rights law should take into account child development. The Convention on the Rights of the Child is ambivalent about the universal, bio-physical features of child development. During the drafting of the Convention there was never any serious discussion as to whether children all over the globe possess similar bio-physical features at the same chronological age.[13] Nor was the question raised as to whether the extent of our knowledge of child development is based upon the cultural domination of industrialized societies. Yet the answer to these questions may be essential when seeking to protect children against harmful treatment and punishment.

When considering the effects of torture, or cruel, inhuman and degrading treatment and punishment, international human rights lawyers rarely explore fully the importance of the development of the child. This is partly because international human rights law is accustomed to describing a particular punishment or treatment as contrary to the prohibition on torture, or inhuman or degrading treatment and punishment per se. For understandable reasons human rights fora do not examine a particular treatment or punishment on a sliding scale taking into account issues of maturity and development. It is also partly because, although the European Court of Human Rights reiterated in *Soering* v. *United Kingdom* that all the relevant circumstances of the case are to be taken into account, including the age and sex of the victim,[14] other child specific factors, including the psychological effects of a particular trauma, do not appear always to be fully considered.[15] Human rights appears to lack an appropriate model for the physical, psychological and social development processes of children.

Children in general are uniquely dependent, both physically and emotionally, on other people for their survival. Although adults may be emotionally reliant upon close relationships, a child often will be totally dependent on a 'primary care giver' for protection and survival. Often this dependence translates into the child's being traumatized on two fronts: they experience 'direct trauma' when faced with a traumatic experience and 'indirect trauma' as a result of treatment perpetrated against people essential for their survival. In essence, a child can be vicariously traumatized. Children of tortured parents often develop serious symptoms because of this vicarious involvement.

Cognitive development is of particular importance when attempting to understand young children's reactions not so much to torture and inhumanity but to cruel and degrading treatment and punishment.[16] A child may experience the same event as an adult but perceive it in a completely different manner and be unable to assess it cognitively. Indeed, while adults may have the ability to isolate the effects of a particular event on their personality, and thus to moderate its impact, children may lack the necessary development and experience for such a perspective, and so will be unable to moderate their suffering. Consequently, events can be more frightening and disturbing, and hence 'cruelty is more terrifying'[17] for children.

Although there are rigorous debates over cognitive development,[18] it is generally accepted that there is a significant difference between the cognitive, emotional and physical development of 2-year-old and 17-year-old children. Such an assumption is not dependent upon embracing Piagetian views that young children are universally incompetent.[19] The universal legitimacy accorded to the concept of children's rights by the global adoption of the UN Convention on the Rights of the Child 1989 implies that children are not to be dismissed as irrational. In this post-Convention on the Rights of the Child-era children's 'experiences must be seen as profound sources of knowledge'.[20]

While an adult may be severely affected by a traumatic experience and as a result suffer some personality alteration, a child's personality, in the absence of pre-existing development, may not only be altered, but actually developed by a traumatic event. Any or all of a child's cognitive, moral, psychological and social cognitive development may be permanently altered by a traumatic event. Because children have not yet had the opportunity to develop their emotional, moral or social foundations fully, they are particularly vulnerable to traumatic experiences and this vulnerability has to be taken into account by human rights fora. Hence the physical and mental characteristics of childhood, as well as the effects of any treatment or punishment on children, is critical in determining whether a specific measure amounts to torture, or cruel, inhuman or degrading treatment or punishment. These psychological differences between children and adults have been misapplied in the past as reasons for denying the granting and exercising of the participatory rights of children; however, such differences may assist in preventing children suffering what could amount to prohibited standards of treatment and punishment.

The fourth dilemma is whether the approach to cruel and degrading treatment and punishment for children is a universal one or whether it should take into account issues of cultural relativity. As Ennew observes, the issue of cultural relativity is not merely how to make universal standards universal but 'how to avoid superimposing one set of concepts on another when transcribing ethnographic data from one culture to another'.[21] There are wide variations between what is accepted as benign and harmful treatment. 'Many Euro-American child-care practices, even those seemingly benign as sleeping arrangements in which infants have separate beds and rooms, are seen as ill-informed at best and uncaring and abusive at worst by many of the world's societies.'[22]

The issue has arisen in relation to female circumcision and arose implicitly in relation to corporal punishment. In *Costello-Roberts* v. *United Kingdom* the applicant had been hit by the headmaster of a private school with a rubber soled gym shoe when he was only seven years old.[23] By a bare majority the European Court of Human Rights found that the slippering which Jeremy Costello-Roberts received was not sufficient to amount to either a breach of Articles 3 or 8 of the European convention.[24]

In reaching their conclusion the European Court, a body concerned only with the protection of human rights within its own region, considered and cited the provisions of the UN Convention on the Rights of the Child. However, the body which is entrusted with interpreting the UN Convention on the Rights of the Child universally, the Committee on the Rights of the Child, reached the opposite conclusion.[25] The Committee, in its report on the United Kingdom's implementation of the Convention on the Rights of the Child, was concerned 'that privately funded and managed schools are still permitted to administer corporal punishment to children'. According to the Committee this 'does not appear compatible with the provisions of the Convention'.[26]

Surprisingly the Committee does not mention the judgement of the European Court of Human Rights[27] and this produces a rather strange result. According to the European Court of Human Rights the United Kingdom is free to allow parents to have their children hit in private schools, but according to the UN Committee on the Rights of the Child such a 'freedom' breaches international law.

In fact the Committee on the Rights of the Child went even further and considered physical punishment of children generally and particularly within the family.[28] Austria, Cyprus, Finland, Norway and Sweden regard parental corporal punishment as an abuse of the physical integrity and the rights of the child. The Committee on the Rights of the Child drew the United Kingdom's attention to the fact that it is 'worried' about the national legal provisions dealing with reasonable chastisement which ... may pave the way for subjective and arbitrary interpretation'. The Committee on the Rights of the Child concluded that the legislative and other measures relating to the physical integrity of children do not appear compatible with the Convention including Article 37, the article which, inter alia, prohibits cruel and degrading treatment and punishment. On the basis of these findings the Committee recommended that physical punishment of children in families be prohibited.[29] So that at the present time the European Court of Human Rights permits a punishment which the Committee on the Rights of the Child deems degrading or cruel.

Torture – The Public and the Private Spheres

Taking account of child development and issues of cultural relativity would still leave children vulnerable to torture, cruel, inhuman and degrading treatment and punishment if traditional views of state responsibility for human rights violations prevail. The traditional view of international law is that states can only be held responsible for actions which occur in the public domain when proven to have been committed by state officials. As children spend much of their time in the private domain this has had a significant restrictive impact on the protection of children.[30] Consequently there is a need for an expansion if not a reconceptualization of the protection of human rights in the private sphere, if children are to be properly protected against prohibited practices. Such a reconsideration is also consistent with Scheuner's observation that, '[a] changing social situation exposes the individual not only to infringements coming from the State but also to an increasing social pressure exercised by social groups and power'.[31]

The traditional viewpoint of international law is reflected in the definition of torture incorporated in the UN Convention against Torture and Other Cruel, Inhuman and Degrading Treatment and Punishment 1984, which defines torture as,

> any act by which severe pain or suffering whether physical or mental, is intentionally inflicted on a person for such purposes as obtaining from him or a third person information or a confession, punishing him for an act he or a third person has committed or is suspected of having committed, or intimidating or coercing him or a third person, or for any reason based on discrimination of any kind, when such pain or suffering is inflicted by or at the instigation of or with the consent or acquiescence of a public official or other person acting in an official capacity. It does not include pain or suffering arising only from, inherent in or incidental to lawful sanctions.[32]

The focus of the definition is solely on the public sphere and reflects an approach which has been accepted since the Roman period.[33] Opsahl, however, described this narrower view of the potential of human rights which considered everything 'in order' as long as there is not any interference by a public authority, as an 'outdated laissez faire concept'.[34] Admittedly, it is made clear by Article 1 that the definition is only applicable in relation to the Torture Convention and is without prejudice to wider definitions in domestic or other international instruments.[35] Nevertheless, a definition of torture incorporated in a major human rights treaty is bound to have its effects beyond the specific treaty regime itself.

The Human Rights Committee has contributed to the erosion of the sharpness of the public/private divide in its revised General Comment on Article 7. In its General Comment the Human Rights Committee observed that the protection of Article 7 'goes far beyond torture as normally understood ... it is also the duty of public authorities to ensure protection by the law against such treatments even when committed by persons acting outside or without any official authority'.[36] The Human Rights Committee would appear to have been influenced by the jurisprudence of the Inter-American human rights machinery particularly by the cases of *Velasquez Rodriguez*[37] and *Godinez Cruz* v. *Honduras*.[38] It may also have taken into consideration the Inter-American Convention on Torture 1985 which although it was adopted only a year later than its United Nations counterpart, clearly perceived that the dangers of torture lay not only within the traditional public sphere.[39]

The European Commission also suggested, nearly a quarter of a century ago, that states indirectly may be responsible for violations by private agents.[40] In the *Swedish Engine Drivers Union Case* the European Court of Human Rights pointedly commented that 'This does not however imply that the State may not be obliged to protect individuals through appropriate measures taken against some form of interference by other individuals, groups, or organisations'.[41] This approach was in fact adopted in *X and Y* v. *the Netherlands* which arose because of an unintended gap in Dutch law whereby a 16-year-old mentally disabled victim of rape was unable to initiate criminal proceedings because Dutch law required the filing of rape proceedings by victims over the age of 12[42] and lacked any provision whereby a parent could file proceedings on child victims who were regarded as mentally incompetent.[43] The case has major implications for the protection of individuals within a wide range of other private institutions.[44]

The Inter-American Commission has gone further, and in its report on the situation of human rights in Guatemala stressed that governments are under a duty to prevent and suppress violence 'whether committed by public officials or by private individuals, whether their motives are political or otherwise'.[45] This is consistent with the Convention on the Rights of the Child, which arguably extends the responsibility of states for actions within the private sphere. Article 19 of the Convention on the Rights of the Child obliges States Parties to take all appropriate measures to protect children from all forms of violence, injury, neglect and abuse, thus clearly taking the intra-familial abuse of children out of the exclusive private sphere into the public sphere. The Convention on the Rights of the Child also extends the states' duties beyond prevention, investigation, and prosecution to rehabilitation.[46]

The cumulative significance of these developments is that international and regional human rights fora ought to develop jurisprudence which obliges states to put in place an effective legal system which does not tolerate the torture and arguably cruel, inhuman, degrading treatment and punishment of children, whether inflicted as a result of state responsibility in the public or in the private spheres.

International and Regional Jurisprudence

The notion that specific treatments and punishments are unacceptable to the international community reinforces the value of life and the dignity of human beings. Conversely, human rights fora in ruling that specific treatments and punishments do not amount to torture, or cruelty, inhumanity and degradation under international law may unwittingly add weight to the argument that such actions are legitimate and appropriate forms of behaviour. Although the UN Committee on Human Rights has observed that 'it may not be necessary to draw sharp distinctions between the various forms of prohibited treatments or punishments',[47] where children are concerned such distinctions may be helpful, particularly since it is the application of the concepts of cruelty and degradation which may have the greatest potential for children.

It would not be helpful to attempt to provide an exhaustive list of what constitutes torture, or cruel, inhuman and degrading treatment and punishment for children, as the depths of evil know no limit, and because of the obvious dangers of such a list. It may, however, be useful to begin to explore specific situations. It may also be valuable to define the essential nature of each of these forms of punishment and treatments, as there may be potential in developing the notion of privacy to combat lesser forms of punishment and treatment.[48]

The prohibition on torture is enshrined in a wide variety of global and regional human rights instruments, and is articulated in the Universal Declaration of Human Rights 1948 and reiterated in child-specific form in the Convention on the Rights of the Child 1989, 'No child shall be subjected to torture or other cruel, inhuman and degrading treatment or punishment'.[49] The prohibition on torture, inhuman and degrading treatment and punishment is arguably a part of international customary law,[50] and its prohibition is a part of those rules of international customary law which have attained the status of *jus cogens*[51] and are therefore binding on states regardless of their treaty commitments or persistent objections. The normative status of cruel treatment and punishment is, arguably, not as clear-cut.[52]

There are not any circumstances which justify employing such practices, and the international community regards it as so fundamental a right that states are not free to derogate from it in declared public emergencies. The prohibition applies to all individuals. The intention or motivation of the agent is also 'irrelevant'.[53] Neither can an order from a superior officer or of a public authority be invoked as a justification.[54] This is the reason for much of the secrecy which surrounds the perpetration of torture.[55]

Much of the jurisprudence on actions which amount to prohibited treatment and punishment is drawn from decisions of the European Court and Commission on Human Rights interpreting Article 3 of the European Convention on Human Rights and Fundamental Freedoms.[56] Generally, the European Court has held that the ill-treatment must attain a minimum level of severity if it is to fall within the scope of Article 3. 'The assessment of this minimum is, in the nature of things, relative; it depends on all the circumstances of the case, such as the duration of the treatment, its physical or mental effects and, in some cases, the sex, age and state of health of the victim, etc.'[57] Similarly one factor alone may be regarded as insufficient but may contribute to the violation of standards when considered cumulatively with other factors.[58]

The ambit of the prohibition has frequently been subject to analysis in relation to adults generally[59] and more recently to women specifically,[60] but there has not been, with the exception of corporal punishment, a thorough consideration of such treatment and punishment in relation to children. A particular treatment or punishment may not be prohibited when imposed on adults but it may amount to cruel and degrading behaviour when perpetrated against children. Life imprisonment without possibility of release, for example, is prohibited in the Convention on the Rights of the Child for those who have committed crimes under the age of 18. This prohibition appears in the same paragraph as the prohibition of torture, cruel, inhuman and degrading treatment and punishment, raising at the least the argument that the two may be equated.[61]

More problematic is the possibility that specific treatments and punishments may be acceptable in relation to older children but are unacceptable when perpetrated against younger children. International human rights law is accustomed to viewing groups of individuals as a class, such as a class of adults, a class of women or children, but not to considering the attributes of individual members of that class.

The advantage of probing the ambit of the definition of torture, cruel, inhuman and degrading treatment as it applies to children, is that it may also serve to reinforce other treaty duties placed on states. Where a child, for example, has not been notified of the whereabouts of a family member, in contravention of Article 9(4) of the Convention on the Rights of the Child, the resulting anxiety could amount to a prohibited level of suffering.

'Grounded only in the scream of his victim, for whom it is all real',[62] it is arguable that the same standards of measuring what constitutes torture apply equally to adults and children.[63] Torture has been described as 'an aggravated and deliberate form of cruel, inhuman or degrading treatment or punishment'[64] which brings about 'the disintegration of an individual's personality, the shattering of his mental and psychological equilibrium and the crushing of his will'. A government may acknowledge that torture has taken place, as with Turkey, but it will not acknowledge that torture occurs as a matter of routine or administrative practice. In Turkey during 1990 and 1991 Helsinki Watch (now Human Rights Watch) received 'dozens of reports of police torture of children under 18'.[65] The prohibition on torture, cruel, inhuman and degrading treatment and punishment is not limited to institutional deprivations of liberty, but when children are deprived of their liberty they may become more vulnerable to such treatment and punishment. Hence during the drafting of the Convention on the Rights of the Child, Venezuela proposed that the imprisonment of children per se constituted a specific form of abuse to which Article 39 and the right to rehabilitation would automatically apply. It would be an understatement to record that the proposal did not meet with the approval of the majority of states.[66]

The difference between torture and inhuman treatment and punishment derives principally from a difference in the intensity of the suffering inflicted, with torture considered the more serious. The European Commission of Human Rights has described inhuman treatment as that which 'deliberately causes severe suffering, mental or physical which in the particular situation is unjustifiable'.[67] However this merely poses the question of what is unjustifiable. Zekia proffered the example of a mother who for interrogation purposes is separated from her suckling baby. They are kept apart in adjoining rooms so that the mother can hear the hungry screams of the baby. This he characterized as inhuman treatment, the mother by being agonized and the baby by being deprived of the urgent attention of the mother.[68]

Torture and inhuman treatment are of a different character than degrading treatment. Treatment or punishment of individuals may be degrading if 'it grossly humiliates him before others or drives him to act against his will or conscience'.[69] If the treatment is considered to be inhuman than it is also degrading. However, the converse is not necessarily true; a finding of degrading treatment does not necessarily mean a finding of inhuman treatment as in *Tyrer* v. *United Kingdom*, where a punishment of three strokes of a birch for a 15-year-old school boy who assaulted a school student was considered to be degrading but not inhuman.[70]

The UN Rules for the Protection of Juveniles Deprived of their Liberty, although non-binding, provide authoritative guidance on the content of the concept of degrading from the child's perspective: the wearing of specific forms of clothing could be degrading.[71] Rule 36 provides that to the extent possible, juveniles should have the right to use their own clothing and all clothing should be suitable for the climate and not be degrading.

Degrading treatment also refers to both mental and physical acts. In *Tyrer* the European Court of Human Rights stated that it was sufficient if 'the victim is humiliated in his own eyes, even if not in the eyes of others.'[72] The European Court pointed out that a punishment does not lose its degrading character because it is believed to be an effective aid to the control of child crime.

The treatment does not have to have long lasting effects but 'feelings of apprehension or disquiet'[73] are not necessarily sufficient to bring the punishment within the sphere of 'degrading'.[74] However, in *Tyrer* the Court found that his punishment 'whereby he was treated as an object in the power of the authorities – constituted an assault on precisely that which it is one of the main purposes of Article 3 of the European Convention on Human Rights and Fundamental Freedoms to protect, namely a person's dignity and physical integrity'.[75] Welcomingly the European Court of Human Rights in *Tyrer* appeared to be heading in the direction of finding all institutional child corporal punishment as degrading. According to the Court the institutionalized nature of the violence was further exacerbated by the 'whole aura of official procedure attending the punishment and by the fact that those inflicting it were total strangers to the offender'.[76]

In *Costello-Roberts* v. *United Kingdom*,[77] the applicant alleged breaches of Article 3, degrading punishment, and Article 8, privacy in the sense of bodily integrity. It is arguable that the threshold of the level of suffering is lower under Article 8 than under Article 3, but 'not every act or measure which may be said to affect adversely the physical or moral integrity' of children will give rise to a finding of invasion of privacy. This will depend upon whether the adverse effects on a child's integrity are 'sufficient' to bring it within the scope of Article 8.

There is a paucity of international jurisprudence on the definition of cruel treatment and punishment. This is in part because the prohibition on cruelty, despite reference to cruelty in *Ireland* v. *United Kingdom*, is omitted from Article 3 of the European Convention on Human Rights under which most of the cases defining prohibited standards of treatment and punishment have been brought. The lack of clarity over the definition also stems from the fact that international human rights fora adjudicating under treaties which prohibit cruelty rarely consider it in isolation. In *Velasquez Rodriguez*, for example, it was held that 'prolonged isolation and deprivation of communication amounted to cruel and inhuman treatment because they were harmful to the psychological and moral integrity of the person and a violation of the right of any detainee to respect for his inherent dignity as a human being'.[78] Some guidance can be sought from American domestic jurisprudence, where it was found that punishment is cruel if it 'is not graduated and proportioned to the offence'.[79]

The Human Rights Committee acknowledges that solitary confinement, according to the circumstances, may be contrary to Article 7 of the International Covenant on Civil and Political Rights, which prohibits such treatment and punishment if it is not used for the purposes of preventing escape, protecting health or maintaining discipline.[80] Isolation as a punishment has particularly severe effects on children. It is arguable that all forms of solitary confinement for children, as distinct from segregation, regardless of conditions and duration, amount to cruel punishment when applied to children. This has important implications, as there are not any treaties which expressly prohibit the imposition of solitary confinement for children, although restrictions in relation to adults and children do exist in non-binding rules.[81] If solitary confinement amounts to cruel punishment when applied to children then regardless of the arguments of *jus cogens*, all of the States Parties to the International Covenant and the Convention on the Rights of the Child would be prohibited from imposing solitary confinement on children.

It may also be that, as with adults, the entire system of imprisonment may amount to inhuman and degrading treatment and punishment. The findings on Jamaican lock-ups reported by Human Rights Watch raises this possibility. 'Children told us that the cells were often overcrowded; that they were forced to defecate into waste buckets that often overflowed in their cells; that sewage systems outside the cells were inoperative and revolting; that they slept on wet floors without any form of bedding; that insect and vermin infestation was rampant; that the food was often spoiled, served at odd times of day and rarely sufficient; that they were not permitted to see a doctor; and that they were not provided with an opportunity to exercise, read, play or work and were hardly ever allowed outside their cells.'[82] Similar issues arose in Tatuape in Sao Paulo in December 1992, for example, in FEBEM's notorious Unidade de Acolhimento Preliminar which housed approximately 250 boys though its official capacity was only for 70. The boys were not segregated according to age and type of offence, and boys who had committed petty thefts shared cells with rapists and murderers.[83]

In seeking to prevent children being subjected to prohibited forms of punishments consideration has to be given to the fact that specific groups of children may be more vulnerable to prohibited forms of treatment and punishment. These include children living and working on the street and children in internal armed conflicts. The characterisation by some that poor children are delinquent or criminal contributes to violence against children, combined with a tradition of police abuse and a lack of confidence in the justice system. The United Nations Rules for the Protection of Juveniles Deprived of their Liberty recommends that detention before trial should be avoided to 'the extent possible', and where such detention is utilized 'the highest priority' should be given to 'the most expeditious processing of such cases to ensure the shortest possible duration of detention.'[84] This seeks to avoid practices in Jamaica, where police 'routinely' take children to 'places of safety', alternative residential institutions designed for young people. Whilst detained in lock-ups children are subjected to physical and some-times mental abuse during interrogations and are beaten and/or placed in dark cells, often in solitary confinement, as methods of discipline.[85]

In states in which there are armed conflicts or lesser forms of tension and strife, children as a class of individuals may also be vulnerable. Children may become caught between two powerful groups, the government security forces and the paramilitary groups.[86] In Liberia, Human Rights Watch has documented cases of children tortured to force them to join INPFL, Prince Johnson's armed opposition group,[87] and some children were subjected to ill-treatment after they had joined the forces. Children were sometimes '*tabayed*', which temporarily paralyses the arms.[88] In other states where there is a lower level of tension and strife children may be vulnerable to prohibited forms of treatment by virtue of the legislative framework. Emergency legislation in Northern Ireland allows children to be detained incommunicado in adult interrogation facilities for up to 48 hours, and they can also be detained without charge for up to seven days.[89] The reservations which the United Kingdom government has attached to Article 37(c) of the Convention on the Rights of the Child, and the derogation after *Brogan* v. *United Kingdom*[90] to Article 5(3) of the European Convention on Human Rights means that such detentions are difficult to challenge under international law.

Conclusion

From the late Middle Ages until the second half of the eighteenth century torture was a part of ordinary criminal procedure in many European states, 'regulary employed to investigate and prosecute routine crime before the ordinary courts'.[91] We have come a long way since torture was accepted as a judicially approved legal practice.[92] Similarly, specific forms of treatment and punishment, such as flogging, which was widely accepted, have since become prohibited. Perhaps the time has come to reevaluate children's ill-treatment from a multi-disciplinary approach questioning certain received wisdoms. Although according to the legend when Pandora opened the box all human ills flew forth, there is another version of the legend. This tells of how all the blessings of the gods escaped except hope, which lay at the bottom.

Notes

1   This chapter is also being published in *17 Law and Policy* 377. The author is grateful to the Baldy Centre for Law and Social Policy of the State University of New York at Buffalo for inviting her as a Visiting Scholar and for providing such a stimulating environment for research.

2   See UN Convention Against Torture and Other Cruel, Inhuman or Degrading Treatment or Punishment 1984; see also Burgers and Danelius (1988), *The UN Convention Against Torture*, Kluwer.

3   See further Van Bueren (1995), 'The International Protection of Family Members' Rights as the 21st Century Approaches', **17** *Human Rights Quarterly*, 732 at 740.

4   See further below.

5   In Liberia child soldiers committed atrocities 'often women were raped by friends of their sons'. Human Rights Watch, Children's Rights Project, *Easy Prey, Child Soldiers in Liberia 1994*.

6   The word cruel is omitted from the European Convention for the Prevention of Torture and Inhuman or Degrading Treatment or Punishment 1987 which is consistent with the Council of Europe's approach incorporated in Article 3 European Convention Against Human Rights 1950.

7   'Torture constitutes an aggravated and deliberate form of cruel, inhuman and degrading treatment and punishment.' Article 1(2) Declaration on the Protection of All Persons from being Subjected to Torture, and Other Cruel, Inhuman or Degrading Treatment or Punishment 1975.

8   *Denmark et al.* v. *Greece*, Report of 5 November (1969); Yearbook XII, 186.

9   For a critique of the traditional approach see Van Bueren, Deconstructing the Mythologies of International Human Rights Law in Gearty and Tomkins (1996) (ed.), *Understanding Human Rights*.

10   These may also be reconceptualised as forms of slavery.

11   See also below McBride, *The Violation of Economic, Social and Cultural Rights as Torture or Cruel, Inhuman or Degrading Treatment or Punishment*.

12   Cassesse (1991), 'Can the notion of Inhuman and Degrading Treatment be Applied to Socio-Economic Conditions', *EJIL*, **2**, 141.

13   Such issues were never discussed either in the formal or informal working groups. The author represented Amnesty International at the United Nations during the drafting of the Convention on the Rights of the Child.

14   Judgment of European Court of Human Rights 7 July (1989). Series A Vol 161 para. 100.

15   See for example the discussion of *Sargin* v. *Federal Republic of Germany* in Van Bueren (1995), *The International Law on the Rights of the Child*, at 215.

16   See generally Pincus (1976), *Death and the Family*, Faber and Faber.

17   Record of an interview by Jill Peasley with Dr. Naomi Richmond. Institute of Child Health, University of London. Project for Care of Children in War and Disasters.

18 See for example Flavell, Miller and Miller (1993), *Cognitive Development*; Rosser (1994), *Cognitive Development: Psychological and Biological Perspectives*.

19 In particular Piaget, who first completed a doctorate in zoology, emphasised age related qualitative changes for example arguing that children under seven are pre-operational, lacking basic logical competence. Piaget (1926), *The Language and Thought of the Child*; Piaget (1929), *Judgement and Reasoning in the Child*, and Piaget (1930), *The Child's Conception of Physical Causality*.

20 Alderson and Goodwin (1993), 'Contradictions within Concepts of Children's Competence', *International Journal of Children's Rights* **1**, 303 at 309.

21 See above Ennew, 'Shame and Physical Pain: Cultural Relativity, Children, Torture and Punishment'.

22 Korbin, 'Child Maltreatment in Cross-Cultural Perspective: Vulnerable Children and Circumstances', in Gelles and Lancaster (1987) (eds), *Child Abuse and Neglect: Biosocial Dimensions* at 35.

23 Judgement of European Court of Human Rights. Series A. No. 247, 24 March (1993).

24 For a more progressive approach see the Educational Code of Namibia which provides that although students 'are expected to comply with legitimate disciplinary measures, they have a right to protection from the corporal punishment, verbal abuse and unjust or excessive punishment.' See UN Doc CRC/C/C Add. 12, 22 January 1993 at 69–70.

25 UN Doc CRC/C/15 Add. 34, January 1995.

26 Ibid.

27 According to Yuri Kolossov, a member of the UN Committee on the Rights of the Child, the European Court judgement was discussed by the legal advisers of the United Kingdom and members of the Committee on the Rights of the Child (in conversation with the author July 1996).

28 *Op. cit.*

29 *Op. cit.*

30 The same is also true of women see Mckinnon (1989), *Towards a Feminist Theory of the State*. See also below Chinkin, The Torture of the Girl Child.

31 Scheuner, Fundamental Rights and the Protection of the Individual Against Social Groups and Powers in the Constitutional System of the Federal Republic of Germany, in *Rene Cassin Amicorum Discipulorum Liber* III, (1971) at 255.

32 Article 1(1).

33 See for example Ulpian's definition: 'By quaestio [torture] we are to understand the torment and the suffering of the body in order to elicit the truth.' See in general Peters, (1985), *Torture*.

34 *Airey* v. *Ireland*, European Court of Human Rights, Series A. No. 32 (1979) at 22.

35 Article 1(2).

36 UN Doc HRI/GEN/1.

37 4 Inter-American Court of Human Rights Series C. (1988).
In *Velasquez-Rodriguez* v. *Honduras* the Inter-American Court determined that an illegal act which breaches human rights and which is not directly imputable to the state, because it is an act of a private person or because the person responsible has not been identified, can lead to international responsibility of the state not because of the act itself but because of the failure 'to prevent the violation or to respond to it as required by the Convention.' The Court also concluded that where human rights violations by private parties are not seriously investigated the parties are in a sense aided by the government making the state responsible on the international plane.

38 5 Inter-American Court of Human Rights Decisions and Judgements. Series C. (1989).

39 Article 2.

40   *X* v. *Ireland*, 14 Yearbook of the European Commission of Human Rights (1971) at 188 and 198.

41   Judgement of the European Court of Human Rights, 6 February (1976), No. 20, Series A at 42.

42   *X and Y* v. *Netherlands*, Judgement of European Court of Human Rights, 26 March (1985), Series A, No. 91.

43   The Dutch government argued, inter alia, that Article 8 of the European Convention on Human Rights could not be interpreted to require a state to create criminal procedures where civil remedies were available.

44   The European Court of Human Rights found that a specific article of the Convention, in this case Article 8, 'may involve the adoption of measures designed to secure respect for private life even in the sphere of relations of individuals between themselves'.

45   OAS Doc OEA/Series L/V11.53. *Report on the Situation of Human Rights in the Republic of Guatamala*, 1981.

46   Rehabilitation under the Convention on the Rights of the Child has a much broader application than is found in the UN Convention against Torture and Other Cruel, Inhuman or Degrading Treatment or Punishment 1984, which only places a duty on States Parties to provide 'as full rehabilitation as possible' for acts which amount to torture, cruel, inhuman and degrading treatment and punishment as defined by the Convention. The duty incorporated in the Convention on the Rights of the Child is for any form of neglect, exploitation or abuse.
See also para. 1(a) General Recommendation 19, 1992:
'That states take all legal and other measures which are necessary to provide effective protection of women against gender based violence, including, inter alia:
(a) ... violence and abuse within the family...'
In para. 1(c) the Committee expressly recommends such protective measures as including rehabilitation and support services for women who are either at risk of violence or victims of such violence.

47   UN Doc CCPR/C/21/Add. 1.

48   Van Bueren, 'Crossing the Frontier – The International Protection of Family Life in the 21st Century', in Lowe and Douglas (1996) (eds), *Families Across Frontiers*, Kluwer.

49   In Van Bueren (1998), *International Documents on Children*, Kluwer/Nijhoff, Second Edition.

50   See in general Schwarzenberger (1957), *International Law*, Vol. 1. 26–7; Parry (1965), *The Sources and Evidence of International Law*; D'Amato (1971), *The Concept of Custom in International Law*.

51   Report of the UN Special Rapporteur on Torture, UN Doc E/CN.4/1991/17 para. 278. For *jus cogens* see Hannikainen (1988), *Peremptory Norms in International Law*; Sztuch (1972), *Jus Cogens and the Vienna Convention on the Law of Treaties*. Weil criticises the theory as it forces states to accept 'the supernormativity of rules they were perhaps not prepared to recognise as ordinary norms', in *Towards Relative Normativity in International Law*, 77 *AJIL* 413, 427 (1983).

52   Cruel treatment and punishment was intentionally omitted from inclusion in Article 3 of the European Convention on Human Rights. See, however, the inclusion of cruelty in the discussion on torture in *Ireland* v. *United Kingdom*, as the Court found that the treatment 'did not occasion suffering of the particular intensity or cruelty implied by the word torture', Series A. No. 25 at (1993), 67 para. 167.

53   See *Velasquez Rodriguez op. cit.*

54   The European Court of Human Rights emphasized this point in *Ireland* v. *U.K.*, *op. cit.*, 'The Convention prohibits in absolute terms torture and inhuman or degrading treat-

ment or punishment, irrespective of the victim's conduct.' Article 3 makes no provision for exceptions ... there can be no derogation therefrom even in the event of a public emergency threatening the life of the nation.' European Court of Human Rights. See also Doswald-Beck, 'What does the Prohibition of Torture or Inhuman or Degrading Treatment or Punishment Mean? The Interpretation of the European Commission and Court of Human Rights' **25** *Netherlands International Law Review* 1978, 24. The same perspective is also adopted by the Human Rights Committee of the International Covenant on Civil and Political Rights. 'Even in situations of public emergency ... this provision is non-derogable ...' See also Article 4(2), International Covenant on Civil and Political Rights.

55 See Millet (1994), *The Politics of Cruelty*, at 18.
56 'No one shall be subjected to torture or to inhuman or degrading treatment or punishment.'
57 *Ireland* v. *United Kingdom, op. cit.*
58 *R.* v. *McCormick* 1984 where the Court of Criminal Appeal of Northern Ireland described the cumulative effects of 'overcrowded detention quarters, a lack of proper washing facilities, absence of heating in winter, lack of hot water, poor lavatory facilities, unsatisfactory dental treatment, close restriction of letters and visits and the extreme manner of separating detainees from their families' as torture.
59 See the discussion in Rodley (1987), *The Treatment of Prisoners Under International Law*, Clarendon Press.
60 See for example Charlesworth, Chinkin and Wright (1991), 'Feminist Approaches to International Law', **85** *American Journal of International Law,* 613.
61 Article 37(a) Convention on the Rights of the Child.
62 Millet, *op. cit.* at 35.
63 However, there is not always agreement between human rights fora as to which classification specific treatments and punishments should be applied. The European Commission and Court of Human Rights disagreed over the nature of interrogation techniques employed by British officials in Northern Ireland. The European Court of Human Rights overruled the Commission in ruling that the treatment amounted only to 'inhuman and degrading' treatment and did not amount to torture.
64 Article 1, Resolution 3452 (XXX). General Assembly of the United Nations, 9 December, 1975.
65 And see Helsinki Watch (1992), *Nothing Unusual, The Torture of Children in Turkey.*
66 Van Bueren (1995), *The International Law on the Rights of the Child*, at 225.
67 *Denmark et al.* v. *Greece* Report of 5 November 1969; Yearbook XII at 186.
68 Separate opinion of Judge Zekia, *Ireland* v. *United Kingdom.*
69 *Denmark et al* v. *Greece op. cit.* at 186.
70 *Tyrer* v. *United Kingdom* Series A No. 26, 1978. Police officers birched the boy at a police station where, several weeks after the original incident occurred, he was forced to remove his trousers and underwear and bend over a table while two policemen held him and another birched him. The boy was sore for 10 days after the punishment. The European Court felt that the treatment was not inhuman because the punishment was insufficiently severe. The Court did, however, find the punishment to be degrading even though he did not suffer any permanent or long lasting physical effects.
71 Reproduced in Van Bueren (1998), *International Documents on Children, op. cit.*
72 *Op. cit.*
73 *Op. cit.*
74 *Campbell and Cosans* v. *United Kingdom* Series A. No. 48, European Court of Human Rights, 25 February (1982) at 13.

75   *Op. cit.*

76   Another important factor in the European Court of Human Rights decision was the delay between sentencing and implementation of the punishment which caused the boy mental anguish because of the anticipation of the punishment and pain.

77   *Op. cit.*

78   *Op. cit.*

79   *Weems* v. *U.S.* 217 US 349, 1910. Thus, a sentence of 12 years in chains at hard and painful labour and lifetime surveillance for the crime of falsifying an official document was declared cruel because it was 'excessive and out of proportion to the offense.'

80   UN Doc CCPR/C/21/Add. 1.

81   Rule 32(1) Standard Minimum Rules of the Treatment of Prisoners prohibits 'close confinement' unless it is with the approval of a medical officer.

82   Human Rights Watch/Childrens Project (1994), *Children in Detention in Police Lock-ups in Jamaica*, at 18.

83   Human Rights Watch (1994), *Final Justice, Police and Death Squad Homicides of Adolescents in Brazil*, at 21.

84   Rule 17. Reproduced in Van Bueren, *International Documents op. cit.*

85   Human Rights Watch/Childrens Project (1994), *Children in Detention in Police Lock-ups in Jamaica*, at 2.

86   For harassment in Northern Ireland see Human Rights Watch, Childrens Rights Project (1994), *The Abuse of Children in Northern Ireland.*

87   Human Rights Watch Childrens Rights Project (1994), *Easy Prey, Child Soldiers in Liberia.*

88   *Tabay* where a person's elbows are tied together behind the back and the rope is pulled tighter and tighter until the rib cage separates because the blood does not circulate.

89   The principal 'emergency' statutes are Prevention of Terrorism (Temporary Provisions) Act 1989 and Northern Ireland (Emergency) Provisions Act 1991. The 1994 Codes of Practice issued under the Northern Ireland (Emergency Provisions) Act 1991 which are non-binding recommend that children should be interviewed only in the presence of a parent, guardian, or some other appropriate person. Under s. 14 Prevention of Terrorism Act children suspected of crimes relating to criminal violence may be denied access to a lawyer for 48 hours hence a 17-year-old may be questioned alone.

90   In *Brogan* v. *United Kingdom* Series A No. 145, (1988) the European Court of Human Rights ruled that a detention of four days and six hours permitted under the Prevention of Terrorism Act breached Article 5(3) European Convention on Human Rights. See further Tanca 1 EJIL (1990), 269.

91   Langbein (1976), *Torture and the Law of Proof: Europe and England in the Ancien Regime*, University of Chicago Press, at 3.

92   See further Peters (1985), *Torture*, Blackwell, 11–67.

5 International Conventions Against Torture and on the Rights of the Child – The Work of Two United Nations Committees

Bent Sørensen

Definition of Torture

The Convention against Torture and Other Cruel, Inhuman or Degrading Treatment or Punishment (Convention against Torture) was adopted by consensus in the United Nations General Assembly on 10th December 1984. It went into force in June 1987 when 20 Member States had ratified the Convention. By 1st April 1996, 89 states out of 184 Member States of the United Nations had ratified. In addition, seven non-Member States had ratified the Convention, thus giving a total of 96 participating States.

The Convention's Article 1 gives a definition of torture:

> For the purposes of this Convention, the term 'torture' means any act by which severe pain or suffering, whether physical or mental, is intentionally inflicted on a person for such purposes as obtaining from him or a third person information or a confession, punishing him for an act he or a third person has committed or is suspected of having committed, or intimidating or coercing him or a third person, or for any reason based on discrimination of any kind, when such pain or suffering is inflicted by or at the instigation of or with the consent or acquiescence of a public official or other person acting in an official capacity. It does not include pain or suffering arising only from, inherent in or incidental to lawful sanctions.

As will be seen, 'pain or suffering arising only from ... lawful sanctions' is not to be regarded as torture in the sense of the Convention. In 1996, many people probably regret this fact; however, it should be remembered that the wording of the Convention originates from the end of the 1970s and the beginning of the 1980s and was adopted by consensus in 1984, at which time the world looked considerably different from today. Had the sentence not been included, the very existence of the Convention could be doubted. In the daily work of the Committee it has turned out that this limitation is of no significant importance.[1]

Article 2 prohibits torture, and the second paragraph of the Article elaborates further on this: nothing, whatsoever, may justify the use of torture. Paragraph 3 of the Article deals with 'due obedience' and states that an order from a superior is no excuse for torture. Thus, the words of the Convention on these points are crystal clear.

The Duties of the States Parties

Articles 3 to 16 describe the obligations the States Parties have taken upon themselves by ratifying the Convention. The most essential duties are as follows:

- not to use torture
- not 'refouler'
- punish torturers
- educate all personnel involved in the care of torture victims
- rehabilitate torture victims
- keep under systematic review interrogation rules, and so on, and arrangement of custody and treatment of persons under arrest and the like.

Moreover, Article 19 of the Convention creates an obligation to report to the Committee on how the States Parties have implemented the provisions of the Convention in their home country's domestic law as well as in practice. This reporting must be undertaken within one year of the ratification, and then every fourth year, *inter alia*, reporting about any amendments made – some of which may have been made as a consequence of recommendations put forward by the Committee.

The Duties of the Committee

Articles 17 and 18 describe the Committee which consists of '10 experts of high moral standing and recognized competence in the field of human rights, who shall serve in their personal capacity'. Members are elected for a period of four years, and can be re-elected. The author has been a member of the Committee since its beginning in 1988.

In summary, the work of the Committee consists of the following:

- receiving, dealing with, criticising and commenting on the reports from the States Parties – all this is done in public
- the work according to Article 20
- the work according to Article 22
- reporting to the United Nations' General Assembly.

Article 20 empowers the Committee against Torture to take active actions: 'If the Committee receives reliable information which appears to it to contain well-founded indications that torture is being systematically practised in the territory of a State Party, the Committee shall invite that State Party to co-operate …'. Such a cooperation may result in the Committee against Torture visiting the country in question to inspect prisons, police stations and the like, with a subsequent report. The work connected with Article 20 is confidential, but the end result, the report, is public. Until now, two reports have been published according to Article 20: Turkey in 1993, and Egypt in 1996.

Article 22 gives an individual the right – if certain conditions have been fulfilled – to put forward a complaint to the Committee against Torture on the violation of the provisions of the Convention in the country where he or she is staying, for example the use of torture, or extradition to a country where there is a risk of being subjected to torture, and so on. Here too, the investigations of particular cases are done *in camera*, whereas the result of the investigations are published, although the names of the persons complaining remain anonymous. Approximately 20 such cases have been published.

The Committee against Torture convenes twice a year, each session lasting two weeks. Until now, the work with the Member States' reports[2] has been far the most important part of the Committee against Torture's workload. From five to ten reports are dealt with each session, and there is no 'waiting-list' for dealing with the reports.

Convention on the Rights of the Child

The Convention on the Rights of the Child (CRC) was adopted on 20th November 1989. It was opened for signature on 26th January 1990 and 61 countries signed the same day, a record in the history of the United Nations. The CRC went into force on 2nd September 1990, when 20 Member States had ratified, and by June 1997, 193 had ratified it. The only missing States are Somalia and the United States of America. This Convention has also set up a Committee of 10 experts.

Their main duties are the same as for the Convention against Torture:

'Examining the progress made by States Parties in achieving the realization of the obligations undertaken in the present Convention.'

The CRC cannot, however, contrary to the Committee against Torture, receive and consider communications from individuals on breaches of the Convention.[3]

The workload of the Committee on the Rights of the Child is enormous. The 10 members have three sessions of three weeks' duration per year and a pre-sessional session lasting one week. At present, 30 State reports are waiting to be dealt with, 80 initial reports are due in 1996, and 57 second periodical reports are due in 1997.

In the Convention, the issue of torture is mentioned in Article 37(a) with the same words as elsewhere in the United Nations system: 'No child shall be subjected to torture or other cruel, inhuman or degrading treatment or punishment.'

Comparison

The elder of the two Conventions, the Convention against Torture, has, twelve years after its adoption, and seven years after it went into force, been ratified only by approximately half of the Member States of the United Nations. Torture is not a popular subject for a treaty. The younger, the Convention on the Right of the Child, has beaten all records with the United Nations, and a little less than six years after it went into force, nearly all of the Member States have ratified it.

The Convention against Torture specifically deals with torture (including torture of children). The Convention on the Rights of the Child specifically deals with children, although torture is mentioned as part of an article.

Both Committees receive reports from the Member States, criticize them and give recommendations for better conditions. The only instrument of power the Committees possess is however the moral pressure, based on general awareness about the problems in the populations, and a raised public international debate. The Committee against Torture can, as mentioned, in certain situations function as a 'superior court', as it receives complaints from individuals about Member States. In practice, the decisions by the Committee against Torture have always been followed.

Until now, the problems on torture have played a minor role in the activities of the CRC. The CRC is completely overloaded with work – nearly suffocated in its own success. The main areas within its work are:

- corporal punishment/flogging: change of law or regulations
- street children: education programmes
- asylumseekers: unaccompanied children
- armed conflicts: child soldiers.

In the Convention against Torture, the work against torture is the central activity area. Torture of children has called for increasing attention in its work. The main areas within the work in the Convention about children are:

- corporal punishment: Article 1
- street children: protection against torture
- impunity of perpetrators
- asylumseekers: Article 3
- armed conflicts: Article 22.

The two Committees cooperate on a secretarial level, and an account of their work is given in the respective Committees, so that the members of each Committee are informed of the work of the other.

Notes

1 Cf. below, Chinkin, 'Torture of the Girl Child'; McBride, 'The Violation of Economic, Social and Cultural Rights as Torture or Cruel, Inhuman or Degrading Treatment'; and Sottas, 'A Non-Governmental Organization perspective of the United Nations' Approach to Children and Torture'.
2 Article 19.
3 For a recommendation of the right to petition for children, see Van Bueren (1995), *The International Law on the Rights of the Child*, Kluwer, 410–11.

6   Torture of the Girl-Child

Christine Chinkin[1]

Introduction

There is a wide disparity between the emphasis given by international human rights law to the prohibition against torture and the reality of its deliberate practice by many states. This chapter first examines this prohibition and the consequences of determining that an act constitutes torture under international law. It suggests that the symbolic weight of labelling an act as torture may be as significant as the formal legal consequences. It then argues that while there is widespread support for the stance that torture must be outlawed, there is less willingness to accept similar consequences for acts that do not fit within the classic concept of torture, even though they manifest the formal elements of torture and the victims suffer similar long-term consequences. In particular many forms of violence deliberately committed against girls and women are by definition excluded and consequently do not attract the opprobrium aroused by torture. Further, since many perpetrators are either indifferent to the age of the victim, or their youth causes them to be targeted, violence is regularly inflicted upon girl-children. While victims of legally identified torture may achieve some release from their suffering through public recognition of the wrongs committed against them, gender-specific acts of violence may be discounted, or regarded as socially or culturally acceptable forms of behaviour. Their invisibility is accordingly perpetuated. The chapter concludes that an extended understanding of the concept of torture that includes deliberate and severe acts of cruelty to girl-children whether committed by public or private actors would facilitate their prevention and eradication.

International Law and Torture

The Legal Prohibition of Torture

International human rights law has placed great emphasis on the prohibition of torture. Within the United Nations human rights system, it is included in the so-called International Bill of Rights through provisions in the Universal Declaration on Human Rights[2] and the International Covenant on Civil and Political Rights.[3] It is also the subject of a widely ratified specialized convention, the United Nations Convention against Torture.[4] Alleged incidents of torture are thus directly subject to the scrutiny of the Human Rights Committee for those states that have accepted its jurisdiction under the First Optional Protocol,[5] and of the Committee against Torture.[6] Torture has been included within the United Nations scheme of thematic special rapporteurs by the appointment of a Special Rapporteur on Torture. Allegations of torture also often form part of the specific mandate of country-based rapporteurs.

Torture is explicitly prohibited by the three major regional human rights instruments,[7] and there are two specialized regional conventions, each with their own enforcement mechanisms.[8] Persons considered especially vulnerable to torture are given additional guarantees through the requirement that the rights enunciated in the above treaties are applied without discrimination, typically on the grounds of 'race, colour, sex, language, religion, political or other opinion, national or social origin, property, birth or other status.'[9] Other treaties explicitly prohibit torture against identified categories of exposed persons, for example children,[10] and protected persons under international humanitarian law. Accordingly torture of protected persons during international armed conflict constitutes grave breach of each of the four Geneva Conventions and Additional Protocols.[11] It is also one of the listed prohibitions of common Article 3 that stipulates a minimum code of behaviour in internal conflict.

The consistent banning of torture in legally binding international instruments has facilitated its acceptance as a norm of customary international law. Detailed standards have fleshed out its content in particular contexts through non-binding 'soft' law instruments that are consistent with the treaties.[12] Its acceptance as a norm of customary international law has been assisted by the widespread ratification of the various treaties, the development of monitoring and enforcement measures through the Human Rights Committee, the Committee against Torture and regional mechanisms, and the application of the standards in domestic courts.[13] These testify to a strongly held *opinio juris* that are asserted to counteract widespread inconsistent state practice.[14] Assertions of non-derogability in times of public emergency,[15] and the non-acceptance of exceptions support claims that the prohibition of torture has achieved the status of a peremptory norm of international law, *jus cogens*, from which no derogation is permissible.[16]

The Definition and Consequences of Torture

Torture is variously defined within the treaties, although there are common elements. Since the United Nations Convention against Torture is widely ratified by states from all regions of the world, this chapter will focus on the definition in Article 1(1) of that Convention. It states that torture is:

> any act by which severe pain or suffering, whether physical or mental, is intentionally inflicted on a person for such purposes as obtaining from him or a third person information or a confession, punishing him for an act he or a third person has committed ..., or intimidating or coercing him or a third person, or for any reason based on discrimination of any kind, when such pain or suffering is inflicted by or at the instigation of or with the consent or acquiescence of a public official or other person acting in an official capacity.

This definition contains a number of specific elements: (i) an act; (ii) causing pain or suffering; (iii) intentionally inflicted; (iv) for the purpose of obtaining information, punishing, intimidating, or coercing the victim or a third person, or for any discriminatory purpose; (v) committed by or with acquiescence of a public official. Although the 'classic' case of torture in custody is clearly envisaged,[17] the Article does not require detention. It also leaves open a number of questions, for example: can torture be committed through omission; do 'disappearances' constitute torture;[18] can acts in non-penal institutions of detention such as hospitals or immigration detention centres constitute torture; what is the difference of degree between torture and 'cruel, inhuman and degrading treatment';[19] can the victim consent to the alleged torture; and what is the obligation upon the state to prevent and punish acts causing pain and suffering committed by private agencies?

The significance of these questions lies in the specific legal consequences of defining an act, or administrative practices, as torture. Acceptance by states of the international prohibition against torture entails obligations within domestic as well as international law. States are subject to the jurisdiction of the international and regional bodies established by the various treaties to which they are parties. This includes allegations of violation by other States Parties without any separate requirement of standing.[20] In the words of the European Court of Human Rights:

> ... unlike international treaties of the classic kind, the Convention [the European Convention on Human Rights] comprises more than mere reciprocal engage-

ments between contracting States. It creates, over and above a network of mutual, bilateral undertakings, objective obligations which, in the words of the Preamble, benefit from a 'collective enforcement'.[21]

The location of the prohibition against torture within the International Covenant on Civil and Political Rights requires states to take the necessary steps for ensuring the right without regard to the available resources.[22] Similarly the Convention against Torture requires states to take legislative and other measures to prevent torture[23] and to make torture a criminal offence punishable in domestic law by appropriate penalties.[24] Under international law national criminal jurisdiction can legitimately be based on territoriality, nationality, passive personality and, following the pattern established by the conventions against terrorism, the presence of the accused within the territory.[25] Continuing the precedent of the terrorist conventions, States Parties are obligated either to exercise criminal jurisdiction over a person accused of torture or to extradite the alleged offender to another state with jurisdiction.[26] On the other hand a person shall not be extradited or returned to a state where there are grounds for believing she or he may be subjected to torture.[27] The customary international law basis for the prohibition has also led to the assertion of civil jurisdiction within national courts, for example in the United States.[28]

One purpose of these provisions is to attempt to ensure that an alleged torturer does not escape legal process through the assertion of a wide jurisdictional base. Another is to assist the victim in finding a safe haven. Nevertheless, as is only too evident, these provisions are routinely not applied and torture continues undiminished and unpunished where those with power consider the practice assists them in its maintenance and in quelling opposition. In light of continued widespread non-compliance perhaps one of the most significant consequences of denoting an act as torture, and thus recognizing that a person has been a victim of torture, is symbolic. Since state elites typically respond to universal condemnation of torture by denying it occurs within their jurisdiction, for victims the label 'torture' is an acknowledgement that the treatment they received is unacceptable and violates the most fundamental principles of law formally agreed by the international community. It is an act of validation that removes any felt guilt or shame away from the victim and places the responsibility squarely on the perpetrators and which may be instrumental in assisting psychological recovery from the harm inflicted. The symbolic effect helps to explain why the prohibition against torture is formally located at the peak of the hierarchy of human rights norms.

Torture is an abuse of power. The torturer seeks the total subordination of the victim through control over the victim's body, thoughts and actions, hence the definitional focus upon psychological as well as physical suffering. One objective of torture is to extinguish the individuality and identity of the person. The effects of torture can continue long after release and may be exacerbated by such circumstances as official denial, public indifference, dislocation through exile or refugee status, or feelings of guilt induced by knowledge of others who did not survive, or belief that submission to torture indicated weakness or led to betrayal. Turning from the victim to the perpetrator, an important element of torture is its commission by public agents. The concept of civil and political human rights is to identify those areas of individual autonomy that are protected from state intervention. The essence of social contract theory is state provision of the framework for political organization while guaranteeing individual freedom. Torture by state officials therefore undermines enjoyment of all other civil and political rights. The acceptance of liberal democratic ideals and fundamental human freedoms through formal adherence to international human rights instruments has too often been countered by attempted state control by any means over those who reject governmental directives. This may come about whether those who represent the power of the state act in the name of fascism, militarism, communism, or any other political or religious ideology. Human rights guarantees, for example of free speech, peaceful association, equal access to law and fair trial processes, are meaningless if state officials can torture with impunity those who dissent, or are accused of dissenting, from their authority. The fear and terror caused among the civilian population by the belief that torture will follow detention are also instruments used by governments in manipulating a compliant populace. Torture through the instrumentality of the state, the very body to which individuals must look for protection under the rule of law, means that the victim has nowhere else to turn. Whether or not the liberal philosophy of human rights law is accepted, this remains as the stark reality for those living under a regime that maintains power through torture. International law remains as the last resort; hence the significance of international vindication of the wrongs committed and of the individual responsibility of the perpetrators.

The Human Rights of the Girl Child

Particular guarantees of the human rights of the girl-child are contained within both the Children's Convention[29] and the Women's Convention.[30] While the age of childhood is defined in the former,[31] the age at which a girl reaches womanhood is not. The legal construct of childhood as ending at age 18 is artificial and may reflect little of the realities of life for many females. In different societies, girls may be married while still under 18 and with little or no regard to their own wishes. Despite marital status they may never be treated by the law as autonomous individuals with access to the same full panoply of civil, political, economic and social rights as their male family members. They may legally remain as 'children' all their lives.[32] The Women's Convention provides for equality in those areas where women's life experiences show discrimination to be most detrimental to their enjoyment of human rights. Since girls are subject to many of these situations, for example restricted access to education, health care and employment, marriage, forced prostitution and trafficking, the provisions of the Women's Convention must be applicable to females under, as well as over, 18 years of age.

However this conclusion may not be beneficial for the girl-child. Although the obligations under both Conventions are framed only in the 'soft' language of taking appropriate measures to achieve their objectives, the Children's Convention identifies rights applicable to children. In contrast, the Women's Convention is not rights-based but has the more restricted objective of achieving equality between men and women through the condemnation and elimination of discrimination. In this it follows the general United Nations human rights treaties that include prohibition of discrimination on, *inter alia*, the grounds of sex. Formally, the human rights movement applies 'as a common standard of achievement for all peoples and all nations ...',[33] but the rights are defined in terms of male experiences and the yardstick for measuring attainment of equality is the lives of men. The general human rights treaties are not readily susceptible to gendered interpretations and fail to take account of the violations of human rights women experience in ways that are different from men and that occur because of gender.[34] The concept that girl-children move from the particular guarantees of the Children's Convention to those of the Women's Convention carries the unfortunate perception that the girl-child does not become fully adult and subject to the mainstream human rights treaties. Instead she becomes a woman, and subject to national laws, practices and traditions that place her in a subordinate position to men.[35]

The substantive and institutional separation of women's rights within the United Nations has contributed to the marginalization of women's rights.[36] Recognition of women's rights as human rights was a primary objective of women's NGOs at the World Conference on Human Rights held in Vienna in 1993 and at the Fourth United Nations Conference on Women in Beijing in 1995.[37] Their campaign led to the reaffirmation in the Beijing Declaration that 'women's rights are human rights' and of the commitment to 'the full implementation of the human rights of women and of the girl-child as an inalienable, integral and indivisible part of all human rights and fundamental freedoms.'[38] Her extreme vulnerability led to the identification of the girl-child as an area of critical concern at Beijing.[39] The Children's Convention and the Women's Convention must be regarded as mutually reinforcing in articulating the human rights of women and the girl-child,[40] and complementary both to each other and to other human rights instruments in the mission to integrate women's human rights throughout all United Nations human rights activities.

Torture and the Girl-Child

Torture is prohibited in the Children's Convention and states also have the duty to protect children from all forms of physical and mental violence, injury and abuse.[41] The double susceptibility of the girl-child to violence is not addressed, that is violence based upon her gender and violence because of her age. Some children are especially vulnerable, for example because they are abandoned, homeless, street children, caught up in armed conflict, disabled or discriminated against because of their identification as belonging to a particular class, racial or ethnic group.[42] The girl-child is vulnerable to violence from the time of conception through her entire life cycle. Son preference, the discriminatory preference for male children, may be based upon religious or cultural constructions of masculinity and femininity, or upon the greater economic value of boy-children. Whatever its roots, it 'often results in violence against and maltreatment of female foetuses and girl-children'.[43] This violence continues through childhood and puberty to womanhood.

Unlike in the Children's Convention, there is no specific prohibition of torture in the Women's Convention. Of itself this does not matter since all provisions in the other human rights instruments must be applied without discrimination, *inter alia*, on the grounds of sex, including the prohibition against torture. However the interpretation given to torture has deflected the attention of the international community away from the pain and suffering deliberately inflicted on women and girls through a failure to perceive such acts as torture, or even as a human rights issue. Violence as experienced by women and girls has not traditionally been identified as violating human rights standards, still less as torture.[44] In many instances it does not even invoke domestic criminal sanctions.

Recent assertions that gender-specific violence violates women's enjoyment of their human rights have begun to break this silence. Gender-based violence has been identified by the Committee on the Elimination of Discrimination Against Women,[45] the General Assembly,[46] and at Beijing as:

> violence that results in, or is likely to result in, physical, sexual or psychological harm or suffering to women, including threats of such acts, coercion and arbitrary deprivation of liberty, whether occurring in public or private life.[47]

Such violence is 'directed at a woman because she is a woman, or [that] affects women disproportionately'.[48] It is an obstacle to the objectives of the Fourth World Conference on Women of development, equality and peace.[49] Governments must condemn such violence and take steps to eliminate it.[50] Although these instruments fall short of defining even extreme examples of gender-specific violence as torture, the parallels between them are evident. Out of the five elements identified in Article 1 of the Torture Convention three are readily satisfied. Both torture and gender-specific violence require acts causing pain or suffering, whether physical or psychological. For acts causing pain and suffering to be defined as torture they must be committed for one of the purposes listed in Article 1 which include intimidation and coercion. In the Declaration on the Elimination of Violence, the General Assembly avowed that gender-specific violence is 'a manifestation of historically unequal power relations between men and women, which have led to domination over and discrimination against women'.[51] This recognition of the structural and systemic nature of gender-specific violence would appear to satisfy the requirement of intimidation or coercion. The targeting of a woman 'because she is a woman' is also discriminatory within the terms of Article 1. The vital distinction between the definition of torture and that of gender-based violence is that the latter covers actions committed by private actors as well as public officials.

The next section examines four locations of violence against girls: the state; armed conflict; the family; and the community.[52] In each case while boys also experience violent abuse, girls suffer forms of violence different from boys, but different factors will frequently inhibit its characterization as torture. The focus of this chapter is on the violence directed most frequently, but not exclusively, at the girl-child. Examples are given for illustrative purposes but it is important to remember that they are not exceptional. Indeed often the only distinctive feature is that they have been documented.

Torture by the State

The classic understanding of torture is by state agents within places of custody and detention. Thus the fifth requirement of involvement of public officials is ostensibly satisfied. Women and girls in detention in both armed conflict and non-conflict situations cannot presume that they are safe from violence by those in positions of authority.[53] In detention particular forms of violence are committed against women and girls that either do not occur, or do not occur as often, to men or boys. The reason for detention may be gender-based, for example expressed opposition to religious based discriminatory laws such as dress codes or required behaviour in public places. The reason for detention is not relevant to the illegality of subsequent treatment by state officials, but it may set the scene for different attitudes towards detainees. Men are more likely to be viewed as important political prisoners in comparison with intransigent women. Female detainees are especially vulnerable to forms of sexual torture, including different forms of rape, sexual abuse, humiliation and harassment.[54] Religious ideology may be used to justify torture, for example the raping of virgins prior to execution in Iran. While such acts are committed against women of all ages, young women, for example students, are often especially attractive targets. Mothers may be tortured through threats and commission of such actions against their daughters. Women's traditional location in the private arena and non-involvement in public life may not protect them from torture. Girls who have not themselves been active in political action may be tortured in these and other ways for information about the activities of male family members about which they may not even be aware. Girls may be tortured as reprisal for the actions of their fathers, husbands and brothers who have evaded capture by the authorities. When women and girls themselves engage in political dissent, they may be subject to even crueller acts of torture because they are perceived as having stepped outside their accepted role and therefore as more dangerous.

While such methods may be used as official methods of torture, for example in questioning, female detainees are also exposed to sexual abuse that is connived in by the prison or other authorities. A woman detainee may be raped by a guard during the night hours. Her cell may be left unlocked allowing access by other prisoners, or officials. A young girl seeking information about a disappeared relative may be raped at the place of enquiry. Police and other agencies may abuse powers specifically bestowed for law enforcement:

> Women were singled out for rape and sexual abuse when the military launched an anti-poaching operation in Zaire's Salonga National Park during April and May 1992. Over a dozen schoolgirls were detained and raped by soldiers and gendarmes forced a man to rape his 18-year-old daughter at gunpoint.[55]

Complaint is difficult and if made the victim may be disbelieved, further abused or her allegation dismissed as the events were not an accepted incident of detention. Sexual abuse by a state agent may be disregarded as falling outside his official duties, as unfortunate but a private action and therefore not torture. Nevertheless in the terms of the definition of torture such acts are deliberately inflicted, cause pain and suffering, almost certainly are intended to intimidate and coerce, are discriminatory, and even when not directly committed by state officials are acquiesced in by them. In the words of Amnesty International: 'When a policeman or soldier rapes a woman in his custody, that rape is no longer an act of private violence, but an act of torture or ill-treatment for which the state bears responsibility.'[56] Even where investigations are carried out into the incidence of torture and prosecutions ensue, these rarely include for rape.

Rape and other forms of sexual abuse are surrounded by myths that perpetuate the view that they are about sex and lust, not violence, humiliation, degradation and pain.[57] These myths include that the woman consented, that she enjoyed or even asked for it, and that the perpetrator was only acting like any man. A woman in detention may see no option but to consent to intercourse with an official. The fear of attack that keeps a woman awake all night is not perceived as a form of sleep deprivation.[58] The fact that a man in custody was tortured is not denied because that torture included sexual abuse, but this may be the outcome for a woman. The effects of rape in custody may be long lasting, including apprehension of subsequent non-acceptance by family and community and ineligibility for marriage. A young girl's social standing may be destroyed through subsequent pregnancy. Silence may deny women any release from the agony.

Torture during Armed Conflict

Violent acts are regularly committed against women during armed conflict,[59] whether international armed conflict or the use by governments of military force to put down internal insurgency. In the case of the latter, governments often allow the military extensive powers that are not subject to civilian legal authorities. This fosters an environment of lawlessness in which rape and other forms of sexual abuse are committed with impunity:

> In Chiapas three sisters aged 16, 18 and 20 were returning to their village with their mother after selling their produce in a local town on 4 June 1994. The[y] … were stopped by soldiers at a road-block, … approximately 10 soldiers raped them. They were warned they would be killed if they reported being raped. The women were so terrified that it was weeks before they told anyone what had happened.[60]

Rape in armed conflict may be seen as a paradigm form of torture. It is a deliberately committed tactic for the intimidation, coercion and humiliation of the enemy. Although men suffer sexual abuse in armed conflict in probably greater numbers than is generally accepted, the targeting of women for acts of sexual violence is discriminatory. These acts are committed by the military arm of the state and by others with the connivance of the military. Large numbers of the world's refugees are women and children, many of whom have fled from the devastation of armed conflict. Such women and girl children are especially defenceless against further acts of sexual violence in return for food, shelter, passage, rations and papers. Rape and sexual violence against refugees who may be trapped in camps for years closely resembles rape in official custody. Officials and other refugees may remain unpunished for acts of violence, especially against unaccompanied women and girls. The particular problems faced by women refugees are now being addressed by UNHCR who have issued Guidelines to assist in identifying and preventing such violent acts.[61]

Far from being widely condemned, the historic persistence of rape and sexual abuse in armed conflict has been ignored and tolerated as part of the inevitable consequences of war. In the context of international armed conflict, the Nuremberg Tribunals did not prosecute rape as a separate violation of the laws of war. Neither was rape included as a crime against humanity.[62] While the torture suffered, for example by prisoners of war, was the subject of prosecutions and recompense, that endured by women forcibly held by the Japanese military in sexual slavery was for decades neither officially recognised nor acknowledged.[63]

The Geneva Conventions of 1949 require States Parties to protect women in international armed conflict 'against any attack on their honour, in particular against rape, enforced prostitution, or any form of indecent assault'.[64] States Parties are obliged to prosecute grave breaches of the Conventions under domestic law. Grave breaches include, *inter alia*, torture, and acts wilfully committed and causing great suffering or causing injuries to body or health.[65] Gender-based violence can readily be read into this definition, but in light of the regularity with which such acts have been committed with impunity, there is concern that their omission will harden their invisibility. Explicit inclusion would have reinforced the unacceptability of such acts. Similarly, common Article 3 prohibits certain acts in a minimum code of conduct for all parties in internal conflict. They include violence to life and the person, cruel treatment and torture, and humiliating and degrading treatment, but again do not spell out rape and other forms of sexual abuse as coming within this interdiction.

Only recently have sexual abuses of girls and women been directly recognized as violations of international humanitarian law. In the context of former Yugoslavia, United Nations agencies, the Commission of Experts, the Security Council and the Secretary-General have recognized that rape occurred on a massive, widespread, systematic and organized basis. Violent acts were committed by all sides against females of all ages, from very young girls to elderly women. Sexual terror was used as an instrument of war. The jurisdiction of the International Tribunal for Prosecution of Violations of International Humanitarian Law in former Yugoslavia includes rape as a crime against humanity.[66] However a crime against humanity is committed against the civilian population, not against an individual woman. This limitation would cause less concern if rape had been included in the grave breaches of the Geneva Conventions over which the Tribunal has jurisdiction.[67] Its continued omission may mean that acts of sexual abuse against individual women will not be perceived either as violations of the laws of war or as forms of torture. Indeed the specification of torture as a separate crime against humanity may imply that even massive, systematic and organized rape including forcible detention for the purposes of rape, does not necessarily constitute torture.

In indictments issued on 26 June 1996 the Tribunal broke new ground. The prosecution alleged 62 counts of crimes committed against girls and women including crimes against humanity, grave breaches of the Geneva Conventions and violations of the laws and customs of war relating especially to rape, torture, outrages upon personal dignity, persecution, wilfully causing great suffering, enslavement and inhuman treatment.[68] For the first time in an international criminal court forms of sexual violence against girls and women have been made indictable explicitly under the rubrics of torture and enslavement as constituting crimes against humanity.[69]

Violence within the Family

The discussion has focused on the gender-specific modalities of torture that may be committed against women and girls by state officials. It may be further argued that the understanding of torture should be extended to cover other acts of violence that occur with far greater regularity to women and girls than does state violence, that is forms of violence within the family, or intimate violence.[70] Western writings tend to assume that domestic violence against women is committed by male partners and child abuse by parents and those acting as parents.[71] The extended family of other cultures may both enlarge the potential scope for violence against women in that it may be committed by other family members acting alone or in collusion, and act to restrain it by limiting the power of any one individual member.[72] The Special Rapporteur on Violence against Women also warns against narrow understandings of the family that exclude and render invisible violence occurring in non-traditional or looser family groupings.[73]

One form of violence is that used by male family members to discipline females of all ages. Acceptable levels of chastisement are recognized in many societies as an appropriate means of asserting proper control over subordinate family members. Even severe levels of violence may not be challenged because they are perceived as culturally, and thus legally, appropriate.[74] Protection against excessive violence is accorded through societal understandings of what is reasonable. However this protection is weakened by changing social and economic circumstances that have undermined communal values and thus accorded greater unchallenged power to individual men.[75]

The Special Rapporteur on Violence against Women has argued that the similarities between extreme cases of domestic violence and torture should be recognised, despite the apparently private nature of the former.[76] Her second Report draws upon the documentation by jurists and experts that shows torture and domestic violence to be comparable in kind, severity and effects. Both the torture victim and the abused girl and woman are isolated and live under a reign of terror. They are debilitated through physical and psychological suffering that prevents the enjoyment of all human rights.[77] Both develop coping mechanisms for survival that come to dominate their existence. It may be thought that, unlike the state detainee, the battered woman or abused child is free to leave. This perception discounts other factors such as the woman's fear of precipitating a bout of deadly violence against herself or her children, the lack of community support services, and economic dependence. Violence within the household is committed intentionally to intimidate, punish, elicit information (whether it exists or not such as confession to an affair that might not have taken place), destroy the victim's self-esteem, extinguish her personality, or to reduce her capacity for work or pleasure.

> As in torture, battering may involve a humiliating interrogation whose purpose is more the assertion of supremacy and possession over the victim than the acquisition of information. Battered women, like official torture victims, may be explicitly punished for infraction of constantly changing and impossible to meet rules. Both may be intimidated and broken by the continual threat of physical violence and verbal abuse; and both may be most effectively manipulated by intermittent kindness.[78]

Another devastating aspect for the victim is that the institution deemed by society to provide protection and nurture becomes the screen behind which violence is concealed. Torture is hidden behind prison walls and is typically officially denied. Similarly, the level of domestic violence is rendered invisible by the family setting, 'the natural and fundamental group unit of society' and itself entitled to protection.[79] Just as the victim of official torture has nowhere else to turn for protection against the state's abuse of its position, the battered girl or woman may have nowhere else to turn for protection against abuse within the family. It is this that provides the nexus required under international law to make states responsible for private acts of violence.

The definition of torture requires commission of the prohibited acts by state officials, or at least instigation or acquiescence by them. Where the state fails to provide legal or practical assistance to prevent or punish perpetrators of domestic violence, it can be said to have tacitly connived in its commission. In many states, law enforcement agencies will not respond to acts of domestic violence, prosecutions are not pursued, violent acts are legitimated (for example the refusal in many systems to criminalize marital rape) and defences such as those of honour reduce or negate criminal liability where there is a claim, whether or not substantiated, of adultery or unfaithfulness.[80] If the state has laws that require complete obedience to male relatives or condone violence against female family members, or it provides no economic support for girls and women who flee from violence, or connives in such violence by failing to enforce prohibitions, then it is aquiescing in it. If customary law reinforces the cultural subordination of women, the state is abdicating its responsibility for individual citizens by signalling that individual males may deliberately cause pain and suffering to women in family relationships without fear of sanction.[81] At Beijing it was recognized that:

> Violence against women is exacerbated by social pressures, notably the shame of denouncing certain acts that have been perpetrated against women; women's lack of access to legal information, aid or protection; the lack of laws that effectively prohibit violence against women; failure to reform existing laws; inadequate efforts on the part of public authorities to promote awareness of and enforce existing laws; and the absence of educational and other means to address the causes and consequences of violence.[82]

In these circumstances women victims of intimate violence have truly nowhere else to turn. The private sanctuary of the family has become a violent prison and the state has failed in its responsibility to provide relief. Failure by the state to exercise due diligence and equal protection to prevent and punish gender-based violence must incur international responsibility in the same way as failure to prevent torture within its places of detention. This extension of state responsibility was articulated in the General Assembly Resolution on the Elimination of Violence against Women.[83]

Recognising the similarities between torture and domestic violence against women and therefore requiring state action for its prevention and condemnation is significant for both boys and girls. Documented evidence suggests a link between violence against women and child abuse. The perpetrator of violence against the mother is likely to turn it against the child if the child attempts to intervene, or is merely witness to the violence.[84] Even if this does not occur the child is likely to suffer stress and studies suggest that a child that is exposed to family violence subsequently experiences behavioural problems.[85] Children with a history of violence at home make up a disproportionately high number of street children.[86] Effective protection for women victims of violence would extend to the children under her care. Advancement of women's equality through the guarantee of economic and social rights would minimize economic dependence on men and enable a woman more easily to leave an abusive situation with her children.[87] Other factors are especially germane to girls. An estimated 90 per cent of victims of child sexual abuse are girls.[88] The young age of marriage for girls in many societies accentuates their economic and other powerlessness and thus their susceptibility to violence within that marriage. This may be further enhanced where there are legal, economic or other social restraints upon such girls returning to their own family home. Further, the realization for the young girl that her mother is subject to such violence is likely to cause awareness of her own vulnerability, and fear for her own future. It also helps to perpetuate the assumption that male domination is a natural state of affairs that in turn reinforces the invisibility of domestic violence.

Incest is a form of intimate violence of particular significance to children, again because of the intimidation, coercion and abuse of trust involved. The 'classic case' of incest is that committed by a father or father figure against the girl-child.[89] Its potential for familial destruction and shame surrounding its occurrence inhibit its reporting, leaving its victims unprotected and once again with nowhere else to turn. As the Special Rapporteur on Violence against Women elucidated:

> ... children victims of incest, are a particularly vulnerable group, as they play no part in decision-making and have no control over their own social situation ... they have no access to protection while they maintain a situation of dependency vis à vis other family members. Often the child victim is too young to rationalize or understand his/her predicament having been coerced under cover of secrecy and familial authority. The divide between male and female and between adult and child is fully exploited.[90]

There is a further irony. Other forms of gendered violence are not rendered culpable by the state because of their alleged acceptability within the particular culture. Incest however is widely regarded as contrary to social, cultural and religious traditions and most states have criminalized incest.[91] Yet it remains widely invisible and therefore uncondemned precisely because it offends against deeply held social and moral mores. Revealing and preventing the incidence of violence against females is socially disruptive, either because it presents fundamental challenges to traditional assumptions about the social roles of men and women, or because it would reveal the breakdown of society's espoused values. In both cases the silenced victim suffers from the act of violence and from the failure of those in authority within the family or the state to provide relief.

International recognition of violence against women as a human rights abuse is important for the well-being and security of children, as well as for women. However the international instruments condemning gender-based violence fall short of identifying such behaviour as torture. The Special Rapporteur goes further by challenging the traditional location of torture in the public arena. This is admittedly a radical conception of torture that questions the view that state violence is inherently worse and more culpable than intimate violence. Acceptance of her approach would entail the consequences in national and international law of labelling an act as torture as outlined above. In particular it would oblige states to take positive legal and administrative measures to prevent domestic violence and to prosecute or extradite its perpetrators.[92] It would also require them not to return a victim of domestic violence to the place where it occurred.

Torture within the Community

Social conditions combine to increase the types of violent acts to which girls are susceptible, often committed with impunity.

> Due to such factors as their youth, social pressures, lack of protective laws, or failure to enforce laws, girls are more vulnerable to all kinds of violence, especially sexual violence, including rape, sexual abuse, sexual exploitation, trafficking, possibly the sale of their organs and tissues and forced labour.[93]

The violence faced by female domestic workers straddles state, familial and community violence. Female workers, many of whom are young Asian and Palestinian girls, are forced through economic exigency to seek domestic work abroad. There are many accounts of the abuses they suffer as a result of their extreme dependency in a foreign state. Passports may be taken from them, earnings withheld, working hours can be excessive and the exposure to verbal and sexual abuse is great. Through poverty, violence, fraud and exploitation many girls become victims of trafficking, and forced prostitution.[94] They are as effectively trapped by their employers in a modern form of slavery, where there is no defence against torture, as those held in state detention.

The Special Rapporteur on Violence against Women submitted two communications to the government of the United Arab Emirates with respect to the case of Sarah Balabagan. Balagaban was aged 16 when she was arrested for stabbing her employer to death after he had allegedly raped her at gun point. Her original sentence of seven year's imprisonment was altered to that of death. After international protest, including from the Special Rapporteur on Extra-judicial, Summary and Arbitrary Executions, it was transmuted to one year's imprisonment and 100 lashes. The UAE government maintained that flogging a 16-year-old girl does not constitute state violence against women because it is a lawful sentence carried out under medical supervision. This evades the question of whether the original circumstances surrounding her offence constituted violence, with many of the elements of torture present, including those of intimidation, and official acquiescence.

Indeed the acquiescence and therefore responsibility may be shared by the worker's own state through its failure to intervene. A Middle East Watch Report published after the restoration of the government of Kuwait in 1991 described a rape crisis in Kuwait 'worse than anything experienced during the Iraqi occupation'.[95] There are many accounts of powerless domestic workers being raped and otherwise violently abused by armed men in Kuwaiti army or police uniform who reportedly asserted that the women 'deserved' their treatment for supporting the Iraqis, or that the men could be excused some excesses because of the difficult time they had recently had. Many domestic workers trapped in Kuwait sought refuge in appalling conditions in various embassies in Kuwait City. Their own countries were unable, or unwilling, to help while their families suffered from their inability to send earnings back home.

There are many other examples of violence against girls occurring within the community. In some countries young girls, including school girls, who defy the demands of religious fundamentalists are abused and even killed. In Algeria women students are at risk if they ignore the prohibition against women travelling on public transport or refuse to wear the veil. In other states self-appointed, male village councils may inflict punishment on girls for allegedly violating social or religious codes of moral conduct.[96] Following the reasoning of the Inter-American Court on Human Rights in the *Velasquez Rodriguez* case the state can be held internationally responsible for its failure to organize or control the structures of public power so as to ensure the free and full enjoyment of human rights, including the right to life, to all persons within the community.[92] The Inter-American Court considered that:

An illegal act which violates human rights and which is initially not directly imputable to a State (for example, because it is the act of a private person ...) can lead to international responsibility of the State ... because of the lack of due diligence to prevent the violation or to respond to it ... .

This duty to prevent includes all those means of a legal, political, administrative and cultural nature that promote the protection of human rights and ensure that any violations are considered and treated as illegal acts.

This reasoning can be applied by analogy to community acts of violence committed against women. Where the other elements of torture are present the offences should be presented as such.

Traditional practices, in particular female genital surgery that is carried out on some 110 million women across over 20 countries, have become the focus of western feminist attention.[98] Accounts such as the following have led to demands that the practice be universally condemned as torture:

> The little girl, entirely nude, is immobilized in the sitting position on a low stool by at least three women. One of them with her arms tightly around the little girl's chest; two others hold the child's thighs apart by force, in order to open wide the vulva. ... Then the old woman takes her razor and excises the clitoris ... The little girl writhes and howls in pain, although strongly held down. Exhausted, the little girl is then dressed and put on a bed. The operation lasts from 15 to 20 minutes according to the ability of the old woman and the resistance put up by the child.[99]

It has proved hard to include female genital surgery within the traditional framework of international human rights law. Indeed it has been excluded from consideration within other international arenas. For example, the World Health Organisation refused for many years even to examine the detrimental health effects on girls of female genital mutilation because it accepted the argument that this was a ritual and cultural matter. Eventually the practice did enter United Nations parlance as a health issue and Article 24(3) of the Children's Convention requires states to 'take all appropriate measures with a view to abolishing traditional practices prejudicial to the health of children'.[100] There are disadvantages to this location within the rubric of providing children with the highest attainable healthcare.[101] It implies that if the health risks were to be eliminated (or significantly reduced, for example by operation in first class medical facilities) the imperative for absolute prohibition would be diminished. The right to health is a social right subject only to weak obligations and implementation measures.[102] It has therefore been argued that female genital surgery should be deemed contrary to the civil and political rights to bodily integrity and freedom from torture,[103] and the practice has been considered by the Sub-Commission on Prevention of Discrimination and Protection of Minorities, through its Working Group on Traditional Practices Affecting the Health of Women and Children. The priority accorded to civil and political rights would enhance the visibility of the practice, assist in demands for its immediate eradication and support claims for asylum or refugee status made by women fleeing from its infliction. The practice fits the definition of torture. It is deliberately inflicted, causes pain and suffering, there is intimidation and coercion and it is discriminatory. Where the state does not criminalize the practice, or fails to make such laws effective, there is official acquiescence.

However categorization of female genital surgery as torture is complex. Unlike other forms of gender-specific violence discussed above, female genital surgery is performed by women on their daughters and grand-daughters who may view it as a prerequisite for womanhood within their society. One of the defining characteristics of torture is the obliteration of the victim's identity or personality. Identity and membership are precisely what the ritual brings to a girl, who may become an outsider in her own community if she has not undergone the surgery. Many women within cultures that practice female genital surgery have rejected the tradition and campaigned strongly against it. Their attempts are obstructed by resentment caused by the label 'torture', which can be perceived as an especially offensive form of cultural imperialism. This may be particularly counter-productive where official torture is widely practiced and seen as something quite distinct.

Conclusions

The chapter has identified a cross-section of acts that are committed against girls and women that fit within the classic definition of torture, except for their commission by private actors rather than state officials. Nevertheless where such acts are committed against females because of their gender they are a manifestation of the 'historically unequal power relations between men and women'.[104]

> In all societies, to a greater or lesser degree, women and girls are subjected to physical, sexual and psychological abuse that cuts across lines of income, class and culture.[105]

In these circumstances gender-based violence is not a private, isolated act but structural and supported by patriarchy.[106] It is acquiesced in by the power systems within the state, including traditional and other forms of law.

Labelling acts as torture requires affirmative responses for their prevention and eradication. This may be harder for even a resolute government to achieve where the perpetrators are private individuals acting within the home or community setting rather than public officials subject to public regulations and codes of conduct. It requires measures for changing deep-rooted cultural and religious assumptions about the gender roles within society.[107] Economic factors often work against the eradication of the violence that is inherent in the commercial exploitation of girls. This shifting of the parameters of human rights law into private relationships is one of the distinguishing and controversial features of both the Women's Convention and the Children's Convention. Thus at Beijing actions for governments include taking:

> ... appropriate legislative, administrative, social and educational measures to protect the girl-child in the household and in society from all forms of physical and mental violence, injury or abuse, neglect or negligent treatment, maltreatment or exploitation, including sexual abuse;[108] and enacting ... legislation protecting girls from all forms of violence, ... and develop[ing] age-appropriate safe and confidential programmes and medical, social and psychological support services to assist girls who are subjected to violence.[109]

The Children's Convention requires states to take all appropriate measures to promote physical and psychological recovery and social reintegration after acts of torture.[110] The measures listed above indicate the wide range of anticipated measures to redress violence against girls and resemble those required in response to torture. Legislative or other prohibitions are not sufficient. States should provide adequate refuges for women and their children, medical, counselling, support and legal services as well as integrative educative programmes for men and women. Security in all places of detention (including temporary camps for refugees or displaced persons) should embrace the concept of internal security for the inmates and not be restricted to external security concerns.

Extending the concept of torture to embrace gender-specific acts of violence including those committed by non-state agencies might be thought to trivialize it. Torture must retain its place at the apex of human rights violations to reinforce its gravity and the need to condemn it wherever it may occur. Governments that practise or condone torture betray the trust the people have placed in them and undermine the structure of society. But violence committed for similar purposes within those structures that society cherishes for the protection of the weak has similar effect. Far from trivializing torture, recognizing the similarities to torture in intimate violence would help release the victims from their humiliation and shame and publicly affirm that they should not have been subject to this treatment. If acts that can be characterized in the same way in terms of the physical and psychological impact upon the victim are not recognized as torture, it renders less relevant the formal prohibition of torture to women and girls.

Notes

1   The author thanks Shaki Sanusi for her excellent research assistance in preparing this chapter.

2   GA Res. 217 A III, 10 December 1948, Article 5.
3   International Covenant on Civil and Political Rights, 16 December 1966, 999 UNTS 171, Article 7.
4   United Nations Convention Against Torture and Other Cruel, Inhuman or Degrading Treatment, 10 December 1984, GA Res. 39/46. The Convention built upon the Declaration on the Protection of all Persons from being Subjected to Torture and other Inhuman or Degrading Treatment or Punishment, GA Res. 3452 XXX, 9 December 1975.
5   Optional Protocol to the International Covenant on Civil and Political Rights, 16 December 1966, 999 UNTS 171.
6   The Committee against Torture was established by the Convention Against Torture, Article 17. It receives initial and periodic reports from States Parties, may seek cooperation from states about which it has received reliable information that torture is being systematically practised and submit observations, and receive inter-state and individual communications where the State Party has separately accepted its jurisdiction to do so; ibid., Articles 19-22. See Byrnes, 'The Committee Against Torture', in Alston (1992) (ed.), *The United Nations and Human Rights*, 509.
7   European Convention for the Protection of Human Rights and Fundamental Freedoms, Rome, 4 November 1950, ETS No. 5, Article 3; American Convention on Human Rights, San Jose, 22 November 1969, 1144 UNTS 123, Article 5(2); African Charter on Human Rights and Peoples' Rights, (Banjul Charter), 27 June 1981, rep. 21 *ILM* 1982, 58 Article 5. Cf., Cairo Declaration on Human Rights in Islam, 5 August 1990, Article 20.
8   European Convention for the Prevention of Torture and Inhuman or Degrading Treatment or Punishment, 26 November 1987, ETS 126; Inter-American Convention to Prevent and Punish Torture, 9 December 1985, rep. 25 ILM 519, 1986.
9   International Covenant on Civil and Political Rights, Article 2(2); cf. European Convention on Human Rights, Article 14, American Convention on Human Rights, Article 1(1); African Charter, Article 2.
10 Eg. The Convention on the Rights of the Child, GA Res. 44/736, 20 November 1989, Article 37(a).
11 Convention for the Amelioration of the Condition of the Wounded and Sick in Armed Forces in the Field, 75 UNTS 31; Convention for the Amelioration of the Condition of the Wounded, Sick and Shipwrecked Members of Armed Forces at Sea, 75 UNTS 85; Convention Relative to the Treatment of Prisoners of War, 75 UNTS 135; Convention Relative to the Protection of Civilian Persons in Time of War, 75 UNTS 287, all at Geneva, 12 August 1949; Protocol Additional to the Geneva Conventions of 12 August 1949 and Relating to the Protection of Victims of International Armed Conflicts (Protocol I); Protocol Additional to the Geneva Conventions of 12 August 1949 and Relating to the Protection of Victims of Non-International Armed Conflicts (Protocol II).
12 See especially the work of the Crime Commission of the United Nations relating to standards of conduct with respect to prisoners under various forms of detention, codes of conduct for law-enforcement officials and medical ethics guidelines; Clark (1995), *The United Nations Crime Commission*.
13 See eg. the reasoning of Judge Kaufman, Circuit Judge, in *Filartiga* v. *Pena-Irala*, US Ct of A, 2nd Cir, 1980, 630 F. 2nd 876.
14 For example, Oscar Schachter argues that where conflicting conduct is 'violative of the basic concept of human dignity' statements of condemnation are sufficient evidence of its illegitimacy under customary international law. O. Schachter,

'International Law in Theory and Practice: General Course in Public International Law', 178 Rec. des Cours 1982 21 at 334–338; cf. Kirgis, 'Custom on a Sliding Scale', 81 AJIL 1987, 147.

15   International Covenant on Civil and Political Rights, Article 4(2); Convention Against Torture, Article 2(2); European Convention on Human Rights, Article 15(2), American Convention on Human Rights, Article 27(2).

16   Charlesworth and Chinkin, 'The Gender of Jus Cogens', 15 *Human Rights Quarterly* 1993, 63.

17   Byrnes, above note 6.

18   *Velasquez Rodriguez* v. *Honduras*, Inter-American CHR, C, no. 4, 9 HRLJ 1988 212 28 ICM 1989 294.

19   *Ireland* v. *the United Kingdom* ECHR ser. A (Judgment of 18 January 1978).

20   International Covenant on Civil and Political Rights, Article 41; Convention against Torture, Article 21; European Convention on Human Rights, Article 24; American Convention on Human Rights, Article 45.

21   *Ireland* v. *the United Kingdom, op. cit.*, para. 239.

22   International Covenant on Civil and Political Rights, Article 2. In contrast the obligation under the International Covenant on Economic, Social and Cultural Rights, 16 December 1966, 993 UNTS 3, Article 2 is to take progressive measures to the maximum of available resources to achieve fulfilment of the stipulated rights.

23   Article 2.

24   Article 4.

25   Article 5.

26   Article 7.

27   Article 3. The association with the definition of a refugee and the requirement of non-refoulement is evident.

28   *Filartiga* v. *Pena-Irala, op. cit.*, however in the United Kingdom, in the *Al-Adsani* case the government of Kuwait successfully claimed sovereign immunity in a case of allegations of torture; *Sulaiman Al Adsani* v. *Government of Kuwait*, Court of Appeal, 12 March 1996 100 ILR 465, cf. *Siderman de Blake* v. *Republic of Argentine* 965 F.2nd (2nd) 699 (1992). Immunity for torture has been removed in the US by the Torture Victim Protection Act 1992.

29   The Convention on the Rights of the Child, GA Res. 44/736, 20 November 1989.

30   Convention on the Elimination of All Forms of Discrimination Against Women, 18 December 1979, GA Res 34/180.

31   Convention on the Rights of the Child, Article 1 provides that a child is a human being under 18 years of age, unless national law stipulates otherwise.

32   Adult women may be subject to laws restricting their legal capacity, in effect subjecting them to guardianship. Under customary law a woman's legal status may be subsumed within that of her family of birth or marriage. Conversely child marriage may mean that a child is a wife. 'Thus we have, "a wife as a child, and a child as a wife".' Armstrong, Chuulu, Himonga, Letuka, Mokobi, Ncube, Nhlapo, Rwezaura and Vilakazi, 'Towards a Cultural Understanding of the Interplay between Children's and Women's Rights: an Eastern and Southern African Perspective', 3 *International Journal of Children's Rights* 1995, 333, 339.

33   Universal Declaration of Human Rights, 1948, Preamble.

34   See further Bunch, 'Women's Rights as Human Rights: Towards a Revision of Human Rights' 12, *Human Rights Quarterly* 1990 486; G. Ashworth (1993), *Changing the Discourse: a Guide to Women and Human Rights*; Kerr (1993) (ed.), *Ours by Right*; Tomasevski (1993), *Women and Human Rights*; Cook (1994) (ed.), *Human*

Rights of Women National and International Perspectives; Chinkin, 'Women's Rights as Human Rights under International Law', in Gearty and Tomkins (1995) (eds), *Understanding Human Rights.*

35 This is recognized in Article 5 of the Women's Convention which requires States Parties to take appropriate measures to modify social and cultural patterns of conduct in order to remove prejudice and to change attitudes with respect to sexist stereotyping.

36 For example, the Women's Convention was drafted by the Commission on the Status of Women rather than the Commission on Human Rights. See further Byrnes, 'The Other Human Rights Treaty Body: The Work of the Committee on the Elimination of Discrimination Against Women', 14 *Yale JIL* 1989, 1.

37 United Nations World Conference on Human Rights: Vienna Declaration and Programme of Action, 25 June 1993, rep. 32 *ILM* 1993 1661; Fourth World Conference on Women, Beijing Declaration and the Platform for Action, 15 September 1995 (hereinafter Platform for Action).

38 Beijing Declaration, paras. 9 and 14; Platform for Action, para. 213; cf. Vienna Declaration and Programme of Action, I para. 18.

39 However this was controversial and the entire text on the girl-child was bracketed in the pre-conference Draft Platform for Action.

40 Cf. Goonesekere, *Women's Rights and Children's Rights: the United Nations Conventions as Compatible and Complementary International Treaties* UNICEF 1992.

41 Convention on the Rights of the Child, Articles 19 and 37.

42 Cf. Platform for Action, paras. 270 and 271.

43 Report of the Special Rapporteur on Violence against Women, its Causes and Consequences, 5 February 1996, E/CN.4/1996/53 para. 91 (hereinafter Second Report). See also Sen, 'More than 100 Million Women are Missing', N.Y. Rev. Books, 30 December 1990.

44 For statistics and description of the violence suffered by women see *Women: Challenges to the Year 2000* (United Nations 1991); *The World's Women: Trends and Statistics* (United Nations 1995); Connors, *Violence Against Women in the Family* (United Nations 1989); Russell (1984) (ed.), *Crimes Against Women: The Proceedings of the International Tribunal.* One of the most moving and horrifying events at the Vienna World Conference on Human Rights was the similar Tribunal on violence against women.

45 Committee on the Elimination of Discrimination Against Women, General Recommendation No. 19, 11th Session, 1992, 'Violence Against Women', UN Doc. A/47/38.

46 'Declaration on the Elimination of Violence Against Women', GA Res. 48/103, adopted 20 December 1993.

47 Beijing, Platform for Action, para. 113.

48 Committee on the Elimination of Discrimination Against Women, General Recommendation No. 19.

49 Platform for Action, para. 112. These were the same objectives as at the World Conference to Review and Appraise the Achievements of the United Nations Decade for Women: Equality, Development and Peace, Nairobi, 1985.

50 Platform for Action, para. 124.

51 Cf. Platform for Action, para. 118.

52 'Preliminary Report on Violence Against Women, its Causes and Consequences', submitted by the Special Rapporteur, Radhika Coomaraswamy in Accordance with Commission on Human Rights Resolution 1994/45, UN Doc. E/CN.4/1995/42 1994.

53   Platform for Action, para. 121.

54   Amnesty International (1992), *Rape and Sexual Abuse: Torture and Ill Treatment of Women in Detention.*

55   Amnesty International (1995), *Human Rights are Women's Right* at 87.

56   Amnesty International (1992), *Rape and Sexual Abuse: Torture and Ill Treatment of Women in Detention.*

57   See for discussion, Graycar and Morgan (1990), *The Hidden Gender of Law.*

58   Sleep deprivation was one of the five techniques used by the United Kingdom authorities in N. Ireland that the European Court of Human Rights found to constitute inhuman and degrading treatment under the European Convention on Human Rights, Article 3; *Ireland* v. *United Kingdom* ECHR ser. A, (Judgment of 18 January 1978).

59   'While entire communities suffer the consequences of armed conflict and terrorism, women and girls are particularly affected because of their status in society and their sex.' Platform for Action, para. 135.

60   Amnesty International (1995), *Human Rights are Women's Right* at 31.

61   United Nations High Commissioner for Refugees, Executive Committee Resolution No. 73 (XLIV) 1993, *Refugee Protection and Sexual Violence.*

62   Charter Annexed to the Agreement for the Establishment of an International Military Tribunal, 5 UNTS 251, Article 6(c).

63   Historians estimate the number of such women to be between 150,000 and 200,000. Dolgopol, 'Women's Voices, Women's Pain', 17 *Human Rights Quarterly* 1995, 127.

64   Geneva Convention Relative to the Protection of Civilian Persons in Time of War, 12 August 1949, Article 27; Protocol Additional to the Geneva Conventions of 12 August 1949 and Relating to the Protection of Victims of International Armed Conflicts (Protocol I), Article 76.

65   See for example Geneva Convention Relative to the Protection of Civilian Persons in Time of War, Article 147; Protocol I, Article 85(3).

66   The Tribunal was established by SC Res. 827, 25 May 1993. Article 5(g) of the Statute of the Tribunal includes rape as a crime against humanity.

67   Statute of the Tribunal, Article 2 lists grave breaches in the same terms as the Geneva Conventions and therefore exclude explicit reference to rape. Cf., Statute of the International Tribunal for Rwanda, Article 4(e) which incorporates rape as contrary to common Article 3 of the Geneva Conventions applicable in non-international armed conflict.

68   Indictment Gagovic & Others ('Foca'), Review of Indictment Pursuant to Article 19(1) of the Statute, 26 June 1996, Case IT–26–23–1.

69   See further *Mejía Egocheaga or another* v. *Peru* (Inter-American Commission on Human Rights) (1996) 1 Butterworths Human Rights Cases, 229 and *Aydin* v. *Turkey* (1998) 3 Butterworths Human Rights Cases 300 for findings of state responsibility for breach of human rights conventions amounting to torture.

70   See further Thomas and Beasley (1993), 'Domestic Violence as a Human Rights Issue', 15 *Human Rights Quarterly* at 36; McKinnon, on 'Torture: A Feminist Perspective on Human Rights', in Mahoney and Mahoney (1993) (eds), *Human Rights in the 21st Century: A Global Perspective*; Copelon, 'Intimate Terror: Understanding Domestic Violence as Torture', in Cook (1994) (ed.), *Human Rights of Women National and International Perspectives* 116; J. Fitzpatrick, 'The Use of International Human Rights Norms to Combat Violence Against Women', in R. Cook (1994) (ed.), *Human Rights of Women: National and International Perspectives*, University of Pennyslvania Press, 532

71   Armstrong et al., above note 32 at 361.

72   Ibid.
73   Second Report, para. 24.
74   This compares with the unsuccessful argument in the *Tyrer* case that corporal punishment of children within schools was accepted as an effective deterrent to deviant behaviour on the Isle of Man; *Tyrer* v. *United Kingdom* ECHR, ser. A, vol. 26 (Judgment of 25 April 1978).
75   Armstrong et al., above note 32 at 359.
76   This section draws heavily upon the Second Report.
77   Committee on the Elimination of Discrimination Against Women, General Recommendation No. 19, 11th Session, 1992, 'Violence Against Women', UN Doc. A/47/38.
78   Second Report, para. 47.
79   International Covenant on Civil and Political Rights, Article 23.
80   See Americas Watch (1991), *Criminal Injustice: Violence against Women in Brazil*.
81   'Violence against women ... derives essentially from cultural patterns, in particular the harmful effects of certain traditional or customary practices ... that perpetuate the lower status of women in the family, the workplace, the community and society.' Platform for Action, para. 118.
82   Platform for Action, para. 118.
83   Cf. Platform for Action, para. 124(b).
84   For instance, 'children whose mothers are battered [are] more than twice as likely than children whose mothers are not battered to be themselves abused, by either their mother's attacker or their mothers'. Second Report, para. 87.
85   United Nations, *Understanding the Problem*, in Davies (1994) (ed.), *Women and Violence*, 6, cited Armstrong et al., above note 32 at 360.
86   Second Report, para. 89.
87   'Improving the woman's legal, economic, social and psychological status results in an improvement of the situation of the child, and in satisfaction of the [Children's] Convention's requirements that the child be protected from physical violence.' Armstrong et al., above note 32 at 359.
88   Second Report, para. 86.
89   Second Report, para. 66.
90   Second Report, para. 68.
91   Second Report para. 66.
92   The Special Rapporteur includes with her report a *Model Law on Domestic Violence* that can be used as a guide by law-makers.
93   Platform for Action, para. 269.
94   See report on the mission of the Special Rapporteur to Poland on the issue of trafficking and forced prostitution of women (24 May to 1 June 1996) UN Doc. E/CN.4/1997/47/Add.1.
95   Middle East Watch, *A Victory Turned Sour, Human Rights in Kuwait Since Liberation*, (September 1991); Women's Rights Project and Middle East Watch, *Punishing the Victim: Rape and Mistreatment of Asian Maids in Kuwait*, (August 1992).
96   For an account of such courts in Bangladesh see: Amnesty International, *Bangladesh: Taking the Law in Their Own Hands: the Village Salish*, AI, Index ASA, 13/12/93.
97   *Velasquez Rodriguez* v. *Honduras*, 28 *ILM* 1989 294.
98   See especially, Hosken, 'Female Genital Mutilation in the World Today: A Global Review', 11 *IJ Health Serv.* 1981 45; Boulware-Miller, 'Female Circumcision: Challenges to the Practice as a Human Rights Violation', 8 *Harv. Women's LJ* 155; Slack, 'Female Circumcision: A Critical Appraisal', 10 *Human Rights Quarterly* 1988, 437;

Engle, 'International Human Rights and Feminism: When Discourses Meet', 13 *Mich. JIL* 1992, 518.

99   Amnesty International (1995), *Human Rights are Women's Right* at 133.
100   See above Van Bueren, Opening Pandora's Box: Protecting Children Against Torture or Cruel, Inhuman and Degrading Treatment or Punishment. This is also reiterated at Beijing, Platform for Action, para. 281 (I).
101   Cf. Platform for Action, para. 124 (I) where actions to be taken by governments include enacting and enforcing 'legislation against perpetrators of practices and acts of violence against women, such as female genital mutilation, ...' without locating the practice in the context of health.
102   The right to health is contained in the International Covenant on Economic, Social and Cultural Rights, 1966, Article 12. Cf. Convention on the Elimination of All Forms of Discrimination Against Women, Article 12.
103   International Covenant on Civil and Political Rights, 1966, Article 2 requires states to respect and to ensure to all individuals within its territory ... the rights recognized in the present Covenant ... . See further Van Bueren *op. cit.*
104   Platform for Action, para. 118.
105   Platform for Action, para. 112.
106   Bunch, above note 34.
107   Cf. Convention on the Elimination of All Forms of Discrimination Against Women, Article 5.
108   Platform for Action, para. 283(b).
109   Platform for Action, para. 283(d).
110   Convention on the Rights of the Child, Article 39.

7   The Violation of Economic, Social and Cultural Rights as Torture or Cruel, Inhuman or Degrading Treatment

Jeremy McBride

Introduction[1]

The concern of this chapter is to explore the possibility that at least some violations of economic, social and cultural rights in respect of children are capable of amounting at the same time to a violation of the international prohibition of torture, inhuman and degrading treatment or punishment.[2] While there is clearly nothing novel in one act or omission being double-counted in this way,[3] it is certainly unusual (except in the case of trade union activities)[4] for it to be suggested that the overlap involves rights from both the civil and political and the economic, social and cultural categories. However, this may well be connected with the fact that the opportunity to complain about individual situations tends to be restricted to the former kind of rights (both at the constitutional and international level) and there would, therefore, be no advantage in claiming before the tribunal that a particular form of treatment is also a violation of a right over which it has no jurisdiction.[5] There may in any event have been some difficulty in perceiving violations of economic, social and cultural rights in these terms both because, unlike civil and political ones, they have not generally been viewed as giving rise to individual legal claims[6] and because of traditional understandings as to the scope of specific rights. Nevertheless the evolution of concepts is calculated to surprise the framers of human rights instruments[7] and there is no reason in principle why a specific situation could not raise issues in respect of more than one grouping of rights. This chapter will consider, therefore, the circumstances in which such an approach might be tenable as regards the economic, social and cultural rights of children, the obstacles that are likely to be encountered when pursuing it and the benefits that might be derived from its adoption.

Meeting the Criteria

Although I am raising the possibility that there is such an overlap here, I do so with a fair degree of caution. Firstly, there is inevitably an innate tendency on the part of lawyers to conservatism and it is certainly very hard to escape from the traditional image of torture and so on, as a form of physical and mental ill-treatment employed by police officers, prison warders and armed forces around the world.[8] Secondly, it is also important to be conscious of the danger of devaluing a concept by seeking to apply it too loosely; while all human rights violations deserve condemnation, it does not follow that they should all necessarily attract the same degree of outrage or, even if this is appropriate, that this can only be expressed by treating the respective sources of opprobrium as essentially identical conduct. There is no doubt that the traditionally acknowledged forms of torture and the like have been amongst the human rights violations which have received the greatest condemnation[9] and attracted special measures to deal with them by way of response.[10] However, while some violations of economic, social and cultural rights may be of a comparable gravity, attempts to ensure that they also get a comparable response[11] by simply labelling them as a torture are unlikely to carry conviction because the traditional understanding is so well-entrenched and it could, therefore, actually prove to be counter-productive. On the other hand a genuine double categorization of a particular situation should not entail any dilution of the elements that need to be established before a violation of the respective rights can be said to exist and it should not be assumed *a priori* that it is impossible in the case of torture and the like. It is appropriate, therefore, to consider whether at least some treatment received outside the police station, prison and barracks is not just as fundamentally reprehensible but does actually have the same character as that which one is accustomed to find inflicted inside them.

In determining whether this is actually the case it is necessary first to establish the likely effects on persons who are deprived of their economic, social and cultural rights and then compare any suffering, whether mental or physical, that may be endured with that which would be expected when assessing whether or not there has been torture or the like in the more traditional contexts. It is perhaps reasonable, when doing this, to proceed on the assumption that the effects of any violation of economic, social and cultural rights will almost certainly be worse for a child than for an adult[12] and that it may, therefore, be easier to establish this element in respect of the former. However, it is probable that they will be grave in many instances whatever the age of the person concerned and the status of being a child will be no more than an aggravating factor that makes a good case only more certain.[13] It is necessary to look for treatment which is, at the very minimum, a gross form of humiliation, rising to the deliberate infliction of severe mental or physical suffering.[14] The latter may have to be particularly intense if it is to be regarded as torture[15] which will also only exist if the infliction of the suffering has some purpose behind it, whether to gain information, to inflict punishment or for some other reason. In approaching this comparison, it needs to be borne in mind that there are many treatments that have been held not to satisfy these criteria, including the 'whacking' of a child with a slipper[16], intimate body searches[17], the failure to recognize a change of sex[18] and prolonged solitary confinement.[19] The last of these indicates that there can be competing considerations which might make the apparently objectionable still justifiable – for example the needs of security in a prison – but the others underline that simply because many human beings might recoil with distaste from certain behaviour does not mean that it will be regarded as unacceptable by a court when measuring it against the international legal conception of torture, inhuman and degrading treatment or punishment. It must, therefore, be expected that this will also be true of at least some of the suffering that inevitably results from a violation of child's economic, social and cultural rights.

Nevertheless it is probable that legitimate comparisons can still be made between the effects of some such violations and what has been recognized as sufficient for a finding of torture and the like; not least because interference with the content of the former rights has actually been a feature of some of the unacceptable treatments to which prisoners and other detainees have been subjected, even though they have not been identified as such. Thus prison overcrowding, inadequate heating and sanitary arrangements, as well as a lack of food and medical treatment have been amongst the situations that have at least been found to be 'inhuman'.[20] For many people comparable situations are, of course, a feature of life outside prison, not least for the homeless and the poor and it is doubtful whether their condition should be regarded as significantly better simply because they retain their liberty.[21] Other circumstances which might possibly be expected to involve similar suffering or degradation could include: certain working conditions, particularly those which exploit children because of their size and nimbleness[22] or other physical characteristics[23] and which necessarily have a deleterious effect on their health and mental well-being; a lack of clothing and facilities for personal hygiene;[24] conditions imposed on those seeking social security benefits which are so humiliating that they operate effectively as a deterrent from seeking them and, therefore, the denial of it to those who ought to receive it;[25] the failure to respond to the plight of those who are disabled and disfigured by mines and other devices of war;[26] and inadequate or incompetent care by the very institutions that are supposed to help those who are weak emotionally or mentally could well be degrading, if not worse.[27] The sphere of cultural rights is perhaps the one where it seems hardest to imagine violations of them as producing the kind of effects with which we are concerned,[28] but even there a failure to accord proper respect for linguistic rights could produce great emotional difficulties, particularly for children who might not be able to communicate in the official language or feel more comfortable speaking their mother tongue.[29] These are, of course, only possible scenarios in which the treatment might result in the requisite degree of suffering or humiliation and there may well be many instances where this cannot be demonstrated. Nevertheless it would not be unreasonable to expect that there will be at least some occasions when the relevant standard is satisfied and it would, therefore, be legitimate to compare the position of a victim of economic, social or cultural rights violation with that of someone who has been subjected to torture, inhuman or degrading treatment.

However, the mere existence of such suffering and humiliation – no matter how distressing for either those directly affected or the concerned outside observer – will not in itself be sufficient to constitute torture and inhuman or degrading treatment or punishment. In the first place it must be borne in mind that, unlike the prohibition on torture and the like, the duty to secure the enjoyment of economic, social and cultural rights is not an absolute obligation for those states that have undertaken to guarantee them; their duty is only framed in terms of doing what they can achieve, in the light of their available resources, albeit with a view to the ultimate realization of all the rights in full.[30] It will undoubtedly be the case that some, if not all, of the deprivations already mentioned are currently beyond the capacity of some states to deal with; no matter how much they care there is simply not enough money to ensure that everyone is properly housed, clothed and medically treated.[31] Nevertheless there is a danger of accepting this sort of defence too readily; although resources are a factor to be taken into account, their non-availability is not generally as clear-cut a matter as it is sometimes presented. It is incontestable that some states are considerably worse off than others but there is also scope for examining the way in which some of the former (as well as the latter) choose to allocate the resources that they do have at their disposal; a preference for military hardware may call into question the assertion that it is impossible to deal with economic and social deprivation.[32] In some instances, however, it could be a reasonable conclusion that a state was doing the best with its available resources and, where this is so, it would not be tenable to claim that the suffering in question is attributable to it.[33] The resource argument can never be a complete and unqualified defence but it could hardly be maintained that, because of the suffering or humiliation being endured, a state has committed a violation of the prohibition on torture and the like, even though it has not actually breached any duty to act with respect to economic, social and cultural rights; the latter remains a prerequisite for the possibility of the former finding even being entertained.

However, even where the possibility of inadequate resources as an obstacle to liability does not arise, there will still be a need to see the prohibition as going beyond this and actually imposing some sort of positive duty to intervene in certain circumstances (such as by providing a better quality of life itself or by preventing neglect within the home situation) for it to be even capable of being applied to a situation giving rise to a violation of economic, social and cultural rights. This might, at first, be considered to be an insurmountable obstacle since torture, inhuman and degrading treatment have generally been conceived of as something that is inflicted on the victim[34] and the guarantee against being 'subjected'[35] to it will, therefore, inevitably be understood in terms of a duty for the state and its agents to do no more than abstain from acting. It would not, however, be stretching the scope of the prohibition excessively to suggest that it may also sometimes require actual intervention. Certainly there is increasingly a tendency to recognize that civil and political rights can have positive as well as negative aspects.[36] The United Nations Human Rights Committee has recognized the need to take positive measures to prevent the occurrence of torture and the like[37] and the European Commission of Human Rights has at least been prepared to acknowledge that a lack of proper medical care could amount to inhuman treatment.[38] There seems to be no reason in principle, therefore, why some of the other failings with respect to economic and social rights do not also have the potential to be regarded as a breach of the prohibition on torture.

Much more problematic, however, will be the need to demonstrate that any suffering or humiliation resulting from a failure to act has actually been 'inflicted' with an element of deliberation and purposefulness. The need for these elements to be established is perhaps most pressing in the case of torture, particularly since they are an express feature of the definitions in the 1984 United Nations and 1985 Inter-American Torture Conventions[39] and they have been sought by bodies interpreting other provisions.[40] It may, of course, be that the deprivation of economic, social and cultural rights is motivated by a wish to intimidate, obtain information, obliterate the personality or to discriminate against a particular group[41] but it is probably not a common feature of them. Deliberation or intent in this sense is not a requirement of the practices that have been found to be inhuman and degrading since this is one of the aggravating elements essential for such treatment to regarded as having crossed the torture threshhold. It may, therefore, be more feasible to claim that the non-observance of these rights is 'only' inhuman or degrading treatment.

However, even if this 'lower' standard can be satisfied, the need for proximity may prove to be the most serious stumbling block to establishing that violations of economic, social and cultural rights also constitute such treatment. Certainly the mere failure to deploy resources might not be viewed as a sufficiently proximate cause of the suffering that ensues from it in respect of any one individual even though it was fairly obvious that this would occur. It would be easy to argue (with or without conviction) that no problem had been anticipated because adequate precautions had been taken or reliance had been placed on other agencies. There are, of course, problems of evidence in all cases of torture and inhuman and degrading treatment but it is unlikely that, as compared with the apparent result of treatment in a police station or prison,[42] the burden of proof could be shifted to the state in relation to decisions at this level. For a violation of the prohibition it will have to be demonstrated that a particular public body was conscious of its act of neglect and that neither it nor its consequences were unintentional. If violations of economic, social and cultural rights are, therefore, to be seen as torture and inhuman and degrading treatment, it will be important to abandon the traditional way of viewing them as situations and turn them into individual cases.[43] The complaint will have to be directed at decisions close to the point of deprivation and not the adoption of social policies no matter how inevitable the consequences may seem. Specific failures to provide assistance, whether in terms of food, clothing or shelter as well as the failure to remove someone from harmful conditions, are likely to be the only situations which will satisfy the need for proximity; culpability will only arise where the official is sufficiently well-informed about the consequences, or alerted to them, that action could reasonably be expected to prevent them occurring. As has already been suggested,[44] it is unlikely that legal, as opposed to moral, responsibility could be imposed on other states or international organizations in a position to help where they fail to do so. It is also improbable that the *Soering*[45] doctrine could be extended so as to prevent someone being removed to a country where they would face undoubted economic and social deprivation, except perhaps where there was an immediately quantifiable threat to the person's life.[46] That apart there is likely to be a considerable gap between the legal and colloquial assessment of a situation.

Even where the conceptual leap involved in double categorization can objectively be made, there are still likely to be difficulties in persuading tribunals to accept that it is appropriate to go down this particular route. It may well be hard for tribunals to recognize that there is genuine comparability between the conventional situations regarded as constituting torture and the like and those which arise out of economic, social and cultural deprivation. The longstanding association of torture and allied violations is with the law enforcement agencies whereas quite different bodies are likely to be involved in complaints relating to economic, social and cultural rights; just as the ill-treatment of wives was once considered by the police as lying outside the sphere of the criminal law, so the suffering that results from the deprivation of economic, social and cultural rights, no matter how intentional, may not be perceived as appropriate for consideration under this heading.[47] There may undoubtedly be some reluctance on the part of the bodies concerned with civil and political rights to engage in the evaluation of social policy that will invariably underlie the decisions to be impugned.[48] It will, therefore, be necessary to demonstrate that the suffering which is the subject-matter of a complaint would not have occurred but for a specifically identifiable act or failure to act. If a sufficiently close proximity of this kind cannot be established, procedural hurdles are also likely to be raised to prevent an in-depth examination of the complaint.[49] It is important, therefore, that allegations of torture and the like arising from this sort of situation are particularly well-focused and do not become bogged down in generalized situations, even though the concern will probably be more on addressing these than individual cases.

Conclusion

The value of pursuing such an approach is at least twofold. In the absence of operative complaint mechanisms for violations of economic, social and cultural rights,[50] other than in the labour field,[51] this would provide a new opportunity to target violations of human rights of a particularly grave character. Individual cases could then be used as a vehicle for addressing a more generalized problem; success with these would demonstrate that economic, social and cultural rights violations are more than situations giving rise to despair. Nevertheless it would be foolish to assume that the cases that can be brought are likely to have a major remedial effect on the deprivation involved. It would, however, be a useful way of tackling some of the more serious problems. At the same time it would be a corrective to the limited perspective that suffering inflicted by law enforcement officers is a more pressing problem than that resulting from systematic neglect. The indivisibility of human rights requires that like situations be treated in the same way.[52]

Notes

1   The principles underlying this analysis may also be applicable to adults.
2   This prohibition is not only a common element of all the regional and global human rights instruments guaranteeing civil and political rights but also of the rules governing both international and non-international armed conflict: see the 1949 Geneva Conventions and the two Additional Protocols of 1977. It is also acknowledged to be a requirement under customary international law; see, e.g. *Restatement of the Law Third, Restatement of the Foreign Relations Law of the United States*, §702 (1987).
3   For instance, an interference with freedom of movement could have implications for freedom of expression: see *Piermont* v. *France* (1995) 20 E.H.R.R. 301; and a breach of procedural guarantees could be that which makes the regulation of property rights unacceptable: see *Bryan* v. *United Kingdom*, Ser. A, No. 335-A (1995).
4   Where unsuccessful attempts have been made to claim the means used to pursue their objectives such as strikes, consultation and collective bargaining within the protection of the freedom of association guarantee within civil and political rights instruments despite their explicit recognition within the provisions of instruments protecting economic and social rights; e.g. see Forde, 'The European Convention on Human Rights and Labour Law', (1983) 31 *A.J.C.L.*, 301.
5   But the ability to claim discrimination before mechanisms essentially devoted to the protection of civil and political rights can be used to protect social and economic rights; see, e.g. *Shuler-Zgraggen* v. *Switzerland* (1993) 16 E.H.R.R. 405 (invalidity pension) and *Zwaan-deVries* v. *The Netherlands, Selected Decisions of the Human Rights Committee*, UN Doc CCPR/C/OP/2, p. 209 (unemployment benefit). Moreover some elements of economic and social rights have also been found in other civil and political rights; see Pellonpää, 'Economic, Social and Cultural Rights' in St. J. Macdonald, Matscher and Petzold (1993), *The European System for the Protection of Human Rights*, Dordrecht, at 855.
6   See Scheinin, 'Economic and Social Rights as Legal Rights' in Eide, Krause and Rosas (1995), *Economic, Social and Cultural Rights: A Textbook*, Dordrecht, 41. This was, of course, only true of attempts to derive them from general guarantees and not of reliance on specific laws implementing them, such as in the field of social security.
7   A notable example is 'family life'; see the discussion in Harris, O'Boyle and Warbrick (1995), *Law of the European Convention on Human Rights*, London, at 312–7.
8   See, e.g. Peters (1985), *Torture*, Oxford, for a historical perspective and the more contemporary account of not too dissimilar treatment being meted out in a wide range of countries which is found in the Amnesty International report (1984), *Torture in the Eighties*, London.
9   The fundamental character of the prohibition is reflected in the refusal to admit derogations from it even in emergency situations.
10 Such as the adoption of specific conventions concerning torture and inhuman and degrading treatment or punishment by the Council of Europe, the Organisation of American States and the United Nations, as well as the establishment of a Special Rapporteur on Torture by the United Nations Commission on Human Rights.
11 Economic, social and cultural rights have generally suffered from weaker mechanisms for their implementation than civil and political rights; see A. Rosas and M. Scheinin, 'Implementation Mechanisms and Remedies', in Eide et al., *op.cit.*, n.6, at 355.
12 This may, of course, be unwarranted in individual cases. The Convention on the Rights of the Child 1989 includes a prohibition on torture and the like but there is no reason to think that a lesser standard than that in other instruments is involved, see Article 37a.

13   It is certainly not intended to suggest that the deprivation of an adult's economic, social and cultural rights is inherently unlikely to satisfy the threshhold requirements for torture and the like.

14   See Rodley (1987), *The Treatment of Prisoners under International Law*, Oxford, ch.3.

15   *Ireland* v. *United Kingdom* (1978) 2 E.H.R.R. 25 but see the criticism of this approach by Rodley, *op.cit.*, n.14, at 83–90.

16   *Costello-Roberts* v. *United Kingdom* (1993) 19 E.H.R.R.112.

17   *McFeeley* v. *United Kingdom*, 20 D.R. 44 (1980).

18   *B* v. *France* (1992) 16 E.H.R.R. 1.

19   *Kröcher and Möller* v. *Switzerland*, 34 D.R. 25 (1982).

20   See Rodley, *op.cit.*, n.14, ch.9.

21   Although it should be noted that Article 10 of the International Covenant on Civil and Political Rights imposes a specific injunction on states to treat all persons deprived of their liberty 'with humanity and with respect for the inherent dignity of the human person'.

22   For example the use of children in the sweeping of chimneys and the manufacture of carpets. See Van Bueren (1995), *The International Law on the Rights of the Child*, Kluwer, 269–71.

23   Such as in child prostitution.

24   The resulting loss of self-respect entails a degradation of the human spirit.

25   In Case 29/69 *Stauder* v. *Ulm* [1969] E.C.R. 419 the European Court of Justice saw the requirement that the names of persons entitled to buy cheap butter be disclosed to those selling it could infringe privacy rights but it is probable that an even more extensive and gratuitous public disclosure of the identity of persons receiving social benefits could undermine their self-respect.

26   Being forced to crawl around on the ground without artificial limbs would certainly be viewed as degrading in a colloquial sense.

27   The neglect of children in local authority homes would be a possible example of this. In those instances where actual brutality was involved the regime would probably constitute inhuman treatment in the conventional sense.

28   But this is perhaps the handicap imposed by the traditional perception of torture and the like.

29   See also the argument about the control over language rights as a form of oppression in Frank Horn (1994) (ed.), *Linguistic Rights of Minorities*, Rovaniemi, 54–71.

30   See, for example, Article 2 of the International Covenant on Economic, Social and Cultural Rights.

31   For the relative capacities of states, see UNDP, *Human Development Report 1994*, New York (1994). Although it may be possible to remedy the existence of shortcomings within a particular country through aid packages, the failure to provide it will not make the possible donor countries legally responsible for the resulting suffering or humiliation; the international prohibition of torture and the like only applies with respect to the state which actually has jurisdiction over the persons affected.

32   For an argument that the 'available resources' concept still entails an obligation to give priority to social welfare, see D.M. Trubek, 'Economic, Social and Cultural Rights', in T. Meron (1984) (ed.), *Human Rights in International Law*, Oxford, 205, at 214–6.

33   This would certainly be so if there were a truly equitable distribution of the available resources but suffering could still not be avoided.

34   See Rodley, *op.cit.*, n.14, at 7–10.

35   The term generally used in the international instruments.

36   See the discussion in Harris et al., *op.cit.*, n.7, at 19–22.

37   These should include arrangements for the supervision of detention, the establishment of complaints mechanisms and the registration of detainees so as to provide an effective machinery of control; General Comments 7(16) and 20(47), HRI/GEN/1/Rev.1, 7 and 30 (1994).

38   E.g. *Bonnechaux* v. *Switzerland*, 18 D.R. 100 (1979).

39   Articles 1 and 2 respectively.

40   See Rodley, *op.cit.*, n.14, at 78–9.

41   The factors identified in the United Nations and Inter-American Conventions.

42   For example, see *Tomasi* v. *France* (1992) 15 E.H.R.R. 1.

43   This has not, so far, been the character of the implementation mechanisms for economic, social and cultural rights but a collective complaints procedure has been established for the European Social Charter, work is being undertaken on a protocol establishing a right of individual petition for the International Covenant on Economic, Social and Cultural Rights and there is an Additional Protocol to the American Convention on Human Rights in the area of Economic, Social and Cultural Rights which permits individual complaints to be made. See further Rosas and Scheinin, *op. cit.*, n.6. The African Charter on the Rights and Welfare of the Child 1990 also has a petition mechanism encompassing both categories of rights. See Van Bueren *op. cit.* at 411.

44   See n.31.

45   *Soering* v. *United Kingdom* (1989) 11 E.H.R.R. 439 in which an extradition decision was successfully challenged where it would have consigned the accused to the 'death row phenomenon' in the United States.

46   Such as where particular medical care was needed and was only available in the removing state.

47   In *Free Legal Assistance Group et al.* v. *Zaire* it was alleged that, where public finances had been mismanaged, a failure to provide basic education and health services was degrading but the African Commission on Human and Peoples' Rights restricted itself to finding violations of the right to education and health even though it did uphold complaints about torture as traditionally understood; AHG/207 (XXII), Annex VIII (1996).

48   But the European Court of Human Rights has stated that 'the mere fact that an interpretation of the Convention may extend into the sphere of social and economic rights should not be a decisive factor against such an interpretation'; *Airey* v. *Ireland* (1979) 2 E.H.R.R. 305, at 316.

49   Cf. the ability to avoid dealing with the position of transsexuals under the European Convention on Human Rights by insisting at a late stage that the rule that domestic remedies be exhausted had not been observed; *Van Oosterwijk* v. *Belgium* (1980) 3 E.H.R.R. 557.

50   Even those mentioned in n.43 that have actually been adopted are not yet operational.

51   On these see Leary, 'Lessons from the Experience of the International Labour Organisation', in Alston (1992) (ed.), *The United Nations and Human Rights*, Oxford, 580.

52   This was recognized in the *Vienna Declaration and Programme of Action, 1993, G.A.O.R., A/CONF.157/23*, para. 5.

8   Are the Rights of Refugee Children Protected Adequately Against Torture?

Louise Williamson

Introduction

I am told that the 1911 edition of the Encyclopaedia Britannica contained an entry on torture which stated that torture was a subject of 'historical interest' alone. Unfortunately in this genocidal century, governments and movements of the right and left have used torture both as a systematic strategy of intimidation and have used or tolerated it in more spontaneous, but equally brutal, forms. In other cases, states have been unwilling or unable to protect their citizens from torture at the hands of certain groups or individuals. Some of these citizens are children, as an eloquent letter sent to the Refugee Council by a seven-year-old child from Poland testifies:

> I am not like any other seven-year-old. I am a gypsy ... Some men attacked me and my mum in the park. I only remember the sudden sharp pain in my leg. When I woke up in hospital my right leg below the knee was missing. The men in the park had cut it off. The fingers of my right hand were also cut off. I do not know the reason. Why do they hate me so much? I will try to be a good refugee here in England.

Since its inception in March 1994, the British Refugee Council's Panel of Advisers for unaccompanied refugee children has supported over 1,000 children and young people[1] who have fled to the United Kingdom from over 40 countries. All too often their stories include having witnessed or experienced at first hand the destruction of their neighbourhood and homes, violence to themselves or people they have known and loved, sexual abuse and rape, being a child soldier or experience of detention or prison. Unfortunately in the case of detention or prison, this is sometimes on British soil.

Why do Children Fall Through the Safety Net?

Geraldine Van Bueren's invitation letter to this symposium posed the question: do children fall through the net of international legal protection because 'they suffer the effects of traumatic events in ways which are different from adults' (and which are then presumably unrecognized)? This is quite likely, given that children's levels of physical, cognitive and emotional maturity differ from those of adults. It is certainly a factor which should be addressed, and more child-focused and child-informed work is necessary to ensure the child's voice and experience are heard.

There are also other possible reasons why children's suffering of torture, cruel, inhuman and degrading treatment might go unrecognized.[2] One reason is that it is too painful for adults to accept evidence of extreme abuse – too painful to admit that adults like us can do such things, and too painful to accept that children experience such undeserved and unnecessary agonies and betrayal of trust.

Sometimes denial springs from an assumption that a child is different from us. How many people would suggest that a grown man be circumcised without an anaesthetic? Yet the potentially abusive nature of unanaesthetised male circumcision in babies has only recently been debated in countries like the US and Britain – amid enormous controversy in some religious circles.[3] Similarly, it is only recently that babies and young children have routinely been given painkillers following invasive surgery in some British hospitals because it was earlier assumed they did not experience pain like adults.[4] Ironically it appears that that is exactly right – they actually experience pain more acutely rather than less. So too the child victims of torture.

However, these musings do not adequately address the situation of children who are the deliberate targets of torture or other abuse as part of a political strategy. That the international community is slow to react or may deny such realities is all too apparent. The failure on 3rd May 1996 to secure a global ban on the use of landmines which have such devastating effects on children provides a very recent example of how political, economic and foreign policy considerations of the powerful are put before humanitarian considerations of the victims of whatever age and in the face of very widespread support for the proposal.[5]

When considering the cruel treatment of children in other countries, there may be certain 'blind spots' where the rights of children 'abroad' are concerned – they are not regarded as being of similar value to 'our' children, and so we do not make a great fuss about them. Such blind spots are also apparent when considering reasons for the unchecked and unrecognized abuse of children 'at home'. And if politicians are not sensitive to the abuse of certain children in their own country, how can they be expected to protect children elsewhere? Of course, it is highly unlikely that all children in a particular society are treated badly. Some will always have the protected status of the vulnerable and valuable future assets they represent, while others will be excluded from that protected group by virtue of class, caste, poverty or other considerations. So in considering this subject, our analysis must take into account political factors.

We are all familiar with the strategy of repressive regimes – and, indeed of democratic governments – whereby the enemy is 'demonised'. At the extreme end, it becomes a patriotic and often divinely approved duty to terrorize, maim or kill innocent people, including children.[6] The process can be seen with the characterization of street children in Latin America as 'vermin' who, it is thought, have to be exterminated. Nearer to home, in the UK we have seen a Home Secretary adjudged at fault when he sentenced two children found guilty of the murder of the toddler, James Bulger, on the basis that he was applying sentencing policy for adults rather than for children – this at least in part in response to public opinion that 'normal' children could not have done such a thing, so these children should not be treated as normal children. Even closer to the subject of this paper is the way in which refugees who seek asylum in the United Kingdom are portrayed as 'bogus' and 'welfare scroungers'; this is then used as justification for denying them the means to live as seen in the government's current policy of refusing welfare benefits and social housing to large numbers of asylum seekers.[7]

There are other situations where children are seen by some to be quite valid targets for abuse, torture and even death – because they are doing an adult job. Both sides of conflicts use children as soldiers – approximately 200,000 in 35 countries in the last decade – and some as young as six years old.[8] Children are used in preference to adults because they are biddable and more easily exploited, often quite fearless and easily indoctrinated. A means of coercion or part of children's 'training' or preparation for their combatant role may well involve being tortured or ill-treated. If captured, child soldiers are likely to face grave penalties for their actions as if they were adults. A frightening, but almost logical extension of this phenomenon was observed in the Rwandan genocide, where children, babies and even foetuses were attacked brutally and killed so that they would not grow up to become the opposition and potential killers.

Some abusive treatment of children may not generally be seen to constitute torture or ill-treatment and so it is important to remember that the number of children facing physical violence and mistreatment – too high though it is – is not the whole story. The number pales into insignificance when compared with the millions of children facing humiliation, fear, suffering and death caused by the deliberate or unintended interference with food supplies and health services. This can occur in situations of war or where economic sanctions are applied, but more often is the result of indirect or structural violence in the form of economic injustice, poverty induced malnutrition and ordinary disease.[9] Such phenomena affecting children would not usually be regarded as constituting torture,[10] and yet the denial of food, drink and medical services to a child in detention would almost certainly be regarded by most people as doing so. All the time our economic and political structures fail seriously to recognize the value of each child and instead treat them as expendable, the serious abuse and exploitation of children in whatever manner will be made easier just because certain children 'do not matter'.

Social psychology, economics and political science provide many insights which can usefully be brought to the debate as to why children's suffering remains on the scale it does and has been marginalized to the extent it has. This is also true of refugee children. Before considering whether the international community's approach is adequate to protect the rights of refugee children, it is important to explore further the question of their marginalization.

Are Refugee Children a Priority?

Marginalization of Refugees Worldwide

Certain groups are clearly marginalized within the world of adults – adults who are so often implied to be the major, if not sole, constituents of 'society'. Refugees and asylum seekers are one such group.

Following the end of World War II, there were millions of displaced refugees in Europe. A conference met in Geneva in 1951 to sign the Convention Relating to the Status of Refugees (hence the 'Geneva Convention'); a Protocol was signed in 1967 removing the geographical and time limitations of the 1951 Convention. According to the Geneva Convention, a refugee is someone who:

> ... owing to a well-founded fear of being persecuted for reasons of race, religion, nationality, membership of a particular social group or political opinion, is outside the country of his [or her] nationality and is unable or, owing to such fear, is unwilling to avail himself [or herself] of the protection of that country.[11]

In 1995, the United Nations High Commissioner for Refugees (UNHCR) estimated the number of uprooted people worldwide to be about 53 million – either refugees who had fled their country or people who were displaced from their own homes but who had not crossed an international border. That meant one out of every 115 people on earth.[12] There are now more refugees than at any other time in history, the vast majority of whom – over 80 per cent – are living in developing countries of the world.

In spite of the massive impact these numbers of people have on the economies, environment and political stability of the regions and countries to which they flee – not to speak of the enormous humanitarian challenge they represent – refugees are often absent, or barely mentioned, in seminal works on global and international issues from whatever perspective.[13] Even in books on the work of the United Nations, the contribution of the UNHCR and the challenge of ever-increasing numbers of refugees get scant mention.[14] Refugees are similarly absent from many basic texts on race, ethnicity and discrimination.

Marginalization of Refugees Who Are Children[15]

It is, in fact, clear that a large proportion of the world's refugees are – and probably always have been – children. It was the problems faced by child refugees from the Balkans which prompted Eglantyne Jebb – founder of Save the Children – to draft a document which formed the basis of the Declaration of the Rights of the Child, subsequently adopted by the League of Nations in 1924.

There is a growing interest among psychologists of the effects on children of traumatic events such as war or intense political upheaval: Boothby, Garbarino and Punamäki to name a few. Some development economists and nutrition and health experts are also interested in large refugee movements and encampments. However, there is a general lack of sustained policy analysis or policy development concerning root causes of refugee movements and their prevention and management, particularly with the needs of children in mind. For example, Loescher and Monahan mention the fact that vast numbers of children have spent all their lives in refugee camps – yet not one chapter of their book is devoted to the situation of refugee children.[16] Camus-Jacques' chapter entitled 'Refugee Women: The Forgotten Majority'[17] mentions children, but fails to recognize that they, of course, are the real majority and does not treat them in their own right. Even Boutros Boutros-Ghali, in *An Agenda for Peace*, mentions the word 'children' just once as a vulnerable group.[18]

In response to pressure in the last decade from refugees and relief workers as to the inadequacy and inappropriateness of programmes of the UNHCR or other non-governmental organizations (NGOs), policies and activities are now more sensitive to the needs of refugee women, usually implying 'women and children'. UNHCR surveys of refugee and displaced populations in 13 countries show that children make up more than 50 per cent of the total number.[19] However, programmes are not necessarily devised with the needs of children being paramount although there are some exceptions, especially where there are large numbers of children who are unaccompanied.

The marginalization of children by the majority of adult decision-makers in the world through the structures they perpetuate and create was a theme taken up in the first World Summit on Children in 1990. Seventy heads of state or government and representatives from 152 countries agreed to draw up national programmes of action for achieving basic social goals with regard to children, to be attained by the year 2000. The need for protection of children in difficult circumstances, particularly those in war situations, was stressed but only passing reference was made to refugee children.

NGOs such as the International Committee of the Red Cross/Red Crescent and Save the Children attempt to keep children on policy makers' agenda at the international level, not only with disaster relief in mind but also preventative programmes. Interestingly, the United Nations Children's Fund's report, *The State of the World's Children 1993*, did not mention refugee children once; but in recent years, there has been a growing emphasis on the effects of war on children. In the past decade, the United Nations Children's Fund (UNICEF) estimates that two million children have been killed in war. In addition, between four and five million have been physically disabled and at least ten million have been traumatized by violence, displacement and loss of family members.[20] Save the Children have pointed out that ten million children in 1994 meant one child in every 200 throughout the world.[21] Many of these children will be refugees.

Marginalization of Children, Especially Those who are Refugees

Academics and practitioners often struggle to ensure children are included in research and policy-making at the domestic level, let alone the international. The Economic & Social Research Council of the United Kingdom (ESRC) has adopted a new research programme entitled: *Children 5-16: Growing into the Twenty First Century*. The programme specification notes 'the relative lack of attention to children across many of the United Kingdom social sciences disciplines' but notes there is a 'growing concern for and interest at a number of political levels', both in the Council of Europe and European Union in response to the UN Convention on the Rights of the Child (CRC).[22]

However, hard though it may have been until recently to promote serious interest in children, refugee and asylum-seeking children are often a forgotten group within the child population. Recent research on refugee children, certainly within the UK, can almost be counted on the fingers of one's hands. It is very policy-oriented and falls into three main categories:[23]

(i)   the psychosocial adaptation of refugee children;
(ii)   refugee children's language acquisition;[24] and
(iii) research, carried out mainly by NGOs, designed to inform service providers.[25]

This research is, of course, welcome and valuable but there are enormous gaps, such as the differences (if any) between economic and political refugees and between refugees and migrants, and the subsequent impact on children; the social networks of refugee children; experiences in the host country which can enhance or impede their development, recovery and adaptation; children's national, cultural and political identity; comparative studies with children raised in the host country or from other cultural/ religious backgrounds; and so on.

It is to be hoped that the optimism of the ESRC noted above will be matched by political commitment to change the status quo, but to summarize so far, there appears to have been a process of multiple marginalization at work for refugee children – within the focus on refugees despite children being the majority, and then also marginalization within any focus on children. Refugee children have been the marginalized among the marginalized in an unjust world.

Unaccompanied Refugee Children

It is important that the particular plight of those refugee children who are unaccompanied is not overlooked, that is:

> … those who are separated from both parents and are not being cared for by an adult who, by law or custom, has responsibility to do so.[26]

Although the proportion of unaccompanied refugee children and young people may be relatively small – estimated at between three and 5 per cent of the total number of refugees[27] – the numbers may not be. For example, more than 3,700 unaccompanied children were provided with special services in Thailand in 1980 alone during the influx of refugees from Cambodia[28] with a further 6,000 in institutions in Cambodia itself.[29] There have been at least 20,000 unaccompanied children from Sudan – mainly boys – in the 1980s and 1990s,[30] more than a quarter of a million children are separated from their parents in Liberia, Angola and Mozambique,[31] and in Rwanda from 1994, an estimated 100,000 children have been separated from their parents.[32]

The circumstances which lead to there being unaccompanied refugee children vary. In some countries, as already indicated, children may be the subjects of political repression in the form of arbitrary arrest, detention and torture. This can be as a result of their own activities or those of their families. There are all too many distressing accounts of politically motivated maltreatment of children in Amnesty International Yearbooks and other sources.[33] As a result, children and young people may need to escape to safety. Elsewhere, it is very easy during war-induced flight for children to be separated from their parents, either by accident or because their parents die, and so the children become unaccompanied. Parents may send their children abroad in order to avoid their facing dangerous fighting or unrest, compulsory military conscription or being abducted in order to become porters or prostitutes for the army. In other cases, parents may take their child to a country of asylum and then return to their country of origin. There have also been instances where children have been removed by aid workers, particularly if it seems likely that a child's whole family or village has been destroyed.

Serious attempts have been made by the UNHCR and international NGOs to address the particular vulnerability of unaccompanied refugee children and to ensure that appropriate provision is made for them.[34]

New Developments for Children, Including Refugees

The potential for recognition of refugee children's needs in their own right has been increased by the 1989 UN Convention on the Rights of the Child (CRC). All articles apply to all children, but Article 22 specifically addresses the situation of refugee children:

> States Parties shall take appropriate measures to ensure that a child who is seeking refugee status or who is considered a refugee ... shall, whether unaccompanied or accompanied by his or her parents or by any other person, receive appropriate protection and humanitarian assistance ... [including help] to trace the parents or other members of the family ... in order to obtain information necessary for reunification ...

In addition, the State's obligation to provide rehabilitative provision is outlined in Article 39, in order to ensure that child victims of armed conflicts, torture, neglect, maltreatment or exploitation receive appropriate treatment for their recovery and social re-integration. Many refugee children, whether unaccompanied or with their families, will be child victims in the meaning of Article 39.

Another relatively new development is the appointment of a Coordinator for Refugee Children by the UNHCR in 1992, part of whose brief is to monitor implementation of the UNHCR Guidelines on Refugee Children adopted in 1988 and which were subsequently updated and expanded in 1994.[35]

The World Summit on Children has already been mentioned, which highlighted the plight of children affected by war. When the CRC was drafted, one of the most contentious issues was the minimum age for recruitment into armed forces and participation in armed hostilities. Article 38 endorses 15 years as the minimum legal age. Concerned NGOs enlisted the interest of the UN Committee on the Rights of the Child which devoted its first day of discussion to the subject: 'Children in Armed Conflict'.[36]

One resulting recommendation was that there should be an optional protocol to the CRC raising the minimum age for recruitment and participation in hostilities to 18 years. The second session of the Working Group to draft the protocol met in January 1996, and although some problems remain, much progress was made. For example, there was general agreement that no-one under 18 years should be subjected to compulsory conscription and that there should be a total prohibition on recruitment of young people under 18 into non-governmental armed groups. The Committee on the Rights of the Child has also to take some credit, together with NGOs, for persuading the governments of both Sierra Leone[37] and Mozambique to release several hundred child soldiers from their ranks for rehabilitation and training.

A second recommendation was that the United Nations Secretary General should be requested to appoint an expert to undertake a study on the impact on armed conflict on children. The study, chaired by Graça Machel, the former Minister of Education of Mozambique and a former resistance fighter, was presented to the General Assembly in 1996 – the first time for a study focusing solely on children – and included a research project specifically on child soldiers. In a speech at the UK UNICEF annual general meeting on 20 November 1995, Ms Machel outlined some of the study's proposals, which she hopes will set the future long-term agenda for the UN. These include declaring children to be 'zones of peace' so that it is a crime against humanity to enlist a child into the armed forces or to use rape as a weapon of war; banning the use of landmines; rebuilding community infrastructure in any humanitarian aid programme; and working towards building a child-centred culture.

Refugee Children and International Instruments

Theo van Boven took the abuse of children's human rights seriously. He commented:

> Every year the Sub-Commission on Prevention of Discrimination and Protection of Minorities solicits and examines information on the treatment of persons subjected to any form of detention or imprisonment. The treatment of children is taken duly into account in the course of these annual reviews. The United Nations also has other activities designed to lessen the incidences of torture in the world. All of these activities have children very much at the forefront of their concerns.[38]

Despite its good intentions, the 1974 Declaration on the Protection of Women and Children in Emergency and Armed Conflict, which calls for all necessary steps to be taken to ensure the prohibition of torture, punitive measures, degrading treatment and violence, particularly against women and children, is a non-binding resolution, and no means for enforcement were included.[39] Of a different order, the 1984 UN Convention Against Torture and Other Cruel, Inhuman or Degrading Treatment or Punishment clearly has more teeth, but how far has it prevented children from suffering these abuses?

Is the Convention Against Torture Effective?

The Convention against Torture and its effectiveness cannot be judged in isolation. There is a panoply of international conventions, declarations and protocols on human rights and the protection of individuals of all ages which, if respected and adequately enforced, would dramatically reduce the incidence of torture and mistreatment, as well as ensure its effects were addressed. Over 80 of these set out human rights for children.[40] Concerning refugee children, the Geneva Convention 1951 and 1967 Protocol, the Declaration on Social and Legal Principles relating to the Protection and Welfare of Children, with Special Reference to Foster Placement and Adoption Nationally and Internationally 1985, the Convention on Protection of Children and Co-operation in Respect of Intercountry Adoption 1993 and the Convention on the Rights of the Child 1989 are obviously all very important. They are also the only international instruments with which I have some familiarity and refer to regularly in the course of my work.

The list of others which also have clear relevance is quite long and includes the following: the Universal Declaration of Human Rights 1948,

International Covenant on Economic, Social and Cultural Rights 1966, the International Covenant on Civil and Political Rights 1966, the International Convention on the Elimination of All Forms of Racial Discrimination 1965, the Convention on the Prevention and Punishment of the Crime of Genocide 1948, the Standard Minimum Rules for the Treatment of Prisoners, and the Beijing Rules. In the preparation of this chapter, I have been very struck by my almost total ignorance of these instruments – as well as of the Convention against Torture itself.

It does not appear to be a straightforward matter for a practitioner to find material outlining the modes of operation and effectiveness of these instruments. Of course, it is not easy to assess to what extent they may have prevented terrible things happening – just as you never know if it was that course of vitamin pills which stopped you getting a cold last winter. Nevertheless, vitamin pills do have readily accessible instructions for use on the bottle, which cannot be said for international instruments! After some – albeit limited – searching, I am still unclear how these instruments have been or might be used in conjunction with local and national efforts to serve the interests of refugee children.

An interesting set of questions then arises:

- Am I looking in the wrong places for information or speaking to the wrong people?
- Why is it that this field of inquiry has never occurred to me before when I have been working specifically with refugee children for ten years?
- Are the Convention against Torture and other instruments unsuitable for use in cases with children? or have they overlooked refugee children? or are they generally ineffective?

This is closely followed by:

- How can we ensure refugee children get as much protection through the instruments as any other person?
- How can we ensure practitioners are informed and confident in using them?
- Are the existing structures adequate to ensure a good flow of information between refugee children, their carers, practitioners who support them, international lawyers and international humanitarian law enforcement bodies so that the instruments can be made a reality for refugee children?

How Should the Convention Against Torture Protect Refugee Children?

The Convention Against Torture clearly has a preventative function.[41] In the case of refugee children, torture and other abusive treatment may be the cause of a child, with or without family, fleeing to safety and becoming a refugee. In that sense, the Convention has not protected the child and steps should be taken to identify the perpetrators so that abuse of other children (and adults) does not occur.

The Convention was drafted with the situation of refugees in mind: 'No State Party shall expel, return or extradite a person to another State where there are substantial grounds for believing that he would be in danger of being subjected to torture.'[42] However, activity should not stop there, with the focus on torture in the refugee's country of origin. Not only is it important that a child's person is respected during flight when he or she is likely to be very vulnerable, but also upon arrival in a country of asylum. Countries of asylum not only have a duty to respect Article 3(1) to ensure a child is not returned to a situation where his or her safety is at risk – they have a duty to ensure a child does not experience cruel, inhuman or degrading treatment or punishment in the country of asylum.

The United Kingdom – A Case Study

Although both signed and ratified, neither the UN Convention Against Torture nor the Convention on the Rights of the Child have been incorporated into domestic law in the United Kingdom. In March 1994 it was estimated that 2000 refugee children were in schools outside the capital; in October 1995 local education authorities estimated that there were 27,000 refugee children in Greater London schools.[43]

Detention of Refugee Children

The first hurdle to claiming asylum is gaining entry to the United Kingdom. Immigration officers are able to detain asylum seekers whose cases they decide are likely to be 'without foundation' or where they suspect the applicant will abscond if granted temporary admission. Unaccompanied children are also detained, in adult detention centres and prisons, together with adults.

Under powers in the Children Act 1989, children can have their liberty restricted without the authority of the court for an absolute maximum of 48 hours. In December 1992 the Immigration Minister said, 'Unaccompanied children are only ever detained by the immigration service if they arrive out of working hours and it is impossible to contact immediately the local social services until the following morning ... The protection of children is paramount in such arrangements.' This policy has subsequently been restated in both the Houses of Lords and Commons. However, since the Panel of Advisers has been operating, it has worked with 54 young people under the age of 18 who have been detained.[44] The majority are held for less than a month, but many have been detained for longer periods – in one case, up to eight months. The Immigration Service is not legally obliged to provide written reasons for detention to detainees or their representatives. In some cases, detention has been considered necessary for reasons such as the child having false documents, because there is doubt about age, or because the child has passed through a safe 'third country' where they could have applied for asylum. Some children are only released after medical reports by independent paediatricians have corroborated their stated age, but even these reports are not always immediately accepted.

Immigration detention centres and prisons with detention facilities such as Rochester and Haslar are very bleak places, full of desperate, frightened adults, some of whom are suffering the after-effects of torture and direct oppression, some of whom may be on hunger strike. There are no separate facilities for children and there are very limited leisure or educational facilities for immigration detainees apart from television. It is clear that children are extremely vulnerable to physical, sexual and emotional abuse. None of the safeguards apply to children in immigration detention which exist for children in secure accommodation for young offenders or young people who are persistent absconders or who present a risk to themselves or others, nor do the safeguards for those living in children's homes apply. The majority of children in such detention have been deeply traumatized by the experience.

The Asylum Determination Procedure

Commitments arising from the Geneva Convention and Protocol apply to all people, regardless of age. Indeed, one of the recommendations which was adopted unanimously by the Geneva Conference, stated that State Parties should '... take the necessary measures for the protection of the refugee's family, especially with a view to ... the protection of refugees who are minors, in particular unaccompanied children and girls, with special reference to guardianship and adoption.'[45]

In the United Kingdom, unlike some European countries, it is possible for children under the age of 18 years to lodge an asylum claim in their own right. However, broadly speaking, they have to satisfy the same criteria for refugee status as any adult applicant, that is they must be able to demonstrate a well-founded fear of persecution. The only slight difference is outlined in an Immigration Rule on unaccompanied refugee children, instituted when the Asylum and Immigration Appeals Act was passed in 1993, and as a result of persistent pressure by NGOs on the government to implement the UNHCR Guidelines on Refugee Children. The Rule states that 'particular priority and care is to be given to the handling of their cases'[46] and goes on:

> in assessing the claim of a child more weight should be given to objective indications of risk than to the child's state of mind and understanding of his or her situation. An asylum application made on behalf of a child should not be refused solely because the child is too young to understand his situation or to have formed a well-founded fear of persecution.[47]

It is stressed that interviews should be avoided if possible, but if necessary, should be conducted with an independent adult present who is not an immigration or police officer: 'If [the child] appears tired or distressed, the interview should be stopped'.[48]

In spite of these provisions, only three unaccompanied children were granted refugee status in 1995 (two of whom had to go to appeal before being granted a positive determination), although others have had what appear to be very good grounds, including torture, rape, beatings and imprisonment. Many commentators have pointed to a steep drop in positive determinations of asylum applications in the United Kingdom – for all applicants, whether single, with children or unaccompanied children. This is seen to be due to a 'climate of disbelief' rather than any change in the nature of the applications.[49] The Glidewell Panel, an independent panel established in 1996 to examine proposals in the Asylum and Immigration Bill, confirmed this view.[50] Chaired by Sir Iain Glidewell, a recently retired Lord Justice of Appeal, the Panel concluded that the then Bill: '... offends in some respects against the spirit of international law; encourages a 'culture of disbelief' which makes individual determination of asylum claims difficult; [and] effectively withdraws appeal rights from some groups of asylum seekers.'[51] Some have inferred that Home Office officials are not allowed to make positive determinations over and above a certain quota (around 20 per cent).[52]

Article 3(1) of the Convention Against Torture has been of great assistance to NGO campaigns in the United Kingdom during the passage of the Asylum and Immigration Bill in its Second Reading in the House of Lords in April and May 1996. The previous Government suffered a defeat on 23rd April when the Lords voted by 143 to 124 to exempt torture victims and those who have fled from countries with a recent record of torture from the Act's new fast-track appeals procedure and 'white list' provisions.[53]

If a fair and just system for dealing with asylum claims is not in place, there is always going to be a serious concern that some people will be removed from the UK to situations of danger; this could include families with children or unaccompanied refugee children.

Right to the Essentials of Life

Every child has the inherent right to life,[54] to an adequate standard of living[55], to benefit from social security[56] and to be free of discrimination on the basis of a parent's status.[57] To allow children to live in destitution because they are asylum seekers, especially in a developed industrial society, should be seen as inhumane treatment. However, this is what the United Kingdom Government has been doing since 5th February 1996, when social security regulation changes for certain asylum seekers were introduced. Asylum seekers who apply for asylum in-country and those appealing against a negative decision have lost all entitlement to Income Support, Housing or Council Tax Benefit; they have no means of paying for food or accommodation. Some have dependent children, and included in the number are 16- and 17-year-old unaccompanied refugee young people living independently. Entitlement to free school meals, uniform grants for school children and concessionary fees for English language and vocational courses will be lost. Social Fund payments will not be made because these are dependent on Income Support being payable, and crisis loans will not be payable because asylum seekers will have no means of repaying them.[58] Local authorities have duties to children 'in need' under the Children Act 1989, but not all asylum seekers know of this, and it has to be said that some social services departments have been very reluctant to assist unaccompanied young people. Following the changes and after eight weeks of monitoring, the Refugee Council had provided direct services to 383 people affected by the cuts, 84 of whom are children. The true figure, including all those not known to the Refugee Council, is likely to be much higher.[59]

These changes will have a devastating effect on the health and welfare of asylum-seeking children and their families.[60] Refugee community groups who provide a great deal of support and advice to asylum seekers will themselves be hard-hit, staffed as they often are by asylum seekers. The British Medical Association is concerned about a rapid rise of TB, for example, as people live on the streets and have no access to medicines.

Family Reunification and Adoption

Where a child has loving family members able to provide a home and care for them, it is cruel to keep the family apart. However, that is exactly what happens to some asylum seeking families, split among various countries to which they have fled. Despite vigorous diplomatic efforts in some instances, it is not always easy to effect family reunification, even when 'swaps' of families are possible. Family reunification is also very difficult for unaccompanied refugee children. If they are not granted refugee status (which confers the right to family reunion) but are granted only 'Exceptional Leave to Remain', they have the right to apply for family reunification only after four years – a very long time in the life of the child. Application for family reunion earlier can only be made in 'exceptional cases' and at the discretion of a senior civil servant.

The United Kingdom Government entered a reservation to the CRC specifically on this issue, thereby giving priority to immigration law over family reunion. The right was reserved to '… apply such legislation, in so far as it relates to the entry into, stay in and departure from the United Kingdom of those who do not have the right … to enter and remain in the United Kingdom … as it may deem necessary from time to time.'

This would appear to fly in the face of underlying principles of the Convention, such as the child's best interests and the right of family reunification, as well as those underlying the 1989 Children Act in domestic legislation. The UN Committee on the Rights of the Child made a number of concluding observations on the United Kingdom Government's report of progress in implementing the UN Convention on the Rights of the Child in 1995. *Inter alia*, the Committee recommended 'that a review be undertaken of the nationality and immigration laws and procedures to ensure their conformity with the principles and provisions of the Convention.'[61]

The results of such a review – if, indeed, one has been carried out – have yet to be made known.

In fact, the United Kingdom is not alone in this respect. In a recent study on the rights of refugee and migrant children in the European Union (EU), reports to the Committee from EU members and subsequent recommendations by the Committee were scrutinized.[62] When considering refugee and migrant children, the Committee 'repeatedly raises the question of whether national legislation is compatible with the Convention.'[63] The harmonization of strictly applied asylum procedures in 'Fortress Europe' certainly does not make family reunification easier.

There are also cases known to the United Kingdom branch of International Social Service where refugee children have been legally adopted in this country before thorough attempts have been made to trace relatives abroad – relatives who have subsequently made themselves known and who have opposed the adoption.[64]

Racism and Bullying

For many refugee children, one of the greatest shocks about life in the country to which they have fled for safety is the racism and bullying they face. Some abuse is directed at them for being of a minority ethnic group, some for being refugees. Taunts of 'Flee! Flea! Refugee!' and 'Bogus! Bogus!' have been reported in playgrounds across London. In an oral submission to the Glidewell Panel, Sajida Malik of Newham Monitoring Project told of her experience in working with school children. She said 'I was horrified by the things I heard young children talking about. When we raised the issue of asylum seekers and refugees they talked about them in the context of being bogus – welfare scroungers, beggars, dirty and disgusting.'

Many schools have firm anti-bullying and anti-racist policies, and have made creative attempts to induct newly arrived refugee students into their classes. However, schools cannot be held responsible for the anti-refugee public utterances of Government ministers and the media or for the policy measures targetting asylum seekers in ever more punitive ways all of which can give rise to the type of views expressed by the children above.

Concluding Remarks

Economic injustice and disparities in power have made certain groups of children particularly vulnerable to abuse, whether by malnutrition or physical violence and torture. There are also the unpredictable and uncontrolled outbreaks of violence by government or other forces against civilians, including children. Children, and particularly refugee children, have been marginalized in past decades. International instruments, though worthy statements of intent, have often proved inadequate to protect many victims of injustice in the world, none more than children. However, there have been a number of impetuses in recent years which appear to be shifting this balance. The 1989 UN Convention on the Rights of the Child, the 1990 World Summit on Children, the work of the Committee on the Rights of the Child, UNHCR's revised Guidelines on Refugee Children 1994, UNICEF's Anti-War Agenda 1996 and the UN Study on the Impact of Armed Struggle on Children are creating a momentum for change – change to put the protection of children and the upholding of their rights at the centre of international concerns.

It is also vital that the right to asylum for refugees – for children as for adults – is upheld, rather than being eroded. The portrayal of asylum seekers as 'bogus' which we are seeing currently in the UK is a trend replicated in many other countries. The downgrading of brutal treatment at the hands of state authorities must be challenged with its tendency to regard torture and mistreatment as not 'serious enough' to warrant the granting of asylum. So must the ill-treatment of asylum-seeking children in their countries of asylum, in particular their detention and denial of the economic means to live in dignity.

Great strides in child health have been made in the previous decades by simple preventative programmes. What is now needed for the international body politic, rather than post hoc reporting mechanisms, are child-focused early warning systems, informed public opinion, good investigative journalism, support for lawyers and human rights organizations, and the strengthening of the civic culture and its international links. Clearly, NGOs and those in government with responsibility for policies affecting children must press for the very best for refugee children on the basis of existing domestic law and the CRC. Other international instruments on refugees are of great potential use, but they should be reviewed in the light of the Convention on the Rights of the Child. It is also clear that their means of operation need to be made more accessible to those who have direct responsibility for protecting refugee children from torture – some of the most vulnerable and marginalized children of all.

Notes

1   By mid-October 1997, the Panel of Advisers had worked with over 2,000 unaccompanied asylum-seeking children and young people.
2   For examples of such treatment, as part of a sustained policy rather than isolated incidents, cf. 'Children Under Attack by Governments', *Amnesty Action*, January/February 1988, 2.
3   Bunting, 'GMC [General Medical Council] to debate circumcision', *The Guardian*, 20.4.96, p. 12. Richards, The Ill-Treatment of Children, Some Developmental Considerations, *op. cit.*
4   See Doyal, Can Medicine Be Torture? The Case of Children at 155.
5   In the intervening period, progress has, of course, been made on this issue. A draft treaty banning the use of anti-personnel landmines was drawn up and agreed by 97 states in Oslo in September 1997. It was subsequently signed in Ottawa in December 1997 and is now open for ratification. However, the vital issue of mine clearance, as opposed to a ban on use, has received far less attention.
6   Cf. Keen (1986), *Faces of the Enemy: Reflections of the Hostile Imagination*, San Francisco: Harper and Row.
7   Portrayal of asylum seekers and refugees in the UK media is usually in 'problem' or negative terms, with little coverage of human rights situations from which refugees

have fled. Cf. Paul Coleman, 'Survey of Asylum Coverage in the National Daily Press', in *Runnymede Bulletin*, Dec 1995/Jan 1996.

8   Save the Children (1994), *Children at War*, London, SCF, 9–11.

9   This argument is developed in: Kent, *War and Children's Survival*, University of Hawaii Institute for Peace, Occasional Paper No. 2, 1990.

10 See above McBride, The Violation of Economic, Social and Cultural Rights as Torture or Cruel, Inhuman or Degrading Treatment, at 107.

11 Article 1A(2), 1951 UN Convention Relating to the Status of Refugees.

12 Office of the United Nations High Commissioner for Refugees, *Refugees at a Glance: A Monthly Digest of UNHCR Activities*, Geneva, UNHCR, July 1995.

13 Cf. for example: Clements & Ward (1994) (eds), *Building International Community,* St Leonards/NSW (Australia), Allen and Unwin; Commission on Global Governance, *Our Global Neighbourhood*, New York: OUP, 1995; Evans (1993), *Cooperating for Peace: The Global Agenda for the 1990s and Beyond*, St Leonards/NSW (Australia), Allen and Unwin; Kung and Kuschel (1993), *A Global Ethic: The Declaration of the Parliament of the World's Religions*, London, SCM Press.

14 Cf. for example: Bailey and Daws (1995), *The United Nations: A Concise Political Guide*, Basingstoke and London, Macmillan (3rd edn.); Childers (1994) (ed.), *Challenges to the United Nations: Building a Safer World*, London, CIIR; Roberts and Kingsbury (1994) (eds), *United Nations, Divided World*, Oxford, Clarendon Press (2nd edn. with minor corrections). An exception is: Secretariat of the Independent Commission on International Humanitarian Issues, *Winning the Human Race?*, London and New Jersey, Zed Books, 1988, Ch. 5 ('Vulnerable Groups'), 78–138.

15 In this paper, a child is taken to be: '… every human being below the age of eighteen years unless, under the law applicable to the child, majority is attained earlier' (Article 1, 1989, UN Convention on the Rights of the Child).

16 Loescher and Monahan (1990), *Refugees & International Relations*, Oxford, Clarendon Press, 1.

17 Camus-Jacques, *op. cit.*, 141–57.

18 Boutros-Ghali (1992) *An Agenda for Peace*, New York, United Nations, 46.

19 UNHCR, *A Monthly Digest of UNHCR Activities*, Geneva, UNHCR, March 1995.

20 UK Committee for UNICEF, *Children in War*, London, UK Committee for UNICEF, November 1995, 1.

21 Save the Children, *op. cit.*, 3.

22 ESRC (1996), *The Children 5–16 Research Programme: Growing into the Twentieth Century*, ESRC, Swindon, 3–4.

23 Candappa and Rutter (1996), *Extraordinary Childhoods: Social Roles and Social Networks of Refugee Children*, research proposal.

24 Cf. Further Education Unit, *Refugee Education & Training*, London, FEU; Rutter (1994), *Refugee Children in the Classroom*, Stoke-on-Trent, Trentham Books. There are further examples of work not specifically directed to refugee children, but to children as speakers of other languages, among whom will be refugee children, cf., Blackledge (1994) (ed.), *Teaching Bilingual Children*, Stoke-on-Trent, Trentham Books.

25 Cf. Jones and Rutter (1998) (eds), *Mapping the Field*, Stoke-on-Trent, Trentham Books; World University Service (1996), *No Place to Learn: The Educational Experiences of Young Refugees*, London, WUS.

26 United Nations High Commissioner for Refugees (1994), *Refugee Children: Guidelines on Protection & Care*, Geneva, UNHCR, 121.

27 Williamson and Moser (1988), *Unaccompanied Children in Emergencies*, Geneva, International Social Service, 9.

28   Ressler, Boothby and Steinbock (1988), *Unaccompanied Children: Care & Protection in Wars, Natural Disasters & Refugee Movements*, New York and Oxford, OUP, 104.
29   Ibid., 11.
30   Save the Children, *op. cit.*, 13.
31   Ibid.
32   Ibid.
33   For an account of politically motivated maltreatment of children in several countries, cf. Boyden and Hudson (1985), *Children, Rights and Responsibilities*, London, 5–6.
34   Cf. UNHCR (1994), *op. cit.*, Chapter 10, pp. 121–30; Williamson and Moser, *op. cit.*
35   Further guidelines were issued by UNHCR in February 1997 entitled: 'Guidelines on Policies and Procedures in dealing with Unaccompanied Children Seeking Asylum'.
36   This took place on 5 October 1992.
37   UNICEF, *Children in War*, 20 November 1995, 2.
38   Van Boven (1982), *People Matter: Views on International Human Rights Policy*, Amsterdam, Meulenhoff, 159. Van Boven was the director of the United Nations Division of Human Rights, 1977–1982.
39   See Van Bueren (1995), *The International Law on the Rights of the Child*, at 331.
40   Ressler et al., *op. cit.*, 246–61.
41   See Article 2(1), 1984 UN Convention Against Torture.
42   Article 3(1), *op. cit.*
43   Rutter, *op. cit*, 45.
44   By mid-October 1997, the number of young people in detention known to the Panel of Advisers since its inception had reached over 100. A report on the issue, *Children Behind Bars*, will be published by the Refugee Council in 1998.
45   IV B(2)
46   Para. 350 of House of Commons Hansard, 395, 1993.
47   Para. 351 of House of Commons Hansard, 395, 1993.
48   Para. 352 of House of Commons Hansard, 395, 1993.
49   Recent reasons for refusing asylum claims included: 'Your enemies had ample opportunity to kill you, but did not do so'; 'Those who are currently detained in Ethiopia are kept in comfortable cells'; 'The Secretary of State noted that the soldiers were firing wildly within the house, and he considered that the killing of your brother therefore was not necessarily a deliberate act', quoted in *Exile*, January/February 1996, No. 90, 1.
50   The Glidewell Panel published its report on 15 April 1996.
51   The Asylum and Immigration Bill completed its passage through Parliament in July 1997 and entered into force on 1st September 1997.
52   Dunstan (1996), *Slamming the Door: The Demolition of the Right to Asylum in the UK*, London, Amnesty International, 41–2. See also: Grenier (1996), *The State of Asylum*, London, Refugee Council.
53   So-called 'white list' countries would be designated as posing 'no serious risk of persecution' for their citizens.
54   Article 6 Convention on the Rights of the Child.
55   Article 27 Convention on the Rights of the Child.
56   Article 26 Convention on the Rights of the Child.
57   Article 2 Convention on the Rights of the Child.
58   The Asylum & Immigration Bill received Royal Assent on 26 July 1996. In addition to a clause on Child Benefit, asylum seekers' rights in regard to social housing were further reduced and the social security changes introduced in February by regulation were included in the primary legislation.

59 'Benefit Cuts Leaves Asylum Seekers on the Streets', *Exile*, March/April 1996, 4.

60 For a detailed exposition, cf. Ayotte, *No Refuge for Children*, London, Refugee Council and Save the Children, January 1996 (revised edn). Subsequently, following a High Court ruling and guidance from the Department of Health, it became clear that local authorities continued to have limited responsibilities for destitute asylum seekers under a number of pieces of legislation, notably 1989 Children Act, 1990 NHS and Community Care Act and 1948 National Assistance Act. The new Labour government of May 1997 promised a review of measures affecting asylum procedures, the result of which, as at April 1998, is still outstanding.

61 UN Committee on the Rights of the Child (1995), *Concluding Observations on the Report of the UK Government*, Geneva.

62 Chapter 16, 'Migrants, Refugees and Race' in Ruxton (1996) (ed.), *Children in Europe – A Guide to Legislation, Policy & Practice*, London, NCH Action for Children.

63 Ibid.

64 Following the symposium, a well-publicised case of a Bosnian child, Edita Keranovic, hit the headlines. See, for example, Daly, 'No peace for the war babies', *The Independent Tabloid*, 19.2.97, 2–3.

9 A Non-Governmental Organization Perspective of the United Nations' Approach to Children and Torture

Eric Sottas

Introduction

I have been asked to give an NGO perspective on the issue of the UN approach to children and torture, so I would like to begin by first giving you some idea of the strategy that The World Organisation Against Torture has adopted, a large part of which is tied into the United Nations system. I then hope to address some questions which are currently under review among NGOs involved with the work of the UN and child torture.

The World Organisation Against Torture (OMCT), created in 1986, is today the principal coalition of NGOs fighting against torture, with over 200 affiliated organizations and thousands of NGO partners.

The World Organisation Against Torture Programme for Children

During the third General Assembly in 1991, in Manila, OMCT decided to set up a specific programme fighting against the torture, forced disappearance, and summary execution of children.[1] This decision rested on two observations. Firstly, our database revealed that the number of victims of such violations was not only extremely high – particularly in the case of summary executions – but that it was increasing. Naturally growth could be, in-part, explained by the rapid expansion of our network, which might simply indicate a more accurate account of reality rather than a real modification in behaviour. Secondly, there was also a change in the social profile of minors, particularly in Latin America. While in the 70s and until the mid 80s child victims of torture and summary executions generally came from families of political opponents, or from ethnic, national or religious minorities, the 80s saw an increase of street children among the victims.[2]

This development has underlined the link between the effects of global recession and OMCT presented its research on this question during The Second Paris Conference on Least Developed Countries in 1989. We argued that structural violence induced by profound social inequalities could, in effect, act as a drag on economic development.[3] The mechanism would thus imply that purely legal measures would be fruitless without a multi-sectoral approach including social, economic, cultural, political and legal measures. However, it appears important to make very clear at this point, in order to avoid any confusion, when I come to discuss the definition of torture, that OMCT has never considered social problems even of extreme cruelty such as hunger or utter penury within the framework of torture. On the other hand, we consider that certain economic policies, even conceived with the best will in the world, are principal factors in violence against certain sectors, particularly street children. We consider that these factors engender and nurture the development of torture. This must be taken into account in any strategy which aims to combat the torture of children. Thus, the Children's Programme of OMCT comprises five axes, both interdependent and complementary.

An Urgent Appeals Programme Specific to Children

The procedure for immediate threat of torture or other grave abuses is based on the following logic: the first hours after an arrest are crucial. If the authorities know that they will have to answer for their abuses, then torture is less likely to happen, or can be stopped. Thus, for the success of the programme two aims are crucial. These are the speed of reaction (24 hours maximum) and alerting organizations who can influence the case.

As with all our programmes, institutionalized evaluation has been central to change. OMCT firmly believes that modern management techniques must be part of the strategy against torture: a small number of people fighting with clearly established goals and co-ordinated objectives is infinitely more powerful than an infinite number of well meaning, dedicated but disorganized ones.

If under evaluation a better method of fighting torture were to be found, then we are duty bound to adopt it. This is unfortunately something that provokes resistance in many organizations in the non governmental sector. Final goals such as an end to torture are difficult to measure, thus there is a tendency to treat the process as sacrosanct. If torture can be better fought using what would initially appear to be radical or unorthodox approaches, then we have no right to reject them simply because they have not been tried before. We must never be guilty of displacing the end goal in favour of a tried and trusted process.

The results of evaluation have meant that we are increasingly turning to the internet to increase speed, distribution and targeting. Distribution: from a base of around 1500 bodies receiving the information at the end of last year, we are now being distributed to over 90,000 bodies.

Targeting: it is clear that groups are interested only in information that relates to their mandate. If we want maximum impact we must ensure that is all they receive.[4] In terms of the actual urgent appeals, the results are, quite frankly, disturbing. We have documented cases of torture and summary execution of children from all over the world and the figures show that the programme answers to a need. In 1993 and 1994, we documented 14 cases, in 1995 this jumped to 19. In 1996, up to the beginning of June we have already launched 21 appeals.[5]

Urgent Medical, Social or Legal Assistance

As the world's largest network of organizations involved in the struggle against torture, a combination of its specialization and its structure makes it unique in its ability to deliver emergency assistance to victims at great speed. With representatives in more than 95 countries, mostly based in the South, qualified and reliable agents are already in place and ready to verify a case. Because verification takes place in the field, funds can be despatched at great speed. Indeed, in order to accelerate the process, funds are often advanced by the member organization. Verification in the field is done without charge. The administrative charges at the centre are minimal – the money goes to those most in need. This assistance is given to both children and adults. Strict criteria have been developed over the years.[6]

It is important within the discussion, to point out that OMCT considers that children who have witnessed the torture of their parents or others and have become traumatized as a result, fall within the criteria as direct victims and in no sense as either indirect or dependent. It is a very clear example of a network operating very effectively within its specialization and one of which I am extremely proud.

Analytical Reports Concerning States Parties Reports to the Committee on the Rights of the Child

In reports representing some 20 pages OMCT presents observations to underline, for the experts, any element relevant to the examination of the implementation, by a member state, concerning torture, rehabilitation, summary execution, disappearance, as well as the application of justice to juvenile offenders.

OMCT is often the sole organization providing a consistent channel of reliable information on grave violations against children to the Committee. OMCT country reports are designed to bring about change. By underlining contradictions in government reports and examining the wider issues of deficiencies in legislation, the juvenile justice system, and highlighting urgent cases, the reports present concrete recommendations for change.

The results are demonstrable. On the 29/30 May, Nepal presented its report to the Committee on the Rights of the Child. Very few paragraphs of the government report were dedicated to juvenile justice and unsurprisingly, no mention of torture. The recommendations of the Committee when presented with good information are firm, detailed and lengthy on the subjects of torture and juvenile justice.[7]

Research and Seminars

In addition, OMCT carries out specific research and seminars on the protection of children from torture, other forms of inhuman or degrading treatment, summary execution and forced disappearances. During its general work, time is always allotted to 'vulnerable sectors' and investigations or presentations on children on torture are always part of regional meetings.[8]

The Lobbying of Economic Institutions

States at the national level, and intergovernmental institutions at the international level, are developing strategies which encompass human rights criteria. For example, the German Government has introduced criteria of positive conditionality, giving development aid priorities to countries where the education and health expenses represent an increasing share of the national budget and where military expenditure is decreasing. Similarly, the World Bank is currently re-evaluating some of its programmes to consider the effect on vulnerable sectors, like street children.

Issues Concerning the Convention and the Committee on the Rights of the Child

OMCT, along with other groups has put considerable effort into lobbying for the need for this kind of emphasis. After this overview of the programmes of OMCT, I now want to address some issues that are currently under review. The principle issue of this chapter will be whether a specific definition of torture for children is necessary? But I would also like to deal more briefly, with three other questions: denunciation and prosecution of the torturers of children; compensation; and the rehabilitation of child victims.

Do We Need a Specific Definition for Child Torture?

Article 37(a) of the Convention on the Rights of the Child 1989 contains an obligation for the States to ensure that no child is subjected to torture or to cruel, inhuman or degrading treatment or punishment. It will be noted that the Convention provides no definition. Definitions can be found in the Declaration on the Protection of all Persons from Being Subjected to Torture and other Cruel, Inhuman, or Degrading Treatment or Punishment,[9] and the Convention Against Torture and Other Cruel, Inhuman or Degrading Treatment or Punishment.[10] Both give definitions in Article 1. However, the definitions are not identical, and only the definition contained in the Convention Against Torture is considered as a minimal rule for States Parties who are bound by Article 4 of the Convention Against Torture to legislate, so that the acts referred to in Article 1 should be defined as acts of torture and punished as such.

As OMCT has very frequently observed during examination of the reports of States Parties to the Convention Against Torture, many states either fail to adopt any definition on the subject, or define torture in terms which differ from those used in the Convention. To the extent to which the definition adopted by the state is broader than that of the Convention, the difference in wording is not only acceptable, but frequently also desirable. On the other hand, it is frequently the case that more restrictive definitions reduce the protection of potential victims and frequently prevent the prosecution of those presumed responsible.[11]

Whilst there are problems with states that have ratified the Convention Against Torture, it is even more likely that further problems may arise with states who have not ratified, (the number of states who have ratified the Convention on the Rights of the Child is far greater than the number of states ratifying the Convention Against Torture).[12] Those states who are party to the Convention on the Rights of the Child, but not the Convention Against Torture, may use more restrictive concepts than those provided by the Convention Against Torture.

In fact, the absence of a definition of torture is related to the spirit of the Convention on the Rights of the Child. The Convention contains three different types of provisions. Firstly, provisions concerning specific rights of the child, which are already explicitly defined in other instruments.[13]

Secondly, those rights relating to all human beings which apply equally to children.[14] And, finally, those rights specific to children not expressed in other international instruments.[15] The absence of a definition of torture in the Convention on the Rights of the Child may thus be explained by the structure of the instrument. However, two questions remain. First, what definition of torture is applicable and, secondly, is the definition given in the Convention Against Torture completely appropriate to the case of children? Furthermore, it is worth noting here, the need for a better definition of cruel, inhuman or degrading treatment or punishment. We can see the need with regard to the numerous States Parties to the Convention on the Rights of the Child who accept practices of 'chastisement' not only within the scope of the family, but also within educational establishments – corporal punishment inflicted in the 'best interests of the child'.[16] Thus we can ask if it would not be appropriate to draft a definition concerning the torture of children, which would differ from the definition for adults.

Degree of Pain

Both the Convention Against Torture and the Declaration consider only severe pain or suffering as components of torture. This provision leaves a certain margin of interpretation which may, in some cases, turn out to be excessive.

The courts, and certain national legislators, have thus been led to clarify what exactly is meant by the term 'severe'. In the case of a child it should be noted that pain or suffering which might be considered as relatively light for an adult, may provoke an extremely disturbing state of anxiety or stress, resulting from the age of the victim. Moreover, it is necessary to take into account that if corporal punishment of adults is generally prohibited (with the notable exception of Islamic countries applying *sharia*) the same is not true for children. Corporal punishment is still predominantly accepted within educational establishments and within the family, by law. It is also important to note in this regard that certain codes make provisions for extremely low sanctions should the child die during a light beating.[17]

Corporal punishments are, moreover, not the only matter of concern with regard to definition. Prison sentences or periods of solitary confinement could provoke in a child suffering of very different level than that of an adult.[18] Furthermore, the conditions of detention, despite the provision of the Convention on the Rights of the Child, the United Nations Guidelines for the Prevention of Juvenile Delinquency (Riyadh Guidelines) and the United Nations Standard Minimum Rules for the Administration of Juvenile Justice (The Beijing Rules), are very often appalling.[19] We register every week, cases documenting extreme levels of violence involving children in detention (rape, physical abuse, food deprivation and so on). These problems are generally linked to infrastructural prison conditions notoriously insufficient and provoking appalling levels of overpopulation.[20] In such circumstances, it is not possible to take into account only the duration of the sentence, to judge if the suffering provoked by detention is acceptable. We believe therefore, it should be made clear that the degree of suffering or pain be established taking into account the age of the child, the effect of stress experienced, the milieu of detention and so on, rather than on the basis of an examination, which claims to be objective, of the gravity of the suffering inflicted.[21] This point seems to me important, in as much as, frequently, the perpetrators of such acts deny that their actions could have provoked grave suffering or acute pain in the sense of the Convention or, indeed, that they had deliberately intended to inflict such suffering.

The Intention of Those Responsible

The Convention also makes clear that pain or suffering must be inflicted intentionally. As far as children are concerned, it seems to me, that this concept is far too restrictive. OMCT registers every year, a very high incidence of cases of violence inflicted by fellow detainees upon children, who are being held in the same cells with adult criminals. The staff in charge of such detention centres must be aware of the grave and pressing danger to which children are exposed, particularly the very young. The fact that they may not have intentionally sought to inflict pain or suffering on these children does not seem to me to be a relevant element for excluding torture from such cases. I consider that to the extent to which torture is applied to children, it is necessary to take into account not only intention, but also what is clearly gross negligence.

The Status of the Perpetrator of Torture

The Convention provides that the term 'torture' applies only to pain or suffering 'inflicted by or at the instigation of or with the consent or acquiescence of a public official or other person acting in an official capacity.' This notion, which aims to avoid confusion between private violence and the violence of representatives of the state services also gives rise to problems if the victim happens to be a child. Contrary to an adult, who is autonomous, the children are legally subjected to the authority of his/her parents or of a guardian. Unfortunately, such persons, who should protect the child and help its development, are sometimes the ones at whose hands she/he suffers the worst violence.

During a Colloquium organized in India, by OMCT, in January 1992, the issue of forced child labour (as part of payment debt contracted by parents) was addressed in order to clarify if certain forms of it could be considered as an act of torture. The severity of the violence was not called into question. We looked at two types of violence. Firstly, violence that was a result of the harsh work and secondly, chastisement inflicted for attempted escape. The latter chastisement sometimes resulted in permanent handicap, yet the perpetrators were not state agents, rather they were the 'employers' of children whose parents had given their 'consent'. In the same vein, one can cite the violence suffered by child slaves in Sudan and children given by their parents to 'holy men'(Marabouts) in Mauritania who, in addition to forcing them into the life of a beggar, inflict serious ill-treatment, yet again, these are not agents of the state.

It is interesting to note the opinion of the Human Rights Committee which in General Comment 20 on Article 7 of the International Convenant on Civil and Political Rights 1996, would seem to consider that violence inflicted on children, in the framework of educational and medical institutions, falls within the prohibition of torture, held within the Covenant.[22] This, undoubtedly is the result of pressure exerted by NGOs. This opinion seems to suggest that pedagogical measures which employ violence and result in an acute state of stress or suffering can be considered to be torture. This implies firstly, that the perpetrators of the violence do not inflict violence for a pedagogical end, but rather a punitive or discriminatory one. If this is the case, then the intention of the perpetrators has to be considered, not from the perspective of the perpetrators themselves, but rather, from that of the child. Whilst the perpetrator may consider that his or her intention may be to educate, the child feels that he or she has been punished. The Committee on Human Rights, by labelling these actions as torture, seems to adhere to the latter interpretation of intention.

Secondly, the Committee admits an extensive interpretation of the concept of 'public official' or 'person acting in an official capacity' because the perpetrator in this case, can be anyone working in a teaching or medical institution,[23] and having authority over the patient or child. It seems that for the Committee, the fundamental element is that the perpetrator acts not *on behalf of the state*, but abuses their authority *recognized by the state*. A teacher or a nurse inflicting torture, could be considered to be a perpetrator of torture, even if they do not act as an official of the state.

Is the Situation of Parents so Different?

Would it not be relevant to consider that the child is under the authority of parents in a framework recognized by law and thus, abuses of this type where severe pain is intentionally inflicted, constitute torture?[24] The question is admittedly, extremely contentious, because it enlarges the scope of torture enormously. But, that said, the present definition is unsatisfactory. In the case of children, it may be appropriate to consider suffering intentionally inflicted, by a public agent or by any other persons legally invested with authority over the minor concerned, as torture.

Exclusion of Torture for Pain Arising from Lawful Sanction

Article 1 of the Convention Against Torture states that torture does 'not include pain or suffering arising only from, inherent or incidental to lawful sanctions'. It will be noted that Article 1 of the Declaration on the Protection of all Persons From Being Subjected to Torture and other Cruel, Inhuman or Degrading Treatment or Punishment adds a corrective, stipulating 'lawful sanction, to the extent consistent with the Standard Minimum Rules for the Treatment of Prisoners.' This was not included in the definition of the Convention Against Torture. Nevertheless, the current interpretation stresses that lawful sanction should not be considered solely at the national level but also should consider the international standard. If a national law authorises a sanction that is prohibited by an international instrument the sanction cannot be considered lawful. Unfortunately, in the case of children, the prohibition of sanctions at the international level are not very clearly defined; both the Riyadh Guidelines and the Beijing Rules are written with very general language and provide general measures and principles and not clear rules.

While it is obvious that one may not consider as torture, the suffering resulting from legitimate sanctions, the latter should, however, be proportionate both to the crime committed and the personal situation of the person. There is hardly need to stress the fact that as far as children are concerned this question is especially important, in view of the particular psychological development of children which restricts their responsibility.

A double question arises in terms of the age limit from which a child can be held responsible for criminal acts and the age from which they can suffer sanctions, and of what type. Different judicial systems present an extremely diverse choice of resolutions, according to tradition, culture, and the like. Article 40(3)(a) of the Convention on the Rights of the Child calls for 'the establishment of a minimum age below which children shall be presumed not to have the capacity to infringe the penal law.' Furthermore, Article 4(1) of the Beijing Rules recommends:

> In those legal systems recognising the concept of the age of criminal responsibility for juveniles, the beginning of that age shall not be fixed at too low an age level, bearing in mind the fact of emotional, mental and physical maturity.[25]

These very general approaches do not permit the possibility of addressing certain abuses however obvious.[26] It seems to me, that at the international level, a minimum age of criminal responsibility should be established. Below this age there would be no criminal responsibility. Above this age, sanctions could be foreseen, but clear restrictions could be outlined over the sanctions which would never be applied to minors.

Article 37(a) of the Convention on the Rights of the Child already contains such measures forbidding capital punishment and life imprisonment without possibility of release. This is, however, unsatisfactory. In one sense, because it does not forbid life imprisonment as such, but only in the case where there is no possibility of release. In another sense, because no account is taken of the age of the child. If, for instance, we accept penal responsibility above 12 years, it will appear reasonable to introduce a distinction between sanctions applied to a 12-year-old and a 17-year-old. I believe that further work needs to be done to clarify what type of sanctions can and cannot be imposed on a child. What interests OMCT is among those which should not be applied to children, and which should be considered as torture.

In conclusion, it seems to me that the Committee on the Rights of the Child should, in General Comments and during the examination of specific reports, outline its own doctrine and jurisprudence relating to the torture of children as well as notions currently undefined in terms of cruel, other inhuman or degrading treatment.

Prosecution of Alleged Perpetrators

Torture in principle, is a crime which must be prosecuted *ex officio*, as is stipulated by Article 12 of the Convention Against Torture. However, this principle is largely ignored by State parties as was underlined by OMCT in observations to the Committee on the Rights of the Child in its report on Guatemala.[27] In Guatemala, in order to initiate legal action against a torturer, the victim must file a complaint. In practice, most of the victims do not file a complaint, either because they are not aware of the procedure, or they fear (justifiably) reprisals. In the case of Guatemala, which has ratified the Convention against Torture, it is possible to denounce the violations under Article 12. However, it is still open to question whether the principle of prosecution *ex officio*, for the crime of torture, which is enshrined in the Convention Against Torture, is of the status of *jus cogens,* particularly when the victim is a child. It seems to me, that even if the legal system of a country provided for prosecution *ex officio* in the case of torture, in the case of a child victim, there will be insurmountable difficulties to establish the facts and make a strong case. It would therefore seem important to establish, in all the countries that have ratified the Convention, independent institutions to monitor the detention conditions of minors and ensure their protection. These institutions would also be empowered to inform the competent judicial authorities of any violation to enable the said authorities to investigate the matter. In case of a refusal, the institution in question should have a right to appeal to a higher authority, so that child victims of torture are removed from the hands of their torturers as rapidly as possible. Such institutions should, however, be able to count upon the support, both at the regional and the international level, of an authority to which cases may be submitted.

One of the major weaknesses of the Committee, set up by the Convention on the Rights of the Child, lies in the limit to its competence to the examination of the periodic reports of states and it has no power to deal with communications concerning specific cases. The existence of special rapporteurs on such subjects as torture and other cruel, inhuman or degrading treatment or punishment or on extrajudicial, summary or arbitrary executions and the sale of children, child prostitution and child pornography as well as the working group on forced or involuntary disappearances, is not enough to remedy this serious limitation. It is consequently necessary, to find, as rapidly as possible, other means to provide the Committee with the competence to receive individual communications.[28]

Sanction and Compensation

It would seem logical that torturers should suffer an increased sanction if they torture a child. As was detailed by OMCT in its Sri Lanka report amongst others, certain codes would seem to foresee the opposite.[29]

Mrs Skelton from Lawyers for Human Rights South Africa, highlights the story of a 15-year-old boy who was suspected of having stolen a television from a neighbouring farm. He was caught by a white farmer who welded his hands to a work bench before dousing him in petrol and setting him alight. He suffered severe burns. The farmer was prosecuted for attempted murder and convicted. Lawyers for Human Rights took instructions from the family with regard to the action they wanted. The family indicated that their concern was not that the farmer should go to jail, more that they were interested in damages. After discussion with the State, R40,000 was paid to the family.[30]

This example demonstrates one of the problems of compensation specific to child victims. Compensation, in my view, should not be dictated by a child, or by her or his family but established, taking into consideration the damage suffered and the remedies which are in the best interest of the child.

Rehabilitation

Article 39 of the Convention on the Rights of the Child obliges States Parties to take 'all appropriate measures to promote physical and psychological recovery and social reintegration of a child victim of: any form of neglect exploitation or abuse; torture or any other form of cruel, inhuman, or degrading treatment or punishment; or armed conflict'. It is interesting to note that in their reports most States Parties to the Convention on the Rights of the Child fail to detail such programmes, if indeed they have established them.

The International Secretariat of OMCT welcomed, in its report to the Convention on the Rights of the Child, the efforts of the Colombian Authorities for the establishment of a specific programme for child victims of violence, including torture.[31] It is vital that the Committee insist on the obligations outlined in Article 39 and monitor the type of measures taken for the rehabilitation of child victims of torture.

In conclusion, eradicating torture and summary executions of children which constitute an increasing phenomenon, should be one of the principle objectives of the Committee on the Rights of the Child, if not the priority. However, the Convention protects a vast totality of rights and all make enormous demands on the time of the Committee. No mechanism permits the presentation of individual cases and they are only examined in a general sense during the presentation of the periodic reports. The Convention Against Torture obviously allows a concentration on cases of torture, including cases of child torture, and has an individual communication procedure. Unfortunately, however, the number of states having ratified this instrument, represents only half of those who have ratified the Convention on the Rights of the Child. Those who have accepted the competence of the Committee to deal with the latter cases is even more limited.

These measures, however, are but one side of the protection of children from torture. They must be backed up by political and economic measures to reduce the frightening phenomenon of marginalization of an increasingly significant sector of the population. Growing violence against street children will not cease until all children are integrated into society, and this presupposes both a revolution in attitude and the way we approach structural reform.

Notes

1 Manila 91, International Symposium 'Democracy, Development and Human Rights' OMCT, Geneva 1992, 231 pages.

2 Brazil: Between 1979 and 1982, 4611 children were killed according to the official Parliamentarian Investigation on the extermination of children and adolescents, May 1992. The Senior Military School published a report entitled *1990–2000 Decada vital por um Brasil moderno e democratico* which affirmed that by the end of this century the street children will become the major penal problem for the country and due to the powerlessness of the judicial system the army has to find a solution to 'neutralise' the street children. OMCT has received a large number of urgent appeals since that time relating to street children in Brazil.

3 *The Least Developed Countries: Development and Human Rights* by Eric Sottas 1990, OMCT, Geneva, 152 pages.

4 See OMCT Annual Report 1995.

5 It is important to note that in most cases this involved several child victims.

6 Seminar on Torture and the Medical Profession, IRCT, Istanbul 22-24 October 1992. Presentation *Emergency Assistance to Victims of Torture*, Istanbul Criteria OMCT, Eric Sottas in *SOS Torture* Number 36-37, December 1992.

7 OMCT report on Nepal presented to the Committee at the 12th Session May–June 1996.

8 See *Extraction et Enfants* a study on violence against children based on the responses of 300 NGOs, globally, on a questionnaire on this issue. June 1993, OMCT, Geneva.

9 Adopted on 9 December 1975, by the General Assembly of the United Nations.

10 Adopted by the General Assembly of the United Nations on 19th December 1984.

11 See OMCT periodic report on Senegal at both the Committee Against Torture and the Committee on the Rights of the Child concerning the absence of a definition of torture in the legal system of the country and its consequences, *SOS Torture*, Number 55.

12 On 1 May 1996 187 states had ratified the Convention on the Rights of the Child against 96 that had ratified the Convention Against Torture.

13 Article 32(2)(a) of the Convention on the Rights of the Child requires States Parties to determine a minimum age or ages for permission to employment. This question is governed by International Labour Organisation (ILO) Convention 138, 1973. Moreover, besides these conventions of a general scope, no less than 9 ILO conventions determine the minimum age for employment in specific activities; ILO Convention 59 of 1937 (Industry); ILO Conventions 33 of 1932 and 60 of 1937 (non industrial employment); ILO Convention 10 of 1921 (Agriculture); ILO Convention 123 of 1965 (Underground work); ILO Convention 7, 1920 (Sea work); ILO Convention 15, 1921 (Trimmers and Stockers); ILO Convention 58, 1936 (Sea Work); and ILO Convention 112 of 1959 (Fishermen).

14 For instance, Article 14 of the CRC.

15 The preamble of the CRC asserts the need for legal protection before birth.

16 See OMCT CRC Report on Nepal, Sri Lanka and United Kingdom.

17 However, whilst Section 7 of the Nepal Children's Act forbids the practice of torture, it makes an exception in the case of beating 'in the interests of the child':

> *Provided that, the act of scolding and minor beating to the child by his father, mother, member of the family, guardian or teacher for the interests of the child himself shall not be deemed to violate the provisions of this section.*

What is meant by a 'minor beating' is not defined.

Should the beating result in serious injury Chapter 9 of the Muluki Ain (on battery and assault) states that if hurt, injury or grievous hurt when imposed by the above mentioned persons:

while beating his ward using simple force for the benefit of the ward [child] himself **shall not be held responsible for the result of his act** [emphasis added].

Should the beating result in the death of the child, Chapter 10 of the Muluki Ain section 6 states:

If death is caused *while beating or doing something else for the benefit of the deceased by his teacher or guardian,* **he shall be punished with a fine of up to 50 Rupees** [emphasis added].

See OMCT CRC Report on Nepal, Session 12 May 1996.

18   See above, Van Bueren, 'Opening Pandora's Box: Protecting Children Against Torture or Cruel, Inhuman and Degrading Treatment or Punishment'.

19   These are found in Van Bueren (1998), *International Documents on Children*, Kluwer, Second Edition.

20   For example, The prison of Fianarantsoa, Madagascar, has available space for 400 people. At the end of 1992, 1400 adults and children were detained there; the FEBEM detention centre (centre for the detention of minors), Sao Paulo, Brazil, in 1993 had space for 90 but a population of 250. *Exaction et Enfants* see *supra*.

21   See above Van Bueren, *op. cit.*

22   The prohibition in Article 7 relates not only to acts that cause physical pain but also to acts that cause mental suffering to the victim. In the Committee's view, moreover, the prohibition must extend to corporal punishment, including excessive chastisement ordered as punishment for a crime or as an educative or disciplinary measure. It is appropriate to emphasise in this regard that Article 7 protects, in particular, children, pupils and patients in teaching and medical institutions.

23   See below, Doyal, 'Can Medicine be Torture'?

24   See above Chinkin, 'Torture of the Girl-Child'; Van Bueren, *op. cit.*

25   Reproduced in Van Bueren, *International Documents*, *op. cit.*

26   See OMCT CRC Report on Pakistan concerning the possibility opened to the courts to regard puberty as the age of criminal responsibility.

27   See OMCT CRC Report on Guatemala, 3-4 June 1996.

28   See Van Bueren (1995), *The International Law on the Rights of the Child*, at 410 which recommends the creation of a right of individual petition.

29   The Penal code states:

Section 320. Whoever voluntarily causes grievous hurt for the purpose of extorting from the sufferer, or from any person interested in the sufferer, any property or valuable security, or of constraining the sufferer or any person interested in such sufferer to do anything which is illegal, or which may facilitate the commission of an offence, shall be punished with imprisonment of either description for a term which may extend to twenty years, and shall also be liable to fine or to whipping.

Section 321. Whoever voluntarily causes hurt for the purpose of extorting from the sufferer, or from any person interested in the sufferer, any confession or any information which may lead to the detection of an offence or misconduct, or for the purpose of constraining the sufferer or any person interested in the sufferer to restore or to cause the restoration of any property or valuable security, or to satisfy any claim or demand, or to give information which may lead to the restoration of any property or valuable security, or to satisfy any claim or demand, or to give information which may lead to the restoration of any property or valuable security, shall be punished with imprisonment of either description for a term which may extend to seven years, and shall also be liable to fine.

OMCT/*SOS-Torture* notes that the stipulation of Section 321 of the Penal Code is less harsh in penalising the perpetrator of torture, specially when the victim is a child, when compared with the other sentence inflicted on a person who voluntarily causes grievous hurt to extort property or to constrain to an illegal act.

Punishment in Section 320 is for twenty years, while under Section 321 it is only seven years. Moreover there is no minimum sentence for the act of torture, which leaves open the possibility of light sentencing.

30   See the description of the case in the Intervention of Mrs Skelton in *Africa a New Lease on Life, op. cit.*
31   See UN Doc. CRC/C/add.3/192 and 193.

10   Can Medicine be Torture? The Case of Children

Len Doyal

Introduction

Modern medicine has saved enormous numbers of lives and made others more tolerable than they would otherwise have been. Contemporary images of medical technology remain icons of scientific progress while other technologies have become tarnished through association with ecological imbalance and disaster. These same images, however, are also associated with a darker picture of clinical practice which is summed up by some of its most common expressions: 'inject', 'venepuncture', 'cannulate', 'intubate' and so on. Such words often instil discomfort precisely because that is what they are associated with – greater or lesser amounts of pain. When such pain is at its greatest and medicinal relief is inadequate, it is not uncommon to say, if only to oneself: 'That was just plain torture.' Were there no more to torture than the infliction of pain then most clinicians would indeed be torturers. But they escape this condemnation for two reasons.

First, torture is ordinarily thought of as the infliction of suffering on a person for instrumental reasons which have nothing to do with the needs and interests of that individual – for example, the political security of the state or the emotional gratification of the torturer. The suffering which patients experience is supposed to be administered in their own best interests – to help rather than to harm them.

Second, an individual who is tortured has no say in the matter. Yet in medicine, any harm which is inflicted should only occur with the consent of the patient. Given clear information about the nature and extent of the suffering which they will endure, patients choose it as a lesser evil than the consequences of going without treatment. But what if this choice – and the information and understanding that should inform it – are compromised or missing altogether? The situation then becomes more complicated, especially if we recognize that the suffering involved can extend beyond the physical to encompass mental distress resulting from being forced to do or experience things which in ordinary circumstances would be refused. Whatever the good intentions of clinicians, the psychological impact on patients of being forced to have painful and sustained medical treatment might well approximate torture – especially if no legal redress is available for the suffering and indignity they have endured.

The fact is that children are sometimes given painful and distressing medical treatment without consultation and/or against their wishes. Moreover, they often lack clear legal redress in national and international law.[1] To the degree that their consequent physical and mental suffering is extreme then it is reasonable to claim that a point will come when the result should be described at least as cruelty and possibly as torture.[2] This chapter will explore the moral and legal boundaries of this allegation. In so doing, I will argue that if we draw the definition of torture too narrowly – only to encompass extreme acts of individual violence done for political reasons – then we risk devaluing the significant suffering of children who can be subjected to physical harm, and mental distress with what may be good intentions. The focus here will be forced medical treatment which has been imposed on children through the power and influence of their clinicians, their parents or both. The defining characteristics of poor paediatric practice as regards consent for treatment will be outlined, along with a critique of the relevant law in the UK and elsewhere.

The issue of the moral boundaries of the right of children to give their informed consent to medical care is important for anyone concerned more generally about the torture of children throughout the world. Indeed, the devaluation of suffering to which children have not agreed in a medical context may help to explain the lack of concern often shown about the plight of children who are tortured in the more conventional sense or who are refugees from such torture. Our moral outrage at torture will be proportional to our belief in the human rights of those who suffer it. For whatever else it might be, torture is above all else a violation of such rights. If human rights are unjustifiably qualified because of age, a slippery slope to moral insensitivity seems inevitable. If we will tolerate the moral and physical abuse of children in hospitals – erstwhile safe havens of care – then it is hardly surprising when this attitude is generalized to children who are tortured or killed around the world or who are political refugees from such violence.

Background

The moral tension surrounding much thinking about informed consent in medicine and children is illustrated by two of my most vivid memories about my daughter when she was very young. First, when she was about four and before she had become particularly verbal, she sat down beside me while I was washing the dishes, looking very serious. She announced that she wanted to discuss 'a very important problem'. She then cupped her chin in her hands and said (literally): 'Daddy, you're driving me crazy. Don't you know that I'm too young to read. Why do you keep trying to make me? I've got other things I want to do before I have to go to school.' After I picked up the dish I dropped, my primary response was guilt – the academic father expecting too much of his child. But I was also delighted that she could express herself and her desires with such clarity and conviction. Suffice it to say, I stopped pressuring her to learn to read and turned my attention – also unsuccessfully – to her ballet lessons!

Second, when she was six and presumably more mature, a horse bit her. Our doctor said that she ought to have a tetanus injection. My daughter made it clear to both him and her mother (who was with her at the surgery) that she was not going to do so under any circumstances. When both adults tried to persuade her – explaining what the injection was, why it was important for her health and what it would entail – she responded by screaming, punching our doctor on the nose and generally creating havoc. Her mother rightly decided to wait until she calmed down and brought her home. I decided to take over. After a further futile discussion, I marched her to the car and we went back to the doctor's surgery. In the car, she said tearfully: 'I don't want any needles. Don't I have any say?' My response? After even more attempts at persuasion, I and a nurse eventually held her down while the dirty deed was done! She later referred to the episode for years as an example of my 'moral inconsistency'.

At the time, I thought I was right to do what I did. Now – having worked with children in a clinical environment – I am convinced that I was wrong. Although I felt a strong sense of urgency about her need for the injection, both I and her doctor knew that it could have waited until the next day when she was better able to understand its importance and I might have been more successful in communicating the urgency of receiving treatment. On reflection, I didn't use force to restrain her for reasons which concerned her but me. It had been a long day, the general practitioner and nurse were exerting pressure on me to let them get on with it because, no doubt, they had had a long day as well and so on.

I don't wish to be misunderstood. I am not arguing that my daughter and others in her situation and of a similar age and level of maturity should not ultimately be forced to have protection for tetanus or any other potentially life threatening or seriously disabling illness if this is what is necessary to protect them. In such circumstances, coercion and force may indeed be necessary. However, this should only occur when it is clear that children are unable to make competent decisions for themselves, not, just because of the seriousness of the risk which they may confront.

Sometimes when I tell the preceding story about my daughter, there is laughter in the audience. Clearly there would be nothing to laugh about had I described circumstances in which I exercised the same force over an adult, even if I used the same justification. I can assure you that to this day my daughter still does not see the joke. What I did can accurately be described as a father heaping pain, indignity and violence upon a child for the sake of convenience rather than necessity. The only thing that makes this seem acceptable is the fact that it happened in a medical setting.

Herein lies the problem with which this chapter will grapple. On the one hand, children can sometimes make enormously wise decisions about them-selves – even at a very young age. On the other hand, at what point does their potential for wisdom in isolated instances entail sufficient sustained wisdom for us to respect their right to make important medical decisions for themselves, which have serious and permanent consequences? Adults have a responsibility to act in the best interests of children who cannot compe-tently do so for themselves – including allowing clinicians to inflict pain on children who reject it – when they face significant and immediate risks. Yet they also have another and often competing responsibility: to nourish the autonomy of children – to help them to learn to make decisions for them-selves and to take responsibility for their own actions. When we do not take this responsibility seriously in a medical setting and fail to respect the dignity of children through failing to respect their rights, we conspire to inflict emotional pain on top of whatever physical discomfort the child encounters. This can undermine the development of their confidence and self-respect as individuals in ways which have at least a family resemblance to torture in the more conventional sense.

Of course, this analogy can be questioned. However much children suffer in the short term, clinicians do not intend to do them harm, except as an inevitable consequence of treatment. Moreover, clinicians and parents may simply underestimate the degree to which children should be informed about treatment options, along with their maturity to consent to or reject them. It does not follow that such children are being tortured, in the same sense that they would be if deliberate pain were imposed on them in order, say, to obtain politically useful information about their dissident parents.

This is a strong argument. If we devalue the moral content of torture, it may detract from the horror suffered by those who are subjected to it by agents of the state. It is understandable therefore that the relevant United Nations Convention equates torture only with the actions of such agents and not, for example, with the violent abuse of children in other contexts.[3] However, I would still argue that from the perspective of the child, to be forced to have painful medical care without appropriate consultation certainly counts as cruel treatment and may approximate torture – at least for the duration of the treatment. For the child is being made to feel helpless and without a voice in a decision making process about treatment presented as care but which causes unexplained anguish. The child is also being used as a means to an end totally determined by others – ends which the child may be competent enough to reject – and is being made to suffer as a result. Hence the analogy with torture is worth exploring further. By this means we can identify patterns of inappropriate paediatric practice and inhumane, though possibly well meaning, parenting.

Competence and Decision Making by Adults: The Wider Context

All clinicians have a clinical duty of care to protect life and health to an acceptable standard, but they also have a second duty to respect the autonomy of their patients. This means that they must take seriously the right of patients to determine what happens to their bodies in clinical settings. When I first started teaching medical ethics in the UK in the early 80s, most members of clinical audiences could not clearly define the word 'autonomy' and many would scoff at the importance of obtaining informed consent for treatment. 'Doctor knows best' was the byword. Now, the importance of respecting the autonomy of patients has become incorporated into the everyday discourse of medicine and is stressed in all of the moral guidelines for clinical care published by various regulatory and professional bodies.[4] The right of competent adults to self-determination in a clinical setting is no longer seriously questioned within the medical profession.

Morally, this is hardly surprising since it is primarily our cognitive abilities that make us take ourselves so seriously as humans. We can formulate goals and strategies for how to achieve them; can communicate with others about whether or not our actions have been successes or failures; and can expand our conception of ourselves and our world in the process. In short, we are special as humans because of our autonomy – our capacity to conceptualise and to make choices about our future. This characteristically human ability for choice and strategic planning is awesome. No other animal species possesses it to anything like the same degree. Other animals live more or less in the present. Their future directed behaviour is more driven by instinct than chosen by intent.[5]

The contemporary emphasis within medicine on respect for individual autonomy translates into belief in the right of patients to informed consent – to plan and choose their own medical destinies to the extent that this is practically possible. So to the degree that we have rights which are characteristically human – including the right to informed consent – it is because of what we believe makes us special as humans and entitles us to make certain types of claims on each other which we do not, for example, make on animals. If I want others to respect me because I can make considered choices about my life then to be consistent I must respect them. For in principle, they have an equal ability unless they are permanently and psychologically disabled in some fundamental way.[6]

For clinicians, there is a dramatic cutting edge to this argument when adult patients who are seriously ill make decisions not to consent to treatments which are clearly in their interests. Some clinicians find it hard to accept such a choice but respecting the rights of others is always like this. They will do things that we think that they should not do. That's the whole point about rights. To the extent that we take them seriously, they constitute preferences which trump the preferences of others.[7] So clinicians may be frustrated by adult patients who do not comply with treatment. However, little can be done other than trying to educate such patients about why their behaviour might or will damage their health – always assuming (perhaps wrongly) that the clinicians themselves are right about these implications.

Thus we now live in a professional world where adult patients who have not been declared psychologically incompetent to give informed consent to treatment can refuse treatment – even if they will die as a result – and however absurd their choices may seem to those clinically responsible for their care. The law in the United Kingdom and many other countries reinforces this right to medical self-determination.[8] International law does the same.[9]

Intentionally touching another person without obtaining their consent risks a civil, and possibly criminal, action for battery. This can result from competent patients receiving treatments of which they are unaware; from their explicit wishes about treatment being ignored; or from elective procedures being performed which they would not wish while they are unconscious. Of course, many different kinds of informed consent can be given for clinical touching – explicit written, explicit verbal or implied. However, aside from life saving treatments for incompetent adults in emergency situations, consent of some kind should always be obtained.[10]

The moral force of attributing the right to informed consent to adults presupposes that in some sense they are competent to exercise it – that against the background of their value systems they can make coherent and consistent decisions for themselves. However, competence should not be thought of in binary terms – either you are competent to make decisions about your future or you are not. Anyone working in clinical medicine will recognize the over-simplicity of such a mechanistic notion of competence. Because I may be competent to do some things does not mean that I am competent to do all things.[11] Hence, current thinking on the subject rejects global definitions of autonomy in favour of task specific ones. For example, the fact that patients have been compulsorily detained under mental health legislation and deemed incompetent to make decisions about their psychiatric treatment does not entail that they are incompetent to consent to other forms of medical treatment.[12]

In the United Kingdom, the force of this argument was recently felt by a landmark case, *Re C 1993*, where a detained schizophrenic was deemed competent to decide to refuse the amputation of a gangrenous foot.[13] It was decided that despite his mental illness, the patient was competent to make this decision because he was able to understand, remember, reason about and believe information given to him about his specific condition and proposed treatment. It was equally agreed that the patients should be assumed to be competent in these terms unless evidence could be produced to the contrary. This assumption has received support from other influential sources.[14]

Thus far, we have summarized the moral arguments for individuals being able to control what happens to their own bodies as regards medical treatment. But it also makes practical sense to take the right to informed consent seriously. Consider the consequences of doing otherwise. Patients who believe that treatment is being foisted upon them against their will, will in all probability be poor patients.[15] The clinical relationship of trust and the practice of successful medicine go hand in hand, whatever we might think about human rights in the abstract. If we want patients to act like adults and to take their duties as patients seriously then we have to behave toward them as if they were capable of doing so.

It is only through nourishing their capacity for competent judgement that we will optimize the chances of patients acting on judgements which are competent both in principle and in practice. This means respecting their right to consultation, to partnership and ultimately to make decisions about their medical destinies for themselves – whatever we might think of their chosen outcome.

Competence and Decision Making For Children

All of the preceding arguments apply equally to children. Indeed, one way of describing the process of maturation which we associate with childhood is to refer to the manner in which the autonomy of children evolves during their youth. Some children have more ability to exert reasoned control over what happens to them than others. How much such ability they possess in relation to which tasks they attempt to perform will depend on their levels of relevant understanding and emotional confidence, along with the social opportunities which they have to practice both in appropriate ways. It is through the process of such practice – of trying to do new things and having others confirm their acceptability – that they expand their sense of themselves and what they are capable of.[16]

If children are not allowed to try to do new things and to make choices – and mistakes in the process – their growth as persons and as citizens will be artificially limited. Much research has underlined the relationship between the degree of autonomy children possess and the extent to which they are given such freedom: the former reinforces the latter and *vice versa*.[17] It seems clear, for example, that children become more and more helpless and incapable of exerting control over aspects of their lives when they are forced to act in ways over which they have no say. The close relationship between such feelings of helplessness and disabling depression has been well documented.[18] In short, if we believe that children have a right to the chance of flourishing as individuals then respect for their autonomy – as it develops – will be crucial.

It has taken some time for moral and legal opinion to begin to come to grips with the importance of recognizing the existence of autonomy in children, along with their right to exercise as much competent self-determination as they are capable of. Until recently, children were in many ways regarded as the moral property of their parents who completely determined the boundaries over what they could and could not do – what they could and could not make autonomous choices about. The moral justification of this was paternalistic – children had to be protected from the harsh realities of life and from themselves until they were mature enough to know how to deal with both. In practice, of course, such arguments were sometimes employed by adults to make it easier for them to exploit and abuse children.[19]

The idea that children sometimes may be competent to make decisions about some things – even if not about all things – has traditionally received little explicit moral or legal support. Implicit recognition of their abilities did come with the acceptance that children could competently perform a range of vocational tasks. However, since this was designed to permit the continuation of child labour, it was hardly a victory for children's rights! The total control that parents and guardians could exercise over children even during the early part of this century often had disastrous effects on their intellect and emotionality in ways which are well known. Some of the most poignant examples include the fate of young men but more often women who were institutionalized in mental hospitals – sometimes for the rest of their lives – for the offence of challenging the authority of their parents.[20]

In the 1950s, under the influence of various gurus of successful parenting and progressive education, attitudes began to change about the potential of children for autonomous choice. It was argued that those areas of life where children could exercise competent choice should be recognized and nourished. Unless they were given some sense of ownership over their aims, beliefs and choices, children would not develop healthy levels of self respect or the ability to learn properly from their mistakes.[21]

It took the intellectual and political fervour of the 1960s and the accompanying philosophical and political focus on human rights to bring these ideas to medical practice.[22] To illustrate what has happened since and some of the ethical problems these developments pose, our emphasis here will be on legislation and case law in the UK. While there are differences between British law and that found in other jurisdictions, the similarities are sufficient to make the moral arguments of this paper more widely relevant.[23]

In the UK the Family Law Reform Act 1969[24] reduced the age of majority from 21 to 18 and of medical consent from 18 to 16. In doing this, the new Act implicitly underlined the absurdity of equating any specific age with the maturity required to make informed choices about important life events. The past two decades have seen a similar lowering of the legal age of consent for medical treatment in other countries.

The Family Law Reform Act also embraced what had already been accepted as good professional practice. If clinicians believed a child under the age of 16 to be competent to provide such consent – mature enough to understand their condition and the nature and risks of any proposed treatment – then in certain circumstances it was already common for them to provide treatment without parental involvement. This practice was used where care was thought to be in the best interests of underage children but where parents were for whatever reason not available for consultation. The Act made clear that this was legally acceptable without the necessity for a court order.[25]

These provisions of the Family Law Reform Act – and similar legislation in other countries – probably had more to do with protecting the rights of clinicians to exercise their discretion in treating children under 16 than in reinforcing the rights of the children themselves. After 1969, clinicians were still loath to proceed to treatment without parental consent and there was little discussion in the paediatric literature of that time about what should be done when a child disagreed with a parent or a doctor about either elective or necessary care. The presumption was that the child would and should do what the parents and clinician wanted. Most discussion about ethical dilemmas was focused on conflicts of belief between parents and clinicians.[26]

However, there was one exception to this broad paternalist consensus which led eventually to what many believe was clarification about a child's legal right to consent to and refuse medical treatment. In Britain and elsewhere, family planning was the one area of normal clinical work where treating adolescents under the age of 16 without parental consent was agreed to be professionally appropriate.[27] In Britain, doctors prescribed the contraceptive pill and even arranged abortions without parental knowledge or agreement when they believed it to be in the child's best interests. However, little attention was given to such cases until 1985.

In an important legal judgement, *Gillick* v. *West Norfolk and Wisbech AHA*, the argument was further endorsed that clinicians should be able to provide contraceptive advice and access to contraceptives without the knowledge and consent of parents.[28] This result confirmed the widespread professional acceptance of the fact that to inform parents about a young person's wishes for such help without consent would be an unacceptable breach of confidentiality.

The *Gillick* case seemed to provide final clarification in the UK about the legal right of children to give informed consent. A task specific rather than an age specific concept of competence was approved which underscored the legal right of competent children to reject the clinical preferences of their parents. For example, in his judgement, Lord Scarman stated: '... the parental right yields to the child's right to make his own decisions when he reaches a sufficient understanding and intelligence to be capable of making up his own mind *on the matter requiring decision*'.[29] The general message was that a child who is 'Gillick competent' – the phrase now widely used in Britain in this connection – has the same rights to consent to and refuse treatment as adults. The only issue relevant to the exercise of such rights is task specific competence and not age. Again, internationally, other states have come to the same conclusion. For example, Articles 5 and 12(1) of the Convention on the Rights of the Child also emphasize the importance of respecting the particular degree of autonomy that children have reached in the decisions about who can touch them and under what circumstances.[30]

This legal message – and the moral principles which it embodies – were reinforced by another landmark piece of British legislation – the Children Act 1989. This was not primarily concerned with medical treatment; since its key focus was the legal management of children at risk of harm from parents. However, the Act did have to address similar issues about the scope of the child's right to consent to medical examination and to treatment in the context of decisions about their future. On the face of it, the content of the

Act reinforces the principles outlined in the *Gillick* case. Time and again, it refers to the general right of children to be consulted or to give agreement about decisions which are made on their behalf. On medical treatment in particular, the United Kingdom Department of Health Guide to the Act states: 'Children under 16 may also be able to give or refuse consent depending on their capacity to understand the nature of the treatment; it is for the doctor to decide this. Children who are judged able to give consent cannot be medically examined or treated without their consent. The responsible authority should draw the child's attention to his rights to give or refuse consent to examination or treatment if he is 16 or over or if he is under 16 and the doctor considers him of sufficient understanding to understand the consequences of consent or refusal.'[31]

So if we stop the clock in 1990, it would seem that a crucial moral argument was endorsed within the British legal system: if children are competent to give informed consent to specific types of medical treatment then no difference should be drawn between their rights and those of an adult. Competent children should not have medical treatment forced upon them without their informed consent and their right to determine their medical destiny should trump the preferences of all others including their parents and clinicians. Thus for this brief moment in legal history, children did appear in Britain to have the right to refuse any form of medical treatment – including life saving treatment – provided again that they were 'Gillick competent' to do so.[32]

Once it becomes legally accepted that for children competence is task specific and not age specific then no other conclusion seems possible. If adults have the right of consent and refusal then so do competent children. Of course, the rights of those legally defined as adults will remain more comprehensive. Competence to consent to and refuse medical treatment does not entail competence in other regards. When the age of consent to medical treatment has been reached, however, the presumption should be of competence unless there is strong evidence of serious mental impairment. In light of the moral dangers of forcing treatment on a unwilling adult who rejects it in the face of public and professional opinion, there must come a point where the onus is on the clinician to demonstrate the incompetence of children to provide informed consent.

Where to draw the line between the appropriateness of the presumption of competence and the need to check for incompetence associated with youth is clearly a matter of debate.[33] That such a line should be drawn, however, is reasonable in order to protect some children who make an immature judgement to reject treatment when this is clearly not in their best interests. Restricting the right to reject treatment to those young people who are deemed fit to do so in no way undermines the moral and legal significance of this right – provided that the evaluation of fitness takes place in accordance with established professional criteria which are independent of the treatment preferences of the child's parents or clinicians.

Thus if respect for this right makes it unlikely that cruel and degrading treatment will be inflicted on adults then the same will also hold for children. 'Hands off' means 'hands off'. By 1990 the right to informed consent of children professionally accepted as mature enough to give it had become in effect identical to the corresponding right of someone 18 or over. Unfortunately for such children, however, such clarity was not long-lasting in the United Kingdom.

Two cases are of particular relevance in understanding how this situation changed. The first, *Re R* in 1991, concerned a 15-year-old young woman who was suffering from psychiatric illness and was a ward of court.[34] The second, *Re W* occurred the following year and involved a young woman aged 16 with anorexia.[35] They both wished to refuse specific treatments deemed to be potentially life saving. The legal precedent set by these cases was that while Gillick competence made it possible for young persons to provide valid consent to treatment, the same did not hold for refusal – provided that treatment was deemed to be in their best interests by someone with parental authority.[36] This principle continues to apply if the young person believes that the treatment in question is cruel or would constitute for them a form of torture.

Thus, a judicial unwillingness to take seriously the right of young people to consent has thrust us back into a situation where persons of designated authority can force medical treatment on them, no matter how competent they may be to decide otherwise. As one noted legal commentator has stated: 'It seems a strange right which enables a child to say "yes" but not "no"'.[37] This same ambivalence – wanting to designate rights of medical self-determination to competent children yet only when they agree with parental and medical authority about what should be done – can be found in many other national jurisdictions.[38] So where do we go from here?

Can Children be Tortured by Doctors?

One thing is clear. We cannot look to the law for any way out of the dilemmas which the law itself has posed. The problem to be resolved is what morally and professionally can be done to provide maximum respect for children who are competent and who say either that they do not want treatment or that they have had enough of any treatment already administered. Any attempt to deal with this must start with the fact that refusal of treatment may occur in two very different circumstances.

The first concerns elective interventions where the consequences of postponement are not especially dramatic as regards the child's best interest. Here, hospitals should adopt guidelines which make it clear that if a child is Gillick competent and refuses such treatment, their wishes should be respected – irrespective of what parents might say or wish. If this is not done then I can see no reason why the child should not be regarded as at best being subjected to cruel treatment and at worst to torture – depending on the level and permanence of the trauma which the unwanted treatment generates.

The justification of this position is straightforward and, it is submitted, would be unlikely to be overruled by a court despite the legal reasoning offered in *Re R* and *Re W*. It is not in the best interest of mature children to ignore their maturity and thereby to risk undermining their future intellectual and emotional development. If we really expect such children to take responsibility for their lives – to take themselves and others seriously – then we have to take them seriously. This principle is well established in helping young people to comply with medical treatments which they need. Trying to force them to take their medicine through bullying and coercion just does not work. Successful medical practice requires a partnership between clinician and patient and young patients are no exception. To deny a competent child the right to refuse elective treatment would be a breach of that partnership, regardless of whether or not we thought that they were making the correct choice at this point in their lives.

There can be no doubt that elective treatments are sometimes forced on children who have verbally and/or physically rejected them. Clinicians and nursing staff can be under the pressure of time and insistent parents to proceed as quickly as possible with taking blood or giving injections. More dramatic cases can involve children who need elective surgical care but who are not properly told what to expect either about what will be done to them or its consequences.[39] It is for this reason, for example, that in good dentistry the first visit of a child to a dentist will often not involve treatment at all but rather discussion about what is going to be done and why. Similarly in good paediatric surgical units, play therapists will be available who help children act out what they will go through in receiving their treatment – especially operations which might be painful and frightening – before they happen.[40] This has been shown to be effective but must be tailored to the child's age and development. Younger children benefit from the use of dolls and puppets and older children respond positively to videos, diagrams and verbal explanations.[41] However, dentistry is not always done this way and such therapists may not be regularly available in some underresourced paediatric departments.

An unwillingness to respect the descriptions of children of their experience of treatment has probably led in the past to their pain being sometimes underestimated and undertreated.[42] The perception that children tolerate discomfort well and so need less pain relief may be because they have not been given a proper voice in pain management.[43] This in turn can lead to an unwillingness of children to signal their pain when it is important for them do so in order to receive effective clinical care.[44] Any attempt to force elective care of mature children who reject it can only reinforce patterns of bad practice which will perpetuate such problems. Of course, parents can add to the injury through unwittingly further undermining the trust between child and clinician. A comment still often heard in paediatric clinics and doctors' surgeries is: '... if you don't behave then the doctor will give you an injection'! Clearly, such statements will have no force unless the child thinks that the doctor might do so because the parent suggests its appropriateness.

When the right to refuse elective treatment is denied, young people can suffer intensely. Even very young children have an acute sense of their own private space and expect clinicians to ask them before clinical contact is made and to give a general explanation of why it is necessary. They will often react violently if this is not done. Equally, young children are quite capable of understanding why treatment is necessary, what it will consist of and what they can expect to feel like and be able to do afterwards. When such information is not given – or improperly communicated – such children can manifest effective levels of distress. This is not only morally unacceptable in itself; it cannot be justified with reference to the therapeutic interests of the child. Again, proper examination and successful treatment are possibly compromised as a result, as is the child's trust of and willingness to consult health care professionals in the future.[45] Since elective care can always be postponed until the child has been properly informed, why should such interventions not be equated with cruel treatment and, at worse, torture? Such suffering of the child is pointless, harmful and in the long term potentially dangerous.

All of the preceding arguments continue to apply to situations where competent children reject treatments which those with parental authority wish them to have. The fact that someone with such authority deems it appropriate for such treatment to occur does not justify its harmful imposition. Just because an elective treatment is clinically appropriate does not mean that a child with sufficient maturity should not postpone it until he or she better understands or is ready to experience it. Of course, clinicians are rightly wary of interfering with the relationship between parent and child in these circumstances and will try to convince the child that the parent is correct. Yet to conspire with the parent to manipulate or force the child to comply remains morally unacceptable. Moreover, there is no clear legal obligation to engage in such conspiracy since for the reasons already outlined, forced elective treatment can always be argued to be against the child's best interests by his or her other clinicians. In short, competent children of whatever age should be regarded as having the same moral right to refuse elective care as competent adults. Not to respect this right is inconsistent with the duty of care. The issue remains one of maturity and not of age *per se*.

However, the problem still remains about what we do with children who reject life saving treatments. We should be sympathetic to the terrible moral dilemma posed by *Re R*, *Re W* and other similar cases and with the parents and clinicians who are involved. In the two UK cases, there was doubt about the competence of the young women involved. They were potentially placing their lives at risk through their rejection of the treatments in question. While elective care can always be accepted later on, refusing potentially life saving care is to risk making the one uncorrectable mistake. Thus the moral issue is whether or not a competent child has the right to make such an irrevocable and potentially lethal choice.

If the decision of the child is as mature as an adult decision in similar clinical circumstances then it follows from our preceding arguments that it should be respected. As always, the important issue is competence and not age. Where there is any doubt about the requisite maturity to make an informed choice, the child should be protected and treatment should be administered. Unfortunately, these moral arguments are neither reflected in the current state of the law in the UK nor in other states. As regards life saving treatment, young people up to the age of 18 are believed to be equally incompetent.

It is vital that all adults – including clinicians, parents and judges – recognize that sometimes children will be competent enough to decide to reject treatment which can save their lives.[46] Research suggests that even at an early age, many children who are seriously ill can have a good understanding of their illness, treatment options and their probable outcomes.[47] They are, after all, experts on their own suffering for it is they who experience it. While in hospital, they learn much from other children who are in similar circumstances and through conversations with health care professionals. Provided that we are sure that their rejection of treatment is both competent and informed, to ignore it because of their age is no more acceptable than it would be for an adult. With respect to the decision at hand, the child effectively is an adult.

A case in point is children with cancer who have already had unsuccessful courses of chemotherapy and will sometimes get to the stage where they only want palliative care at home. Similar dilemmas are posed by children who have been on long term dialysis and sometimes request that it be stopped knowing full well the consequences. It is understandable that parents and clinicians will often resist these decisions if there is any hope of extended life. The issue, however, is who will ultimately decide the value of life in this situation – the ill children who suffer and make the agonising decision to be allowed to die or parents and/or clinicians who may be acting in their own interests rather than those of the child. The child is the patient – not the parents or the health care team – and this basic reality should never be clouded.

To force treatment – either through physical coercion or manipulation – on such children is at the very least cruel for two reasons. First, they must continue to live in circumstances where they have decided that life is not worth living. To the degree that their mental and physical suffering becomes extreme and for them not worth the price of their resulting quality of life then 'torture' seems to be an appropriate description. Second, not having their autonomy respected by those who supposedly love and care for them, can make children lose whatever dignity they have managed to maintain in the face of illness, causing additional and unnecessary suffering. For a chronically or terminally ill child competently to reject life saving treatment can be a courageous and self-defining act. It should be accepted as such by those in parental or clinical authority with equal courage.

This is not to say that the wishes of all children should always be accepted. The issue remains one of their competence to choose their fate for themselves. Again, if there is any evidence that they cannot understand, remember, reason about and believe relevant clinical information, then they should be treated whatever their views. Here, given what is at stake through an incompetent decision, such competence should certainly not be presumed. There is much that we still do not understand about the degree to which children develop competence to consent to medical treatment in stages. Yet even if such a hypothesis is true – and it is widely debated – it would not follow that all children must go through the same stages at the same time, irrespective of their individual experiences. What does follow is that we must be particularly diligent in assessing the maturity of younger children to refuse clinical care which is necessary and not elective.[48] In short, children should not be judged to be incompetent because they choose death rather than a life of suffering which they cannot tolerate. If they are competent to make such a choice then they should be allowed to make it, despite the distress which this may cause to others.

There is nothing impractical either legally and morally about showing such respect.[49] In a recent landmark case in Canada, a 15-year-old boy with leukaemia was allowed to refuse a life saving blood transfusion on the grounds that he was competent enough to make the decision. He was a Jehovah's Witness. Under the heading 'A Minor's Victory' an editorial in the local paper said, 'The New Brunswick Court of Appeal's decision that 15-

year-old Joshua Walker has the right to consent to or refuse medical treatment is a victory not just for Jehovah's Witnesses, but for us all. Sometimes the decisions an individual makes may seem too hard for society to bear, especially hard if the life and death of a young person is at stake. But even harder to bear would be a society that routinely violates the bodies and souls of its citizens. Joshua Walker has done his part to keep us safe from that'.[50] Before his death, Joshua's doctor who fully supported his right to refuse blood on the grounds of his competence to do so said of him: 'Of all the patients I have ever treated, he is the friendliest, most considerate, most polite and most compassionate person I have ever met. He is a very courageous young man we will never forget.'[51]

The moral reasoning behind this preceding legal judgement should be incorporated in all national and international law concerning the treatment of children. At present, there is no legal barrier in most states to prevent patients like Joshua Walker from having treatment forced upon them. This has already happened in Britain.[52] If this makes the last days of a young person's life one of suffering and indignity, it seems no exaggeration to describe their experience as one of torture. Similar points can also be made about competent children who reject dialysis or those suffering from the intense and chronic pain associated with thalassaemia and sickle cell who also refuse life prolonging treatment which can itself increase their suffering dramatically.

Conclusion

To torture an adult is a terrible moral crime. To do so to a child whose personality and individual identity are still developing commits the crime twice over. This is because of the immediate harm as well as the severe distortion of the child's future psychological development which can also occur. Nothing should be allowed to distract from the particular horror of deliberately torturing a child for political reasons. The torture or cruel treatment of children by agents of the state is especially offensive since it is done for overtly instrumental reasons. This is why some argue that the word 'torture' should be confined to the activity of such agents.

Yet this chapter has argued that the results of torture are not ultimately separable from the kind of harm which can be done to mature children when their rights to agree or refuse medical treatment are ignored. While the latter is not as dramatic and potentially destructive as state sponsored torture, it can still do enormous damage to children both in the short and long term. Even more importantly, it signifies an unwillingness to take the rights of children – and therefore children themselves – seriously. Such attitudes obviously facilitate a willingness to torture and abuse children in other ways and should be morally condemned, even when harm is not intended.

Generally speaking, there is a high regard for the rights of children in paediatric care. Most paediatricians have chosen to work with children precisely because of their respect and concern for their well being. Clinical and moral standards are usually good and children are ordinarily treated with both care and respect. However, this fact should not detract attention from those circumstances where this does not occur, especially when the beliefs of both doctors and parents are insufficiently attuned to the right of competent children to agree to and refuse treatment. So that this does not happen in the future, the law and professional guidelines should be altered where necessary to ensure that:

- Competence to consent to or refuse treatment is decided in the same way for children and adults – the ability to understand, remember, deliberate about and believe the personal implications of proposed specific treatments.
- The explicit consent of competent children should be sought for all elective medical examination and treatment, along with that of those with parental authority. Their right to refuse treatment should always be respected.
- When declared incompetent to give consent, children should still be consulted and be given appropriate information and intellectual and emotional preparation for treatment.
- When a competent child refuses 'necessary' treatment – that which is life saving or which prevents permanent and serious disability – this decision should also be respected provided that: (i) it is sustained; (ii) specific reasons are given for it which are consistent with what is known of the child's values; and (iii) competence is confirmed by a senior paediatrician and child psychiatrist who are not involved with the child's treatment.
- In emergency situations where there is no time for assessment of competence, children under the age of 16 who refuse necessary treatment can be treated against their wishes. When this occurs and treatment is successful, the young person should be given a detailed written explanation of why the treatment was necessary and why their wishes were ignored.
- At the age of 16, all patients should be treated as adults as regards consent to treatment.

To the degree that these principles are ignored by judges, doctors and parents, the medical treatment of children can rightly be said to be cruel, even when the treatment *per se* is successful and little physical suffering is involved. When there is great suffering and the child's self-respect and trust of adults are permanently and severely damaged then medicine can indeed be torture.

Acknowledgements

Many thanks to Lesley Doyal, Vic Larcher, Jenny King and Michael Hird.

Notes

1 Van Bueren (1995), *The International Law on the Rights of the Child*, Kluwer, 310–12.
2 Alderson (1993), *Children's Consent to Surgery*, Buckingham, Open University Press, 166–7.
3 The UN Convention Against Torture and Other Cruel, Inhuman and Degrading Treatment and Punishment, 1984: Article 1(1).
4 General Medical Council (1996), *Good Medical Practice*; British Medical Association (1993), *Medical Ethics Today*, London.
5 Carruthers (1992), *The Animals Issue*, Cambridge, Cambridge University Press, 122–70.
6 Gewirth (1978), *Reason and Morality*, Chicago, University of Chicago Press, 240–8.
7 Dworkin (1981), *Taking Rights Seriously*, London, Duckworth, v–xv.
8 Kennedy, Grubb (1994), *Medical Law: Text and Materials*, London, Butterworths, 87–245.
9 Bailey and Daws (1995), *The United Nations: A Concise Political Guide*, London, Macmillan.
10 Doyal, *Consent for surgical treatment*. In Kirk, Mansfield, Cochrane (1996), *Clinical Surgery in General: Royal College of Surgeons Course Manual*, London, Churchill Livingstone, 131–40.
11 Buchanan, Brock (1989), *Deciding for Others: The Ethics of Surrogate Decision Making*, Cambridge, Cambridge University Press.
12 Miller, The ethics of involuntary commitment to mental health treatment, in Bloch, Chodoff (1991) (eds), *Psychiatric Ethics*, Oxford, Oxford University Press, 265–90.
13 *Re C* 15 BMLR 77.
14 President's Commission (1983), *Making Health Care Decisions*, Washington, 169–71.
15 Redeimeier, Rozen, Kahneman (1983), 'Understanding patients' decisions: cognitive and emotional perspectives', *Journal of the American Medical Association*, 271:72–6.
16 Doyal, Gough (1991), *A Theory of Human Need*, London, Macmillan, 59–69.
17 Newell (1989), *Children Are People Too*, London, Bedford Square Press.
18 Seligman (1975), *Helplessness*, New York, Freeman.
19 Freeman (1983), *The Rights and Wrongs of Children*, London, 1–31.
20 Rose, Psychiatry: the discipline of mental health. In Miller, Rose (1986) (eds), *The Power of Psychiatry*. Cambridge, Polity, 43–84.
21 Eekelaar (1986), The Emergence of Children's Rights. 6 *Oxford Journal of Legal Studies* 161–80.

22   Faden, Beauchamp (1986), *A History and Theory of Informed Consent*, New York, Oxford University Press, 86–100.
23   Verhellen, Changes in the images of the child. In Freeman and Veerman (1992) (eds), *Rights, Ideology and Children*, 78–93.
24   Family Law Reform Act 1969. Section 8.
25   Brazier (1992), *Medicine, Patients and the Law*, Harmondsworth, Penguin, 329–35.
26   Freeman, *The Rights and Wrongs of Children*, *op.cit.*, 255–9.
27   Van Bueren (1995), *op. cit.*, 312.
28   *Gillick* v. *West Norfolk and Wisbech Area Health Authority* 1985, 3 All ER 402, HL.
29   Ibid., 422.
30   Van Bueren (1995), *op. cit.*, 131–50.
31   Department of Health, *The Children Act 1989: An Introductory Guide for the NHS*, HMSO, 1989, 48.
32   Kennedy, *Consent to treatment: the capable person*. In Dyer (1992), *Doctors, Patients and the Law*, Oxford, Blackwell Scientific Publications, 57–61.
33   Freeman, Limits to children's rights. In Freeman, and Veerman (eds), *op. cit.*
34   *Re R* (1991) 4 All ER 177 CA.
35   *Re W* (1992) 4 All ER 627.
36   Kennedy, 1992, *op. cit.*
37   Brazier (1992), *Medicine Patients and the Law*, Harmondsworth, Penguin, 346.
38   Van Bueren (1995), *op. cit.*, 310–13.
39   Alderson (1993), *Children's Consent to Surgery*, Buckingham, Open University Press, 175–87.
40   Price, 'Preparing children for admission to hospital', *Nursing Times*, 27 February, 1991, 46–9.
41   'Preparation of children for hospitalisation and surgery: a review of the literature', *Journal of Paediatric Nursing* 1, 1986, 230–9.
42   Shechter, Allen, Hanson, 'Status of pediatric pain control: a comparison of hospital analgesic usage in children and adults', *Pediatrics* **77**, 1986, 11–15.
43   Royal College of Surgeons, College of Anaesthetists (1990), *Report of the Working Party on Pain After Surgery*, London, Royal College of Surgeons.
44   Fuggle, Shand, Gill, Davies, *Pain, quality of life, and coping with sickle cell disease. Archives of Disease in Childhood*. 75, 1996, 199–203; Alderson (1993), *op. cit.*, 93–115.
45   Alderson, Montgomery (1996), *Health Care Choices: Making Decisions With Children*, London, Institute of Policy Studies, 41–63.
46   Doyal, Henning (1994), 'Stopping treatment for end-stage renal failure: the rights of children and adolescents', *Pediatric Nephrology*, 768–71.
47   Alderson (1993), *op. cit.*, 116–42.
48   Freeman (1992), 'Taking children's rights more seriously', *International Journal of Law and the Family*, 64–9.
49   Alderson, Montgomery (1996), *op. cit.*, 64–84.
50   Watchtower Society, *Awake*, 22 January 1995, 11–13
51   Ibid.
52   *Re E* (1993) 1 FLR 1065.

11 Children and Reintegration[1]

Gisela Perren-Klingler

Introduction

In this chapter I shall make an attempt to unite experiences from very different settings. One is the setting in private practice as a psychiatrist for children, in a rural and conservative part of Switzerland, in which I have worked for 20 years. It is children of Swiss or migrant and refugee origins and their parents who are my patients. The other is different settings in prisons, both in European prisons as a member of the Commission for the Prevention of Torture and Inhuman Treatment in European prisons and in other prisons of the world, such as Israel/Occupied Territories, Latin America and Africa, as a delegate of the International Committee of the Red Cross.

The common theme with the two different populations is the impact of traumatic experiences. Be it the family setting, the school or in society at large, violence seems to affect children more than one would like to imagine. It can be the horrors of family violence, told by survivors of sexual and 'only' violent abuse,[1] the reactions to simple traumatic experiences such as road accidents, avalanches, or it can be secondary traumatization living through the suffering of a parent who has been affected by trauma. It can be also the horrors told and played by refugee children, specially since the war in former Yugoslavia: violence is like an epidemic of which society at large gets slowly conscious. A large number of adolescents in prisons, but also youngsters who are refugees or our own marginalized children and adolescents in our societies can tell their stories of living through violence.[2] One just has to take the time to listen to them. What is special is that in prisons the number of male adolescent offenders is much higher than that of the females. It seems that girls assimilate their traumatic experiences in a way different from boys.

What struck me and still is striking me is that children in prisons are getting less attention than is their right, considering the documents on children's rights of the United Nations and of the Council of Europe.[3] There seems to be a sort of attitude which considers these children as psychopaths so that efforts to rehabilitate and reintegrate them are bound to fail. However, if we consider that many of them have passed through traumatization by violence we should try every step to guarantee their reintegration.

For children one basic right is to have the chance to develop, physically, mentally and spiritually, to learn and to be instructed, according to their capabilities. As a child psychiatrist unfortunately I had to learn that equal rights are very hazardous, and visiting prisons in the world I realize this even more. To illustrate this reality let me share with you some short vignettes:

> Marco's (six years) parents consulted me, because they just had discovered that his sister, Jeannette (eight years) had been sexually abused at age five by an uncle. Their GP had advised them to seek help for her with me. During exploration with mother and daughter it became clear quite soon that there was not only this problem of abuse in the past, but that father was an alcoholic, jobless, violent and approached his daughter when mother was working as a house cleaner. While contacting teachers and social workers around this family I got to know that Marco had a lot of school problems and that he regularly stole expensive toys from shops. The teacher first had told the parents, and father had said, that he would spank his son, so that he would not dare to do it anymore. As Marco did not seem to be impressed by his father's punishments and went on stealing, the teacher had stopped informing the parents and went back to the shop with Marco every time she saw him with an obviously stolen toy. With me Marco made the impression of a normally intelligent child, who had a lot of concentration problems, seemed emotionally very distant, feared his father and rejected any suggestion that stealing was not the best way of getting the toys he wished to get. We tried to introduce a social worker to help the family with Marco's school problems, his stealing and the problem of possible sexual abuse of Jeannette by the father. The family did what they had been doing beforehand several times, they moved to another canton, to a small village where there was no social service at hand ...

With this family setting what is Marco's chance of growing up and not becoming one of these burnt out clients in our prisons? What is Jeannette's chance to grow up and not end in prostitution, delinquency or as a battered wife?

> Marianna, 11 years, was hospitalized in a child psychiatric unit in Northern Germany, where I gave regular supervision. Her problem – or rather the problem of the educators, therapists and the policemen: frequent aggressiveness, out of the blue, where she attacked persons in such a way that containment could be done only by three adults. Nevertheless she managed in a long stay in the child psychiatric unit, to break the nose and the bones of two hands of helpers. When

she ran away the police had the same difficulties, except that they knew how to contain her and bring her back to the unit without mutual harm.

Marianna, child of a single migrant woman from Eastern Europe, had suffered from leukaemia between age two and three. Modern tertiary medical care had succeeded in saving this child's life. However on a social level she had never got the attention and education she would have needed after the medically introduced probably traumatic experiences . Now at age 11 she was refused by every school, every educational place and spent a year in child psychiatry, because this is the only place, in this city, which must accept patients, even if they do not fit the setting.

Strong, aggressive, runaway, will she end in child prostitution or in delinquency?

Joseph, 16 was interviewed by me in the setting of a visit by the Commission for Prevention of Torture and Inhuman Treatment in European to a prison for adolescents. He had repetitively committed some minor delinquent acts. In his family there was a father, jobless and in the prison for adult men of the same city, along with one of his brothers. Two other brothers were trying to survive outside, one with experience of the same juvenile prison, the other with no criminal record. Mother worked as a cleaning woman and had still to look after his little sister age six. So he did not get visits from her as often as he liked and the rules would have permitted. When I saw him, both his underarms were scarred by injuries obviously from self-mutilation with a cutting instrument. Joseph told me that when he was desperate such an action would give him some relief. When I checked in the infirmary the injuries were not even noted in his clinical record and the nurse told me that the habit was to disinfect such injuries with alcohol so that the pain would deter the youngster from doing it again ... Joseph was not seen by the doctor or the psychologist or the social worker. He had completed some missed schooling and now would have been able to start an apprenticeship. However this was not possible because the prison had no such facilities or contacts to the outside to procure this for him.

With this prison setting what is Joseph's chance of growing up and not becoming one of these burnt out prison clients, like his father and brother?

Thomas, 15 was seen by me also in the setting of a visit by the Commission for Prevention of Torture and Inhuman Treatment in European Prisons to a detention centre for adolescents. He was there, because his father had died and his mother was not able to deal with him educationally. He had never commited any delinquent act. For educational reasons he was detained, with delinquents and delinquent drug-addicted youngsters. He had the chance to finish his school in the institution, and start an apprenticeship, but he was scared he would become like the other delinquent boys in his group, and his only hope was, that his mother did everything to get him back home, and he was determined to behave better at home.

Was this deprivation of freedom the sound educational response to his behaviour or was it a risky act or even inhuman and degrading treatment?

What is the common theme, if there is any, with these three boys and the girl? Where are the rights of the child to develop physically, mentally and spiritually, to become an integrated member of the corresponding European societies and prepare for a meaningful life?

Psychosocial Setting

In each of the cases there is what has been called by Martin Baro[4] 'psychosocial destruction'. Baro argues there are three ingredients to it: violence; marginalization social polarization; and institutional lies.

Violence

The presence of violence is evident in all the cases: not only through the behaviour of the chidren but also by the answer of the adult societies who took them into charge. Violence has many negative effects on the psychological development of children and adolescents. Violence can have evident consequences on a physical level: injuries are seen in the normal case. Sometimes however it is applied in such a way that the physical signs are easily overlooked or quickly removed. This is especially the case in situations where violence is perpetrated with a specific purpose, such as in torture. Physical signs of violence must be described by physicians who are trained in forensic approaches and are conscious that their first duty is to protect the victim from retraumatization. They should also be able to let the victim go through a process, what can/should be done about this experience, whether it is worth denouncing it and what would be the price to pay for it, if it is the victim's wish.

Violence always also marks people psychologically,[5] even if there are no physical signs. Threats and humiliations, personal or to family members, separations, craving for a mind altering substance, anxiety about the unknown, all this can be traumatic. Children and adolescents are more at risk than adults, especially if there is no caring social network around them.

Trauma affects children in two different ways depending on whether it is a singular or repetitive occurrence. Type I trauma is a single violent event outside of the normal experience of the person including natural catastrophies (such as floods, hurricanes, avalanches) and the sudden loss of a person. The immediate reaction of persons to it will be described below. Type II trauma is characterized by its repetitive, nearly permanently imminent presence. After the reactions typical for type I trauma, children exposed to type II trauma have to adapt psychologically to this permanent threat. This adaptation leads to specific developmental and personality changes in children. These reactions will be described below.

Marginalization/Social Polarization

Marginalization is linked intimately to violence and each reinforces the other. Marginalization is evident in all four cases: fathers absent or without jobs, mothers who have to carry all the weight of a marginalized family, poverty due to the status of single breadwinners, overwhelmed by tasks of life, ready to decompensate at one or another moment and become violent themselves with their children. The children are marginalized at school, because of concentration problems, missing school hours, frequent illnesses, and they are considered less intelligent than other children. If they are lucky they are taken into psychotherapeutic or family therapy care, and sometimes it is possible to let them have through these measures some of what they miss on a societal/familial level. However poverty is not taken care of in this way. Sometimes such well intentioned interventions are experienced as violent and non respectful interventions, as if the professionals wanted to impose a worldview which is very different from the one the families have themselves.

Institutional Lies

The system says that everyone has legitimate means of accessing the common goods of society.[6] By that theory, every adolescent would have the possibilities to learn according to his capabilities and interests, to use a certain amount of money for his needs and for pleasure. However adolescents who have been living through chronic violence suffer from the effects of type II trauma. They have lost track of a normal school programme, they have concentration problems, they suffer from emotional and behavioural problems, and they cannot get, due to their social background, the support they would need to overcome these problems. In short they cannot satisfy the demands of a higher school or a professional apprenticeship, according to their underlying intelligence. Even if they have been taken care of by the school psychologist, psychomotor, psychotherapeutic or psychiatric approaches, these costly interventions, full of goodwill, have not achieved such change that they would have a real chance of adapting to society. Society has mandated to professionals tasks which can only be taken over by society as an entity. Even the most dedicated professional intervention cannot replace and heal what these adolescents have lived through and missed during their childhood.

A holistic view often fails because of its fragmentation, of its untimeliness and non-coordination. Society which has not been able to protect them as children from the violence of psychosocial destruction, now continues traumatizing them by institutional violence, forced reeducation and/or detention. This ongoing or sequential[7] traumatization is lucidly perceived by them as an institutional lie, as already children have a very clear and acute sense of justice and truth.[8]

Psychological Consequences of Violence

Violence of all origins has traumatic effects on every human being. Persons who have been exposed to it react psychologically with phantasies, changed assumptions and beliefs, attitudes and behaviours. When children are exposed to repeated or chronic violence, their cognitive, intellectual, emotional and spiritual development is affected and often distorted.

Traumatic Reactions

There are two different categories of reactions to trauma: unspecific[9] and specific.[10] Unspecific reactions are reactions which can also be found in other settings, independent from violence. They depend on attributional styles and interpretation of facts and are determined by cultural and social backgrounds. They can be divided into three categories:

- *Disorientation*: every violent event disorients exposed persons. Values, basic trust, space and time are experienced in a different way. Shattered assumptions are one sign of disorientation.
- *Helplessness* is an intense negative emotion and it disrupts the sense of self-coherence: anger, rage, shame and guilt can be the concomitant emotions, depending on culture, the nature of trauma, the personal history and the social setting.
- *Loss experiences* (of persons and ideals) lead to grief and mourning reactions.

Specific reactions are reactions specific to violence and they can be observed in every culture. The three categories are:

- *Hyperarousal* on a physical/psychological level always takes place, as reaction to extreme stress. This can show in lack of concentration, startle response, aggressiveness, sleeping disturbances, restlessness and hyperactivity.

- *Recurrent intrusive memories* can show in 'traumatic play', where the child plays either the victim's or the perpetrator's role, violent acting out, nightmares, flashbacks and 'daydreaming'.
- *Avoiding reactions* (regression, clinging, anxiety, phobic) show that the traumatic event is not yet digested. Dissociation occurs, when a person suddenly is mentally at another place, or even partly another person, is numbed, without any emotion.

The three groups of reactions are linked together, and they reinforce each other, in a vicious circle. Reactions typical for persons who are still in the process of mental and physical development:

- *Intellectual development is changed*, because of concentration problems at school.
- The regressive reactions lead to a *distorted emotional development*, parts of the personality mature faster, while others mature slower.
- Shattered assumptions lead to *mistrust*, specially towards the adult, a specific difficulty to take into account for (re)education and (re)insertion into a 'normal' curriculum.

These children often give an impression of an old-young child, too mature reactions are observed beside very childish, regressed ones.

All these reactions, observed on an individual level, must be understood as part of a specific, often already traumatized culture, the 'Trauma-Culture'.[11] Interpretation of the traumatic events, but also of the reactions are very culture and class specific, and they must be taken into account.

Reactions Specific to Psychosocial Destruction

Sometimes trauma cannot be avoided, even in well organized societies: natural catastrophies, such as avalanches, hurricanes, floods, working and traffic accidents cannot be abolished totally. However, this sort of violence, which causes trauma type I, is less pervasive.

Violence which causes trauma type I will cause nearly all of the reactions mentioned above but they will recede and fade away in a sound social surrounding, as long as caring and competent parents, educators and other community members are present. Most children who are looked after well will recover from such a trauma with minor psychological scars, thanks to their resilience.

Violence which causes trauma type II is always embedded in a social surrounding, in which psychosocial destruction has been or is taking place. It is exactly this societal setting that leads to the chronicity of the traumatic events. Instead of offering help the adult surrounding is marked by the incapacity of parents or teachers, insufficient resources, ignorance, and, as in family violence, secrecy. One of the most pervasive reactions to chronic violence in nearly every society is that it is overlooked, forgotten, negated, repressed but unless violence and its traumatic effects are acknowledged nothing can be undertaken to counteract it. It is also much more difficult for the child to deal with trauma when it it is not recognized. The child starts thinking that what he lives through is part of life and he does everything to adapt and to cope with it.

The psychological impact of type II trauma   To be able to survive physically, mentally and behaviourally these children have to learn how to adapt to such situations. Added to the previously mentioned reactions, at a psychological and behavioural level, they learn to live as if trauma would not touch them. Dissociative reactions, altered emotionality, cognitive distortion and impaired self reference lead to altered behaviour and relationships.[12]

Dissociation is a very important coping skill to survive ill treatment and violence, by anesthetizing body and soul. In dissociation an emotional block and often physical anesthesia protect the children, but at the same time let them become 'inhuman'. Dissociation becomes an integral part of their experience: they learn to deny that terrible things happen – they seem fearless – every time they are exposed to violence they make themselves feel safe by dissociating from their bodies and minds so that they feel neither pain nor anguish. They describe it, as if they were floating out of their bodies, watching themselves from 'above, outside' to what is happening, and having 'outside' some different maybe even pleasurable phantasies. This coping skill is demanded in a controlled way from soldiers, helping professionals in emergency situations and so on. However, children who have to use it often, will suffer from various consequences. Dissociation becomes problematic as soon as the children are the victims of this procedure, as soon as they do not dominate this psychological process. Dissociation is produced even outside of traumatic situations: concentration problems, disengagement, detachment, amnesia, 'daydreaming' all show at school, and soon learning problems follow.

The emotional development continues but not in a harmonious way. Parts of their minds have to mature faster, while others regress or stand still, therefore emotionality is altered.

Control of impulses is difficult because of hyperarousal, and because of unharmonious psychological development. This influences behaviour and leads to violence.

The shattered assumptions about the goodness of the world alter cognition and result in a loss of basic trust and the sense of coherence.[13] This affects relationships, specially with adult persons.

In the struggle to give the experience meaning many children think that they deserve what they live through, their self esteem gets lost, they feel wicked, bad, sometimes guilty, without being able to tell why. So the psychological protection of the 'normal' not traumatized adolescent who knows by checking his guilt feelings, what is right and wrong, is lost. This leads to a sort of moral anesthesia.

With the permanent guilt feelings the right to protect oneself and to anticipate dangers is not learned, and so victims tend to be revictimized.

The social impact of type II trauma   Unfortunately we can observe in many parts of the world social impacts of chronic trauma. The psychological and developmental reactions to trauma are not hidden away, but they show on a large social level, especially when they start to go against common norms of (adult) law and order. As the children cannot know anymore what is right and wrong they develop their own value systems, which very often are not in concordance with the adult society. Child soldiers, street children or the children of the Intifada, have amongst themselves a clear ethical code. They have adapted in a way to the traumatic environment. However, their experiences predispose them to react violently or even criminally to situations they do not like or consider dangerous for themselves or their group. Vandalism or criminal behaviour turn the victim into a perpetrator. And, as for all societies it is easier to deal with perpetrators than with victims and societal injustice and poverty, the causes behind the violent acts are forgotten.

The Child Offender[14]

Many adolescent offenders come from a background, where there is psychosocial destruction. So probably they will have experienced type II trauma, before they have become offenders. And they will display more or less all of the reactions mentioned above. It is evident, that they must be confronted for their offences, and it is of no help to medicalize or psychiatrize their behaviour or personalities, although medicosocial diagnosis is important for planning intervention programmes. The children must be held responsible for their acts. However, the way in which they are confronted mirrors from the very beginning the attitude of society. Will they finally have a chance to heal their reactions to chronic trauma and their experiences due to psychosocial destruction? Will someone listen to the alarm bells they have managed to ring?

From a 'Pathogenetic' to a 'Salutogenetic' Approach

By confronting children with and making them responsible for their acts one marks that it is their acts and not their personalities which lead to the intervention. By not accepting their behaviour one communicates intrinsically the belief that other behaviours are possible. With this attitude a shift is accomplished from a model concerned by deficits, a typically medicalized, pathology-oriented one to a model interested in the resources, the coping capacities, a salutogenetic[15] one. This model has been inspired by aspects of mental health and preventive interventions.

With this more optimistic approach the connotation of every intervention is different, more respectful and less traumatizing. This attitude can also question the concept that offenders need psychotherapeutic interventions in order to overcome their behavioural problems. It helps to get rid of the view that the child is mainly an individual with a problem and that he can be healed of it, an institutional lie.

The development of delinquent behaviour can be considered as a self destructive, but ingenious way for a youngster to cope with psychosocial destruction. If instead we consider that the person has developed many coping skills in a very adverse surrounding, we can be optimistic that there are other, yet unknown possibilities to develop different behavioural skills for a more integrated and meaningful life ...[16]

From the behaviourist point of view removing behaviour leaves a vacuum which will be filled with alternative repertoires. The void must be filled with resourceful, positive behaviour.[17] Training of existing resources helps the child to become conscious of what is already in his or her reach and what he or she still has to learn. With that the cooperation of children can be enhanced, because they can participate actively in finding their own resources.

Managing Sequelae of Trauma and Psychosocial Destruction

If a society has not been able to protect children and adolescents from the effects of psychosocial destruction, this is the very last moment to take care of them in a holistic way. The effects of psychosocial destruction will have to be counteracted on an individual and a group level, and safety and care have to be omnipresent.

Continuous personalized relationship as a cornerstone   A relationship with one adult person and being embedded in a small group of caring adults, and maybe peers, can start building this feeling of being welcome in the world and of being safe and protected. Basic trust can start to develop and with that a sense of self-coherence.[18] With this children can be joined at the actual levels of their distorted development, at the intellectual, cognitive, behavioural and, before all, emotional level. In trauma therapy this attitude is called 'holding capacity' or '*vinculo comprometido*', an engaged solidarity oriented attitude.

Pedagogical Interventions

In many respects the child will have to catch up in his or her development, in other respects he or she will need to let go the stress and strain in order to be a child. The goals of these well planned and concerted interventions are:

- they should provide education for more purposeful life activities.[19]
- they should change or rehabilitate the distorted emotional, psychological and behavioural development
- a new healthy narcissism should be constructed, by giving the notion of being important, respected and valued by representatives of the adult society
- violence should be calmed down, through the steady and caring relationships and through the security and positive connotation and respect of the child as a person
- hyperarousal should be trained into quietness, through self and anger control. Stress and conflict management must be learned, frustration tolerance heightened. Sports and any creative activities can help
- recurrent intrusive memories and acting out can be shared with caring adults and/or in peer groups and integrated as being of the past, under the condition that the new environment is caring and non traumatic. Narratives of traumatic experiences can be helpful in the sense of psychological debriefing and sharing.[20]
- dissociative effects will fade away partly through anger and self-control, through providing and allowing permitted pleasurable activities
- disorientation can be counteracted by slowly buiding up self coherence and some basic trust
- the intensive negative emotions can give way to more positive emotions, as soon as there are positive ways of dealing with the child
- the loss and grief reactions can lead to integration and internalization of wished for ideals and values.

In short the adults will have to help children to overcome their lost childhood. It can never be relieved or compensated. It is also clear that this programme can only be implemented with very dedicated and motivated adult persons, who want to give the child a real chance.

Reintegration to Society and Concern for the Family of Origin

All these rehabilitative, pedagogical, therapeutic and spiritual measures only have a meaning if the way back, that is reintegration to society is prepared. Parents need support to know how to deal with, what to expect of and how to guide their child. Respect for parents who have been marginalized, sometimes for a whole lifetime and still have enabled their children to grow up, is another ingredient. Having the positive connotation that even in a setting of psychosocial destruction parents love their children and want their best might help us to overcome our horror of what has happened to these children and adolescents. It might also make us more humble for what these parents have achieved for their children in much more difficult and adverse surroundings, compared to our own bringing up of children in much more friendly surroundings. I am always struck how traumatized refugee children can integrate into a school setting, provided that there are dedicated teachers who take part at that time.

Conclusion

When we consider European history, or more recently that of South America or of South Africa,[21] children have demonstrated a capacity for resilience. They just need to have the opportunity and develop a psychosocial background. From family violence we know that on the one hand nearly all perpetrators have been victims some time in their life, however only a small percentage of victims become perpetrators. The question is whether societies are ready to give child victims a real chance to be rehabilitated and reintegrate in a humane and meaningful way.

Notes

1   My observations are based on children and young people aged from 14 to 20.
2   Beck-Sander, A. (1995), 'Childhood abuse in adult offenders: The role of control in perpetrating cycles of abuse', *J. Forens. Psychiat.* 6, 3.
3   See Van Bueren (1993), *International Documents on Children*.
4   Baro, M. (1989), 'Political Violence and War as Causes of Psychosocial Trauma in El Salvador', *Int.J Mental Health*, 18, 3–20.
5   Perren-Klinger, G. (1996), 'Human Reactions to Traumatic Experiences', in Perren-Klingler (ed.), *Trauma: From Individual Helplessness to the Resources of Groups*, Berne.
6   Merton, R. and Nisbert, R. (1976), *Contemporary Social Problems*, New York/Chicago.
7   Keilsson, H. (1979), *Sequentielle Traumatisierung bei Kindern*, Stuttgart.

8 De Andrade, Y. (1996), *Psychosocial Trauma: Dialogues with émigré children*. In: Perren-Klingler.

9 Mollica, R. and Caspi-Yavin, Y. (1992), 'The Assessment and Diagnosis of Torture Events and Symptoms', in Basoglu (ed.), *Torture*, Cambridge.

10 APA, American Psychiatric Association (1994), *Diagnostic Statistical Manual IV* (DSM IV), Washington.

11 De Monchy, M. (1991), 'Recovery and Rebuilding: The Challenge for Refugee Children and Service Providers', in Ahearn F.J./Athey J.L. (eds), *Refugee Children: Theory, Research and Services*, Baltimore

12 Briere, J.N. (1992), *Child Abuse Trauma. Theory and Treatment of the Lasting Effects*, London.

13 Antonovsky, A. (1988), *Unravelling the Mysteries of Health*, San Francisco.

14 See note 1 above.

15 Antonovsky, A. (1979), *Health, Stress and Coping*, San Francisco.

16 Cohen, S.L. (1971), *An Investigation of the Utility and Effectiveness of Simulation Techniques in the Evaluation of Disadvantaged Persons ...* UMI Dissertation Services.

17 Shah, S. (1993), 'A Clinical Approach to the Mentally Disordered Offender: An Overview and some Major Issues', in Howells, K. and Holling, C.R. (eds), *Clinical Approaches to the Mentally Disordered Offender*, New York.

18 See note 13 above.

19 Hargreaves, T.W. and Shumway, M. (1989), 'Effectiveness of Mental Health Services for the Severely Mentally Ill', in Taube, D., Mechanic, and A.A. Hohmann, (eds), *The Future of Mental Health Services Research*, NIMH, Washington, DC.

20 Mitchell, J.T. and Everly, G.S. (1993), *Critical Incident Stress Debriefing*, Baltimore.

12 Children Exposed to War, Torture and Other Organized Violence – Developmental Consequences

Edith Montgomery

Introduction

Since World War II, the problem of children's exposure to war and other organized violence has attracted increasing scientific attention.[1] Originally, such experiences were not believed to have long lasting effects on otherwise healthy individuals. However, as childhood consequences were recognized, they were considered completely dependent on parental reactions.[2] Recently more general aspects of the possible impact on child development as such, have been focused on and several studies suggest that childhood experiences of war and other organized violence can have profound developmental consequences.[3]

Traumatic experiences can influence the child's emotional, cognitive and moral development, because it influences its self-image and its expectations of self and environment (its 'inner working model'.[4] As a feeling of security and safety is the foundation of attainment and integration of developmental competencies throughout childhood, traumatic experiences can be of considerable developmental significance.

Psychic trauma

Psychic trauma is defined as '… the mental result of one, sudden, external blow or a series of blows, rendering the young person temporarily helpless and breaking past ordinary coping and defensive operations'.[5] Trauma begins with events outside the child, through which a number of internal, lasting changes is initiated. Terr divides the effects of trauma into two main types: the effect of single events (type I trauma) and the effects of prolonged or repeated extreme external exposures (type II trauma).[6] While a number of reactions are the same disregarding the type of event experienced, the effects of longlasting or repetitive exposures follow a less predictable pattern than the effects of a single event, and can result in enduring personality changes.[7]

Each traumatic event carries with it a range of secondary stressors through its influence on for instance family, housing, school and general life conditions. Adaptation after any traumatic experience therefore must encompass *both* the experience as such *and* the attached secondary stressors. Adaptation after traumatic experiences later in life will to a large extent depend on the success of earlier adaptation as well as on the new experience and the secondary stressors attached to that particular experience.[8]

When the child is exposed to a traumatic event, he or she will try to create meaning in what happens and to incorporate the experience into his picture of self and surroundings.[9] If he doesn't succeed, he is overwhelmed by helplessness, and his experience of control, meaning and coherence in life is shattered.[10] The traumatic experiences are extraordinary, not necessarily because they happen rarely, but because they overwhelm the normal processes of adaptation. The experiences initiate a process characterized by deep physiological, emotional and cognitive change. These functions can be split up, so that the traumatized person can for instance experience intense emotions without clear remembrance of what has happened, or he can remember every little detail without any attached emotional reaction.[11]

After a traumatic experience the traumatized person is rendered into an acute state of arousal characterized by anxiety and fear. Fragmented pictures or other sensations, attached to the experience, penetrate the mind without warning.[12] Even little children, who have been exposed to traumatic experiences so early that they have no verbal memory of them (before about 30 months) can re-experience part of the event and express it in play in a compulsive way.[13] The traumatized person thus will constantly be confronted with his inabilities and will try to avoid the memories and repress them from consciousness. This can result in a restriction of the conscious mind and a retraction from engagement with the surroundings. This restriction becomes a protection against the violent and painful emotions, but results in a lower quality of life, and in the end, worsens the effect of the traumatic situation, as the necessary mental processing and integration of the experience is hindered. These two opposite reactions, re-experience and restriction, make up the dialectic of trauma.[14]

Restrictions of life and activities are 'negative' symptoms, that often are not noticed by surrounding society, or at least not understood within the context of trauma. This can lead to false conclusions. Lack of specific mental symptoms cannot be equated with mental health. In a qualitative investigation of 30 refugee children in Sweden, Gustafsson et al.[15] found, that among children, who had had violent war related experiences, was a group, who did not immediately react with emotional problems, but who much later developed severe symptoms of emotional unbalance. These were children who took great responsibility in the family, who cared for everybody else, and who for a long time succeeded in keeping their own problems and misery to themselves.

Post Tramatic Stress Disorder (PTSD)

Even if reactions after traumatic experiences have been known for a long time, under different names (shell shock, traumatic shock, traumatic neuroses, survivor syndrome)[16] the diagnosis of PTSD was first included for adults in the American diagnostic and statistical manual of mental disorders (DSM) in 1980.[17] In order to qualify for this diagnosis four criteria must be fulfilled:[18]

1 *exposure* to an extreme event outside the range of normal human experience,
2 repeated *re-experience* of the event or part of it,
3 persistent *avoidance* of stimuli associated with the traumatic experience and *numbing* of general responsiveness;
4 persistent symptoms of increased *arousal*.

As regards children, Garmezy and Rutter in 1985 based on existing research, concluded that severe acute traumatic experiences such as might occur in major disasters result in emotional disturbances in some children, but in the majority of such cases, the disturbances are short lived.[19] This was the reason why the diagnosis of PTSD for children was not included until 1987.[20]

There were two main reasons why it was more difficult to determine that children can have post-traumatic stress reactions, than reaching the same conclusion with adults: early research had used *general screening instruments*, not developed to catch stress reactions, and information was primarily gathered from *parents and teachers*, who are known to underestimate the children's reactions[21] – partly due to their own overwhelming stress reactions,[22] partly because it can be difficult even for attentive parents to notice re-experience reactions and emotional numbing in their children, two of the necessary four criteria for the diagnosis of PTSD.[23]

Even if the diagnoses of PTSD is the same for children and adults, the symptoms will often manifest themselves differently in children, dependent upon the age and development of the child. In children the experience of fear, helplessness and terror can be expressed in disorganized or agitated behaviour.[24] Specific for trauma in children furthermore are: compulsory repeated behaviours or monotonous play, in which themes or aspects of the experience is expressed; nightmares without recognizable content; reduced interest in activities the child used to engage in with pleasure; trauma specific fear that is expressed at sensitive times for instance before falling asleep, in the dark, in the bathroom; reduced confidence in self and others; a sense of a severely limited future; and, for small children, loss of already mastered developmental competencies such as cleanliness or language.[25]

From research on children's reactions to war it can be concluded that acute emotional reactions, summarized within the concept of PTSD, are frequent after concrete, war related experiences. Amount and frequency of the experiences, nearness to areas directly involved in combat, and experience of life threat, have been found to be important predictors for the emotional reaction of the children involved.

Developmental consequences of trauma

In developmental terms, the inference from multiple stressful exposures is complicated. When children are exposed to traumatic events, the developmental process is disturbed, and problems of mastering immediate and later developmental tasks arise.[26]

The diagnosis of PTSD focuses exclusively on the traumatic event and the following emotional reactions. How children construct their experience of violence, and the meaning the concrete event has for them, do not enter into the considerations. Children, however, are not passively influenced by their experiences, but actively process and in-cooperate them into an already constructed social context.[27] This social conceptualization is essential in the understanding of the long-term effect of violence on children.

Childhood PTSD research suggests a more or less universal pattern of immediate reactions to traumatic experiences.[28] Whereas the PTSD concept focuses on a specific event, war and other organized violence often is characterized by the continuing presence of a huge variety of different stressors, which together may possibly impact the psychosocial development of children more profoundly. Basically, the effect of war and other organized violence on children has three qualitatively different sources: the children's own *direct experiences* of violence (such as assaults, beatings, witnessing events of violence); *the loss of and separations from* important family members; and the impact of traumatic experiences on *parental responsiveness and role function.*

Empirical findings concerning age of the child in relation to trauma are not synonymous.[29] However, children do tend to react somewhat differently, according to their age. Because of limited cognitive resources and resulting difficulties of understanding and emotional processing of the experiences, particularly pre-school children are sensitive to traumatic events. They feel the most helpless, when confronted with danger, and need the most help from the surroundings, and thus they depend more on the reactions of their parents.[30] They often react with regressive symptoms, cling to their parents, violently protesting when left alone, are afraid of going to sleep, anxious towards strangers and they often experience nightmares. School-children have more cognitive, emotional and behavioural possibilities of coping with traumatic experiences. They often react with problems of concentration, a general state of arousal and fear of the future as well as with psychosomatic symptoms. For the adolescent the greatest consequence of traumatic events can be a forced entrance into too early adulthood. Because they understand the consequences of the events, they are in several ways more vulnerable than school-children. They might use self destructive behaviours as a diversion from anxiety, and they can be pessimistic concerning their own future and marked by a constant expectation of new catastrophes.[31]

Children depend on their parents' ability to project a sense of stability, permanence and competence, and several studies have focused on the buffering role of parents in situations where children are confronted with violence.[32] A direct impact of traumatic experiences on family functioning may, however, include parental loss and subsequent impaired caretaking and/or separation of children from family members. Post-trauma disturbances in parental responsiveness and impairment in parental role function are major sources of secondary stress for children.[33] In chronically violent environments, child-rearing practices may become more authoritarian and restrictive, thus altering parent-child interactions, decreasing opportunities for play, and disturbing family communication. It may compromise the parental roles of disciplinarian, affection giver, and role model, which may influence long-term moral development in children.[34] To live in a context of war and violence furthermore can result in a condition under which the traumatic events and circumstances seem normal.[35] Injustice, assaults and violence thus can become natural and necessary elements in the child's experience of the world and of himself in relation to the world. In violent societies this can influence the general understanding of central human values, and thus give rise to serious problems for the future of such societies.[36]

Traumatic events can destroy the child's experience of security in the world and confidence in other people. The basic trust, developed early in life in relation to the first persons who cared for the child, is the basis of all later human relationships. The traumatic experience can result in a feeling of alienation and the traumatized person can feel cut off from the surroundings, both from intimate family relationships and from more abstract connections with for instance the society, culture and religion. The security of feeling connected with people who cares about the child is the foundation for a healthy personality development.[37] When this feeling is shaken, for instance when the child is witnessing the parents' inability or unwillingness to render sufficient protection during the assaults, the basic trust is broken down, and the traumatized child will loose confidence not only in other people (for instance parents) but also in himself or herself. This breaking down of basic trust may result in future difficulties in forming close human relationships.[38]

Shervin is an Iranian boy who came to a Scandinavian country together with his parents and siblings when he was 11 years old. In his home country, he had spent six months in prison together with the rest of the family, before they succeeded in escaping. In the country of asylum he and his family went for treatment and as part of Shervin's talks with his psychotherapist, he wrote a book about his experiences.[39] Shervin in his book provides several examples of how trust is broken down systematically in prison. In one section he tells about how he had to spend 24 hours alone, away from his family, and without anything to eat:

'Two men came 24 hours later and said: "Are you hungry?" I replied: "Yes." I was very hungry; it was a long time since I had eaten anything. One of them said: "Do you want a glass of water?" I said: "Yes, yes." He drank it himself and said: "It's good." He ate the food I should have had and said: "That was good. It tasted very good. We are going to a restaurant to eat good Iranian food." The other said: "Yes, yes." The first said: "We are going now." "O.K.! That's good". They left and locked the door.'

Shervin also can tell about the situation of being exposed to violence while the parents are witnessing it, without being able to help:

'A man came along. He shouted that I should come out. I was blindfolded but I could see a little below. I bent my head backwards, and then I saw my mother. She was sitting on a chair with a little board. She was writing. I was so happy to see my mother. I ran towards her, but the man beat me hard with a wooden stick across my shins. He hit so hard that the stick broke. I still have scars on my legs from this, and I still can't really play football. I fell after he had beaten me. I cried and tore the blindfolding off. My father and my cousins, my mother and my sisters were all in an open yard and had heard what happened but they could not come to my help.'

Shervin here expresses an understanding of the fact, that the family *could not* help him. This is the child in therapy speaking, and it took him quite some time to reach that conclusion. At the time of the experience, it is most probable that the fact that they *did not* help was the most impressive.

Children of torture survivors

Exposure to torture is one of the most extreme forms of victimization that human beings can experience. Torture has persisted from ancient times and has been used to punish and coerce people, and to extract information from them.[40]

It is now known that the purpose of torture is not only to gain information. The main purpose of torture is to break down a person's integrity and personality in order then to use that broken person to spread terror throughout the community.

Published studies of the prevalence of torture survivors are few. Moreover, the prevalence will expectedly change from time to time and over culture and political environment. In a multi-ethnic group of 187 medically examined refugees arriving in Sweden, Nordström and Persson[41] recently estimated 25 per cent to have been previously exposed to torture. Based on information from 12 Western treatment centres, Baker[42] estimated a prevalence of 5 to 30 per cent in multi-ethnic refugee groups. In a study of 76 Middle Eastern refugees with children three to 15 years old, who were interviewed systematically on arrival in Denmark during two periods in 1992 to 93, 30 per cent (55 per cent of the males, 12 per cent of the females) had been exposed to torture.[43] Consequently more than half of the 99 children living in these families had a tortured mother or father.

That torture produces specific, recognizable psychological effects (sleep disturbances with frequent nightmares, chronic anxiety, depression, memory defects, loss of concentration and change of self-perception) has been well documented in research and clinical practice.[44] These psychological effects of torture interfere with those abilities that are important for proper parenting. A deep change in the protecting quality of the family atmosphere is an effect of torture which has severe consequences for the children.[45]

Children of torture survivors are therefore a particularly vulnerable group who are often severely affected both by their own experiences of organized violence and by that of their parents. Studies of children of torture survivors seem to indicate that they suffer from various psychological symptoms of an emotional, psychosomatic and behavioural nature. Anxiety, sleeping problems including nightmares, psychosomatic symptoms such as stomach pain or headache are frequent symptoms among these children.[46] A follow-up study of a group of children from torture surviving families from Chile, whose parents had been treated at the Rehabilitation Centre for Torture

Victims in Copenhagen three to four years before[47] indicated that the symptoms do not disappear by themselves; on the contrary, more children had symptoms of emotional unbalance and the number of symptoms for each child had raised significantly during this period.

Factual information seems to help children to cope with a stressful situation.[48] Lack of information renders the child a victim of his own imagination which is often worse than the reality. Most torture survivors, however, have not been able to tell their wife and children what has happened to them. The torture experience becomes a barrier between the torture survivor and his family.

> Ali is a 12-year-old boy from Afghanistan. He is the oldest in a group of siblings. When he was around seven years old, his father was imprisoned and tortured. Nobody told Ali why his father suddenly was gone and the boy sensed that he should not ask. He felt his mother's anxiety, and as he was the oldest child living at home, he had to take over some of the practical obligations of the father in the home. The father was away for six months, and after that time he had to hide in his home for about a year. During that period, the military paid frequent 'inspection visits' to the home to look for the father though they did not find him. Ali's sisters were terrified during those visits, which often took place during the night and were violent, with screaming, threats, and throwing things around.
>
> The family decided to escape as the situation grew increasingly tense. The children were not informed; they were told that they were going to visit friends of the family in a neighbouring country. Nevertheless Ali knew, although he said nothing. He knew they were escaping from a dangerous situation and that the escape itself could be dangerous, especially if the younger siblings started to cry on the way. He suppressed his own needs in favour of the family's needs. He also knew, or rather thought he knew, that the family had to escape because of him, lest he be drafted into the army. In this way, Ali took full responsibility for the family's situation.
>
> At arrival in Denmark Ali was anxious and afraid; he was sad and cried a lot, had headaches, a poor appetite, tics, and sometimes enuresis. He tried to isolate himself and withdrew from human contact. The family regarded his behaviour as satisfying: Ali did not bother them, but minded his own business.

In some families, however, the torture surviving parents tend to overburden the children with descriptions of traumatic experiences in order to relieve themselves of the pressure. Too detailed information of experiences like torture however, can also have negative consequences for the child, if the parents do not manage to take care of the child's anxiety, but rather overwhelm it with their own.

> The father in a family from the Middle East had been imprisoned and tortured several times and was suffering from both somatic and psychological effects of

torture when he started treatment at the Rehabilitation Centre for Torture Victims in Copenhagen. He was anxious and emotionally unstable, fluctuated between feelings of anger and depression, he had difficulties sleeping at night, and when he finally slept, he had terrible nightmares. His wife, also herself a torture survivor, also suffered from anxiety and depression, but she had not told her husband of her own traumatic experiences. The two children had witnessed the arrest of and maltreatment of both mother and father by the police, but these experiences were not talked about in the family. Neither had the children received any concrete information about the condition of the father and mother nor the reason for it.

The family was invited to a session at the Centre to talk about current family problems, related to the experiences of the whole family. During this talk the father started a long and detailed explanation of the various torture methods to which he had been exposed. He seemed totally absorbed in his own story, with no regard for the passively listening children and the therapist had difficulty stopping him. The mother told that this situation had repeated itself several times at home, and that neither she nor her husband had managed to help the children process all this information. The children were both very anxious, suffered from sleeping disturbances with frequent nightmares and had difficulties concentrating on their school work.

Being witness to the father's inability to care for his family's needs and experiencing his inability to adapt to the new life in exile changes the child's image of his father. This hitherto powerful figure is, in the eyes of the child, reduced to a weak and vulnerable person, unable to provide the security that the child needs. The process of identification is complicated, and the development of a feeling of personal identity is thus impeded.[49] Living in exile without a firm link to the old cultural values of his homeland complicates the development of identity even more.

The structural changes within the family take place both at the time when the father or mother is taken away and imprisoned and at the time of his or her return. Often it is the father who is imprisoned, and his wife is left to provide for the children, normally without support from the authorities and stigmatized by the husband's activities. Later, when the family is reunited, possibly in exile, the family balance is shifted again. The father has to get to know his children again and take part in their upbringing and in the family life.[50] However, he is often so emotionally unstable, that he cannot cope with that challenge and the wife may be ignorant about the poor condition of her spouse, as it is rare that the wife is familiar with the effects of torture. It is difficult for her to support her husband, whom she might hold responsible for the situation of the family. In some cases she will have developed new and previously unknown capacities during the time of the husband's imprisonment, and when he returns, she does not want to return to her subordinate role in the family. This trend might develop further when the family settles in a Western exile country where women normally take a greater part in the outgoing activities of the family. The low self-esteem of the husband, who has suffered imprisonment and torture, may further deteriorate as a result of this development.[51]

> A Middle Eastern family with four children arrived in Denmark. In the home country, the wife for several years had lived in a very tense and dangerous situation because of her husband's political engagement. The husband had been imprisoned and tortured severely, and directly after his release from prison, they escaped to Denmark. Here the family spent more than a year waiting for asylum in a refugee centre. The mental condition of the husband deteriorated considerably in this period, during which he and the family received no psychological help. After the family had been granted asylum, the wife began to object to the situation. She became angry with her husband, impatient with his way of being as she could no longer recognize the highly educated, intelligent man she had married. This resulted in many quarrels between the spouses which sometimes evolved into violence. The wife's impatience and anger provoked the husband's feelings of not being able to cope with the situation, not being able to take care of his family as he wanted to, and not being the same person as before he was tortured.

Coping with experiences of organized violence

The psychological reactions of children subjected to severe trauma are not uniform, but are related to the context in which the experiences take place. From the existing knowledge, it seems appropriate to conclude that children who have been exposed to war and other organized violence are all influenced by such experiences, but their reactions are dependent upon their physical and psychological health, the presence or absence of parents, family and friends, the material conditions, their earlier experiences, the types of violent experiences to which they are exposed, and the losses these experiences have caused.

Following stressful experience, those children seem to be able to adapt in rather healthy ways, who have cognitive competence, self-confidence, active coping-strategies, a stable emotional relationship to a parent or a parent substitute, and access to a broad social support system outside the family.[52]

In his study of 29 torture surviving families, 46 refugee families, and 53 immigrant families from the same South American population living in exile, Allodi found that there were no significant differences in the psychological reactions of the children within the three groups and that parents largely viewed and reported their children as normal in health and social behaviour.[53] He suggests, that the difference between these findings and those of other similar studies may lie in the presence or absence of parents or parental substitutes and of adequate medical, psychological and social support following the trauma. Long-term follow-up has shown that, even in cases in which the original traumatic experience was very severe, this was not as significant in predicting consequent psychopathology in the child as was failure to provide adequate social support. Parental coping style seems to be essential in this respect.

In a qualitative study of 11 children (three boys and eight girls between five and 13 years old) from five torture surviving families carried out at the Rehabilitation Centre for Torture Victims in Copenhagen in 1989,[54] the intra- and interfamilial context proved to be of central importance for the child's development of a coping strategy. By coping strategy is here understood a specific complex pattern of intrapsychic mechanisms and behavioural patterns which together constitute the child's manner of appraising and dealing with the specific stressful situations.[55] On the basis of the dimensions: active versus passive problem solving; outer versus inner problem solving; and social contact versus isolation; four distinguishable main types of coping strategy were identified in this material: isolation and withdrawal, mental flight, eagerness to acclimatise, and strength of will and fighting. A particular characteristic of this group of children was that several of them were stuck in a once chosen coping strategy which might have been appropriate earlier in the native country, but which was now inappropriate. The lack of support from the surroundings, particularly the parents, had reduced the child's possibilities to revise and develop their coping.

That active, purposive, and courageous coping strategies cannot alone protect children against the negative psychological effect of political hardship was the conclusion of a study of 174 Palestinian women and their 66 children.[56] Punamäki Gitai found, contrary to the hypothesis, that the more active and courageous coping strategies the children used, the higher the level of their psychological symptoms. Mothers' depression were in the same study found to be the most important predictor of mental disturbances in the children.[57]

In their investigation of 40 Cambodian high-school students in the United States who suffered massive trauma during four years in a concentration camp in Cambodia during the Pol Pot regime when they were eight to 12 years old Kinzie et al.[58] found that the role of the family was extremely important in modifying the psychological symptoms. At a follow-up investigation three years later, this function of the family could no longer be identified.[59]

In a qualitative study of 30 children of political detainees in the Philippines[60] the following buffers against the consequences of extreme stress were identified: extensive knowledge of the political beliefs of their fathers, open and democratic life-style within the family, play among the children in the same situation, and emotional group support.

Other studies have pointed to the mitigating effect of structured activities for children's coping with traumatic war experiences.[61] In a study of 44 refugee children in Sweden[62] possibilities for play and school activities served, at least to some extent, as a compensatory factor in the children's experiences of war and violence.

Conclusion

War, torture and other organized violence has a profound influence on children. The acute emotional reactions of children following concrete, war related experiences can be summarized within the concept of Post-Traumatic Stress Disorder (PTSD). Social support, access to support from parents or parental substitutes, open and adequate communication in the family and possibility of participation in play and structured activities can help children cope with such experiences.

Prolonged or repeated exposures can have a profound influence on personality development through its impact on for instance expectations of self and others, meaning in life, basic trust, central human values and morality. Post-trauma disturbances of parental responsiveness and role function renders children particularly vulnerable. As torture has specific, well documented psychological effects that interfere with parenting, children of torture survivors are particularly at risk.

Notes

1   Eth and Pynoos (1985), 'Developmental Perspective on Psychic Trauma in Childhood'. In: *Trauma and its Wake*, edited by Figley, Brunner/Mazel, New York, 36–51.
2   Arroyo and Eth (1985), 'Children Traumatized by Central American Warfare'. In: *Post-Traumatic Stress Disorder in Children*, 1st edn, edited by Eth and Pynoos, American Psychiatric Association, Washington, DC, 103–120. Freud and Burlingham (1943), *War and Children*, Greenwood Press, Westport. Udwin (1993), Annotation: Children's Reactions to Traumatic Events. *J Child Psychol Psychiat* **34**, 115–27.
3   Jensen and Shaw (1993), 'Children as Victims of War: Current Knowledge and Future Research Needs', *J Am Acad Child Adolesc Psychiatry* **32**, 697–708. Macksoud, Dyregrov and Raundalen, M. (1993), 'Traumatic War Experiences and Their Effects on Children'. In: *International Handbook of Traumatic Stress Syndromes*, edited by Wilson and Raphael, Plenum Press, New York, 625–633. Richman (1993), Annotation: Children in situations of Political Violence, *J Child Psychol Psychiat* **34**, 1286–1302.
4   Bowlby (1985), *Separation*, Penguin Books, London.

5   Terr (1991), 'Childhood Traumas: An Outline and Overview', *Am J Psychiatry*, **148**, 10–20.

6   See also Perren-Klinger, 'Children and Reintegration'.

7   Terr (1991), 'Childhood Traumas: An Outline and Overview', *Am J Psychiatry*, **148**, 10–20.

8   Pynoos, Steinberg and Wraith (1995), 'A Developmental Model of Childhood Traumatic Stress'. In: *Developmental Psychopathology*, edited by Cicchetti and Cohen, John Wiley & Sons, Inc, New York, 3–72.

9   Garbarino, Kostelny, and Dubrow (1991), *No Place to be a Child*, Lexington Books, Toronto.

10   Benner, Roskies and Lazarus (1980), 'Stress and Coping under Extreme Conditions'. In: *Survivors, Victims, and Perpetrators*, edited by Dimsdale, Hemisphere Publishing Corporation, New York, 219–58.

11   Herman (1992), *Trauma and Recovery*, Basic Books, United States of America.

12   Terr (1991), 'Childhood Traumas: An Outline and Overview', *Am J Psychiatry*, **148**, 10–20.

13   Terr (1981), '"Forbidden Games" Post-Traumatic Child's play', *J Am Acad Child Psych*, **20**, 741–60. Terr (1988), 'What Happens to Early Memories of Trauma? A Study of Twenty Children Under Age Five at the Time of Documented Traumatic Events', *J Am Acad Child Adolesc Psychiatry*, **27**, 96–104.

14   Herman (1992), *Trauma and Recovery*, Basic Books, United States of America.

15   Gustafsson, Lindkrist, Nordenstam and Nordström (1987), Flyktingbarn i Lycksele. Stenbergska vårdcentralen, Barnmottagningen och Socialkontoret i Lycksele, Lycksele.

16   Trimble (1985), 'Post-traumatic Stress Disorder: History of a Concept'. In *Trauma and Its Wake*, edited by Figley, Brunner/Mazel, New York, 5–14.

17   American Psychiatric Association (1980), *Diagnostic and Statistical Manual of Mental Disorders, Third Edition*, American Psychiatric Association, Washington, DC.

18   American Psychiatric Association (1994), *Diagnostic and Statistical Manual of Mental Disorders, Fourth Edition*, American Psychiatric Association, Washington, DC.

19   Garmezy and Rutter (1985), 'Acute Reactions to Stress'. In: *Child and Adolescent Psychiatry*, edited by Rutter and Hersov, Blackwell, Oxford, 152–76.

20   American Psychiatric Association (1987), *Diagnostic and Statistical Manual of Mental Disorders, Third Edition – Revised*, American Psychiatric Association, Washington, DC.

21   Pynoos, Steinberg and Wraith (1995), 'A Developmental Model of Childhood Traumatic Stress'. In: *Developmental Psychopathology*, edited by Cicchetti and Cohen, John Wiley & Sons, Inc, New York, 3–72.

22   McNally (1991), 'Assessment of Posttraumatic Stress Disorder in Children', *Psychological Assessment*, **3**, 531–7; Udwin (1993), 'Annotation: Children's Reactions to Traumatic Events', *J Child Psychol Psychiat*, **34**, 115–27; Yule and Williams (1990), 'Post-Traumatic Stress Reactions in Children', *Journal of Traumatic Stress*, **3**, 279–95.

23   Pynoos, Nader and March (1991), 'Posttraumatic Stress Disorder'. In: *Textbook of Child & Adolescent Psychiatry*, 1st edn, edited by Wiener, American Psychiatric Press Ltd, Washington, 339–48; Yule (1994), 'Posttraumatic Stress Disorders'. In: *Child and Adolescent Psychiatry*, 3rd edn, edited by Rutter, Taylor and Hersov, Blackwell Science Ltd, Oxford, 392–406.

24   American Psychiatric Association (1994), *Diagnostic and Statistical Manual of Mental Disorders, Fourth Edition*, American Psychiatric Association, Washington, DC.

25   Pynoos, Nader and March (1991), 'Posttraumatic Stress Disorder'. In: *Textbook of Child & Adolescent Psychiatry*, 1st edn, edited by Wiener, American Psychiatric Press

Ltd, Washington, 339–48. Terr (1991), 'Childhood Traumas: An Outline and Overview'. *Am J Psychiatry*, **148**, 10–20.

26   Pynoos, Steinberg and Wraith (1995), 'A Developmental Model of Childhood Traumatic Stress'. In: *Developmental Psychopathology*, edited by Cicchetti and Cohen, John Wiley & Sons, Inc, New York, 3–72.

27   Richman (1993), 'Annotation: Children in Situations of Political Violence', *J Child Psychol Psychiat*, **34**, 1286–1302.

28   Macksoud, Dyregrov and Raundalen, M. (1993), 'Traumatic War Experiences and Their Effects on Children'. In: *International Handbook of Traumatic Stress Syndromes*, edited by Wilson and Raphael, Plenum Press, New York, 625–33.

29   Udwin (1993), 'Annotation: Children's Reactions to Traumatic Events', *J Child Psychol Psychiat*, **34**, 115–27.

30   Pynoos, Nader, and March (1991), 'Posttraumatic Stress Disorder'. In: *Textbook of Child & Adolescent Psychiatry*, 1st edn, edited by Wiener, American Psychiatric Press Ltd, Washington, 339–48.

31   Eth and Pynoos (1985), 'Developmental Perspective on Psychic Trauma in Childhood'. In: *Trauma and its Wake*, edited by Figley, Brunner/Mazel, New York, 36–51. Macksoud, Dyregrov and Raundalen, M. (1993), 'Traumatic War Experiences and Their Effects on Children'. In: *International Handbook of Traumatic Stress Syndromes*, edited by Wilson, and Raphael, Plenum Press, New York, 625–33.

32   Allodi (1989), 'The Children of Victims of Political Persecution and Torture: A Psychological Study of a Latin American Refugee Community', *Int J Ment Health*, **18**, 3–15. Kinzie, Sack, Angell, Manson and Rath (1986), 'The Psychiatric Effects of Massive Trauma on Cambodian Children: 1. The Children', *J Am Acad Child Psych*, **25**, 370–76.

33   Pynoos, Steinberg and Wraith (1995), 'A Developmental Model of Childhood Traumatic Stress'. In: *Developmental Psychopathology*, edited by Cicchetti and Cohen, John Wiley & Sons, Inc, New York, 3–72.

34   Garbarino and Stott, F.M. (1989), *What children can tell us*, Jossey-Bass Publishers, San Francisco. Pynoos, Steinberg and Wraith (1995), 'A Developmental Model of Childhood Traumatic Stress'. In: *Developmental Psychopathology*, edited by Cicchetti and Cohen, John Wiley & Sons, Inc, New York, 3–72.

35   Jensen and Shaw (1993), 'Children as Victims of War: Current Knowledge and Future Research Needs', *J Am Acad Child Adolesc Psychiatry*, **32**, 697–708.

36   Garbarino, Kostelny and Dubrow (1991), 'What Children Can Tell Us About Living in Danger', *American Psychologist*, **46**, 376–83. Macksoud, Dyregrov and Raundalen, M. (1993), 'Traumatic War Experiences and Their Effects on Children'. In: *International Handbook of Traumatic Stress Syndromes*, edited by Wilson and Raphael, Plenum Press, New York, 625–33.

37   Herman (1992), *Trauma and Recovery*, Basic Books, United States of America.

38   Macksoud, Dyregrov and Raundalen, M. (1993), 'Traumatic War Experiences and Their Effects on Children'. In: *International Handbook of Traumatic Stress Syndromes*, edited by Wilson and Raphael, Plenum Press, New York, 625–33.

39   Shervin (1996), *Why suffer from grief?*, International Rehabilitation Council for Torture Victims, Copenhagen.

40   See above Van Bueren, Opening Pandora's Box: Protecting Children Against Torture or Cruel, Inhuman and Degrading Treatment or Punishment.

41   Nordström and Persson (1988), 'Fängelse och tortyr vanliga orsaker till psykiska och somatiska symtom hos flyktingar i Sverige', *Läkartidningen*, **85**, 3560–1.

42   Baker (1992), 'Psychosocial consequences for tortured refugees seeking asylum and

refugee status in Europe'. In: *Torture and its Consequences. Current Treatment Approaches*, edited by Basoglu, Cambridge University Press, Cambridge, 83–106.

43   Montgomery and Foldspang (1994), 'Criterion-related validity of screening for exposure to torture', *Dan Med Bull*, **41**, 588–91.

44   Somnier and Genefke, I.K. (1986), 'Psychotherapy for victims of Torture', *British Journal of Psychiatry*, **149**, 323–29. Somnier, Vesti, Kastrup and Genefke (1992), 'Psycho-social consequences of Torture. Current Knowledge and Evidence'. In: *Torture and Its Consequences: Current Treatment Approaches*, edited by Basoglu, Cambridge University Press, Cambridge, 56–71.

45   Allodi (1980), 'The psychiatric effects in children and families of victims of political persecution and torture'. *Dan Med Bull*, **27**, 229–32.

46   Cohn, Danielsen, Holzer, Koch, Severin, Thøgersen and Aalund (1985), 'A Study of Chilean Refugee Children in Denmark', *The Lancet*, 437–8. Lukman and Bach-Mortensen (1995), 'Symptoms in Children of Torture Victims – Post Traumatic Stress Disorders?', *World Pediatrics and Child Care*, **5**, 32–42. Montgomery, Krogh, Jacobsen and Lukman (1992), 'Children of Torture Victims: Reactions and Coping', *Child Abuse and Neglect*, **16**, 797–805.

47   Weile, Wingender, Busch, Lukman and Holzer (1990), 'Behavioral Problems in Children of Torture Victims: A Sequel to Cultural Maladaptation or to Parental Torture?', *JDBP*, **11**, 79–80.

48   Carli (1987), 'Psychological consequences of political persecution: The effects on children of the imprisonment or disappearance of their parents', *Tidsskrift for Norsk Psykologforening*, **24**, 82–93. Montgomery, Krogh, Jacobsen and Lukman (1992), 'Children of Torture Victims: Reactions and Coping', *Child Abuse and Neglect*, **16**, 797–805.

49   Almquist and Brandell-Forsberg (1989), *Iranska Flyktingbarn i Sverige, Rapport I*, Raedda Barnens rapportserie, Stockholm. Kastrup, Lunde, Ortmann and Genefke (1987), 'Victimization Inside and Outside the Family: Families of Torture-Consequences and Possibilities for Rehabilitation', *PsycheCritique*, **2**, 337–49.

50   Montgomery (1993), 'Children in torture surviving families', *Der Jugendpsychologe*, **19**, 3–11.

51   Kastrup, Lunde, Ortmann, Genefke (1987), 'Victimization Inside and Outside the Family: Families of Torture – Consequences and Possibilities for Rehabilitation', *PsychCritique*, **2**, 337–49.

52   Elbedour, Bensel and Bastien (1993), 'Ecological Integrated Model of Children of War: Individual and Social Psychology', *Child Abuse and Neglect*, **17**, 805–19. Garbarino, Kostelny and Dubrow (1991), 'What Children Can Tell Us About Living in Danger', *American Psychologist*, **46**, 376–83. Garbarino (1992), 'Developmental Consequences of Living in Dangerous and Unstable Environments: The Situation of Refugee Children'. In: *The Psychological Well-Being of Refugee Children, Research, Practice and Policy Issues*, edited by McCallin, International Catholic Child Bureau, Geneva, 1–23.

53   Allodi (1989), 'The Children of Victims of Political Persecution and Torture: A Psychological Study of a Latin American Refugee Community', *Int J Ment Health*, **18**, 3–15.

54   Montgomery, Krogh, Jacobsen and Lukman (1992), 'Children of Torture Victims: Reactions and Coping', *Child Abuse and Neglect*, **16**, 797–805.

55   Lazarus and Folkman (1984), *Stress, Appraisal, and Coping*, Springer Publishing Company, New York.

56   Punamäki-Gitai (1990), *Political Violence and Psychological Responses*, Pampere Peace Research Institute Research Reports No. 41, Jyväskylä.

57   Punamäki (1987), 'Psychological Stress Responses of Palestinian Mothers and Their Children in Conditions of Military Occupation and Political Violence', *The Quarterly Newsletter of the Laboratory of Comparative Human Cognition*, **9**, 116–19.

58   Kinzie, Sack, Angell, Manson and Rath (1986), 'The Psychiatric Effects of Massive Trauma on Cambodian Children: 1. The Children', *J Am Acad Child Psych*, **25**, 370–6. Sack, Angell, Kinzie and Rath (1986), 'The Psychiatric Effects of Massive Trauma on Cambodian Children: 2. The Family, the Home, and the School', *J Am Acad Child Psych*, **25**, 377–83.

59   Kinzie, Sack, Angell, Clarke and Ben (1989), 'A Three-Year Follow-up of Cambodian Young People Traumatized as Children', *J Am Acad Child Adolesc Psychiatry*, **28**, 501–4.

60   Protacio-Marcelino (1989), 'Children of Political Detainees in the Philippines: Sources of Stress and Coping Patterns', *Int J Ment Health*, **18**, 71–86.

61   Gustafsson (1986), 'The STOP sign – a model for intervention to assist children in war'. In: *Children in Emergencies*, edited by Raedda Barnen. Raedda Barnen, New York. Gustafsson, Lindkvist, Nordenstam and Nordström (1987), *Flyktingbarn i Lycksele* Stenbergsak vårdcentralen, Barnmottagningen och Socialkontoret i Lycksele, Lycksele.

62   Ljungberg-Miklos and Cederblad (1989), 'Flyktingbarns psykiska hälsa', *Social-medicinsk tidskrift*, 18–24.

13 The Effects on Children of Witnessing Violence Perpetrated against their Parents or Siblings

Dora Black and Martin Newman

Introduction

The words 'violence' and 'trauma' describe a wide range of phenomena. Some studies define violence to include occasional slapping or physical chastisement of a child. At the other extreme may be rape, serious assault, torture, homicide or genocide. Here we are considering the heavy end of violence. Trauma has been defined as 'the experience of an inescapable stressful event that overwhelms one's existing coping mechanisms'.[1]

In this chapter, we will review the range of psychological reactions to serious violent and traumatic events in which children may be involved. We will review the research literature on the effects of war and civil conflict on children. We consider how children of different ages perceive, process, remember and deal with the images of the events and the effects these memories have on their development and psychological well-being. Finally, we touch on therapeutic strategies available to help them.

We come to this task from the perspective of practicing child and adolescent psychiatrists who spend their time assessing and treating troubled children and their families. One of us (Dora Black), because of a research and clinical interest in childhood bereavement, found herself seeing an increasing number of children bereaved as a result of homicide. Recognizing that these children were not always well served by existing services she founded a special psychiatric clinic for the children and their families in 1993. This clinic, originally at the Royal Free Hospital, moved in 1995 to amalgamate with a similar clinic for adults, as part of the Camden and Islington Community NHS Trust with some funding from the Department of Health through a grant to the national charity, Cruse-Bereavement Care. The Traumatic Stress Clinic sees children and adults who are traumatized as a result of a wide variety of traumas, including homicide, attempted murder, assault, suicide of a family member, abduction, war and civil conflict, accidents and disasters. It serves the whole of the United Kingdom and, as a result of the expertise developed there, we have been asked to advise the United Nations Children's Fund in former Yugoslavia and other non-governmental organizations elsewhere.

Our knowledge and expertise with traumatized children is derived from our clinical practice. For example, we have seen and treated over 350 children where one parent has killed the other. Half of the children either saw the killing, or heard it, or came in on the dead body – sometimes having been left alone in the house after the perpetrator fled.[2] Most of the other children we have seen at our clinic (as is inevitable in UK based practice) have been caught up in personal or relatively small-scale transport and other man-made or natural disasters. We have not had to experience in the West the impact of the scale of disaster in places like Rwanda where UNICEF estimates that there are 95,000 orphans[3] or Skopje, where four refugee camps were, in 1992, 'home' to over 7,000 refugee children from Bosnia.[4] In Rwanda, half the orphans had been threatened with death themselves, a quarter had been injured, a fifth had witnessed rapes and 64 per cent had witnessed massacres. Nearly half had witnessed other children participating in the killings.[5]

Our own experience in Montenegro where, in 1995, Dora Black visited, at the request of UNICEF, a project which offers respite and treatment to Bosnian children from war zones, convinced us that the emotional scars of war inflicted on the children whom we should be seeking most to protect, may be ineradicable. One boy of 14 there was manipulated into revenging his soldier father's death by the latter's commanding officer, who put a gun into his hands and gave him permission or downright encouragement, to kill three prisoners of war. The ensuing severe depression, especially profound when the boy learned later that his father had died accidentally from 'friendly fire', and not from the enemy's, did not respond to medication or psychotherapy and the possibility of his ending his life, or that of others, remains high.[6]

Children's Reactions to Traumatic Events

Children, like adults involved in traumatic events, can react with symptoms of psychological distress. Children's reactions to traumatic events have been under-recognized until relatively recently, possibly due to the use of screening instruments which were not designed to pick up the symptoms in children that may occur after such experiences and also because of over-reliance on the reports of parents and/or teachers, rather than direct examination of the children.[7] However, it is now recognized that children, including pre-school children, can suffer psychological morbidity after traumatic experiences.[8]

Children may suffer from a variety of disorders following a trauma or traumatic experiences.[9] Post-traumatic stress disorder (PTSD), as described in the fourth edition of the *Diagnostic and Statistical Manual* (DSM-IV)[10] and the tenth edition of the *International Classification of Disorders* (ICD-10),[11] has become a focus for recent research,[12] but it should not be considered the only response to trauma. There is still some controversy about this diagnosis. The symptoms described may represent a 'normal' reaction to highly stressful experiences. It is unclear how appropriate it is to use a single diagnostic classification in many different cultures and after many different types of trauma.[13] It may be misleading to use diagnostic classifications based on Western culture in non-Western cultures. The significance of symptoms may vary between cultures – for example, nightmares may be regarded as a symptom of illness or distress in some cultures, yet in others may be taken as messages from ancestors.[14] One of the disadvantages of classification systems is that those individuals whose symptoms do not fit neatly into a diagnostic category may be deemed not to be ill, and therefore not receive appropriate professional help. We need to beware of the 'medicalization of distress'.[15] After all, one cannot be 'cured' of experiencing a traumatic event or of being bereaved.

According to DSM-IV criteria, PTSD is characterized by the following:

i)   at least one symptom of re-experiencing the trauma, such as recurrent and intrusive recollections of the event, recurrent distressing dreams, acting or feeling as if the traumatic event was reoccurring, psychological distress at exposure to reminders of the event, or physiological reactivity at exposure to reminders of the event;

ii)   three or more symptoms of avoidance, such as making efforts to avoid thoughts, feelings and conversations that are associated with the trauma, efforts to avoid people, places or activities that arouse recollections of the trauma, an inability to recall an important aspect of the trauma, markedly decreased interest or participation in significant activities, feelings of detachment or estrangement from others, a restricted range of affect (for example, an inability to have loving feelings), and a sense of a foreshortened future;

iii)   two or more symptoms of increased arousal (not present before the trauma) such as difficulty falling or staying asleep, irritability or outbursts of anger, difficulty concentrating, hyper-vigilance, and an exaggerated startle response.

For a diagnosis of post-traumatic stress disorder to be made in accordance with the DSM-IV criteria, these symptoms should have persisted for more than one month and be causing clinically significant distress or impairment in social, occupational, or other important areas of functioning.[16]

Sleep disturbance, the loss of newly acquired developmental skills, concentration difficulties and memory impairment may all be particularly prominent in children who have experienced trauma. Intrusive thoughts and anxiety may also be common. Re-enactment of aspects of the traumatic event(s) may be seen in play. There may be evidence of 'separation anxiety', fears of situations that remind the child of the trauma, and loss of hope for the future. Impairment of concentration may lead to school difficulties and learning failure. Parents and teachers may not initially realise that children's behavioural problems may be a manifestation of psychological distress.

A different set of criteria for diagnosing PTSD in children under four years of age has been proposed by Scheeringa and his colleagues.[17] This takes into consideration the way young children express their fear and traumatic experiences in play. They propose that reexperiencing can be determined through the nature of the child's play – either post-traumatic with compulsive repetition representing part of the trauma which fails to relieve anxiety and is less elaborate or imaginative, or play reenactment, or nightmares and flashbacks. They note that young traumatized children show a numbing of responsiveness, may display a restricted range of emotions and may lose acquired developmental skills such as toilet training and language. Using Scheeringa's criteria, colleagues at the Traumatic Stress Clinic are currently planning to evaluate young child patients, referred as a result of one parent killing the other.[18]

A person may fail to meet all the criteria for a post-traumatic stress disorder, yet be more distressed than someone who does. It has been estimated that, depending on the type of trauma experienced, the ensuing incidence of PTSD in children may range from 40 to 100 per cent.[19] In our study, we found that virtually all our patients who had witnessed the killing developed PTSD. Only a few of those whom we knew had not been present did, and they were mainly children who had been exposed to chronic and severe violence between their parents prior to the homicide.[20]

When carrying out a psychiatric examination of an individual after a traumatic event, it is important to establish what the person's subjective experiences were, and the significance of these within that individual's inner world, and how it fits into their framework of their self, their world, and others. Other psychiatric disorders such as depression may frequently co-exist with PTSD. Care is needed when making a diagnosis.[21] A diagnosis of PTSD is poorly predictive of capacity to function and not a reliable indicator of a need for psychological treatment.[22] Future editions of the DSM-IV and the ICD-10 may well need to revise the diagnostic criteria as our knowledge about responses to trauma increases.

There is still uncertainty about which factors make some children more likely to develop post-traumatic stress reactions than others. The studies of children's reactions to traumatic events suggest that factors which increase the likelihood of developing post-traumatic psychological morbidity include the degree of exposure to the traumatic event, witnessing death or injury in others, being separated from family and friends, a subjective fear of a threat to life, the active or passive role of the survivor during and after the traumatic event, feelings of helplessness and feelings of guilt.[23] A number of studies have shown that children's reactions to traumatic events are greater when the parents themselves are suffering from severe post-traumatic reactions or are unable to provide emotional support to their children. The younger the child, the more likely he or she is to react adversely to traumatic events. Children may be unable or reluctant to voice their distress when they perceive adults around them to be distressed.

Studies of the effects of trauma on children and adolescents have been made after a range of events, including natural disaster,[24] kidnapping,[25] a sniper attack at a school,[26] witnessing the murder of one parent by the other[27] and children who witnessed the sexual assault of their mothers.[28] Others have looked at the effects of community and political violence[29] and war[30] and a useful review is provided by Jensen and Shaw.[31] Children may also be held hostage, either by someone known to them, or by strangers, either in peace time or during conflict.[32] All these papers and others report the high association between witnessing or experiencing horrific events and developing post-traumatic symptoms.

Other Psychiatric Disorders

Children in situations of war and conflict may be mal- or under-nourished, physically at risk or injured or mutilated. If the infra-structure has collapsed they may not receive education or adequate medical care. They are likely to be inadequately treated for chronic pre-existing conditions such as asthma, diabetes or congenital disorders (cystic fibrosis, for example), may have inadequate housing, especially if they are refugees, and may suffer from the consequences of poverty and displacement. Their parents may be absent, chronically depressed, fearful, injured or physically ill, so that their parenting may be affected. All these factors increase the risk of the child developing a psychiatric disorder.

Children caught up in traumatic events are likely to be separated from familiar caretakers, either through their death, capture or serious injury, or because of evacuation, displacement or maladministration. The effects of this are still uncertain.[33] Reactive attachment disorders,[34] or degrees of separation anxiety, may result in clinging behaviour, crying on separation, hostility to the parent or carer, or sleeping, toileting and eating disturbances, especially in younger children.

The consequences of bereavement have received comparatively little attention. Many studies have focused on clinical populations that cannot be generalized to the population as a whole, and there are few controlled or longitudinal studies.[35] The relationship between childhood bereavement and the incidence of subsequent psychiatric illness is still unclear. Sibling bereavement has been little studied. This is perhaps surprising since we may normally expect sibling relationships to be among the longest lasting in our lives. Applebaum and Burns,[36] in the United States, reported a small study of ten surviving siblings who had lost a brother or sister to accidental death and ten who had lost a brother or sister to homicide from 20 families. The surviving siblings in both groups reported symptoms of post-traumatic stress disorder, with 45 per cent meeting diagnostic criteria according to DSM-III-R.[37] Parents were not necessarily aware of the child's symptoms, perhaps because they were themselves coping with symptoms (35 per cent of the parents met DSM-III-R criteria for PTSD). The surviving siblings in the accident and murder groups did not differ significantly on parent ratings of the surviving sibling's PTSD, the surviving sibling's self-report of PTSD, or their score on the Child Reaction Index, a measure of the severity of PTSD. However, parents of murdered children did report more PTSD symptoms than parents of children who suffered accidental death, and higher levels of parental PTSD were associated with higher levels of PTSD in the surviving sibling. The authors point out that this is a small study, with no proper control groups, and there may have been bias in the recruitment (the majority of the families were obtained through two self-help groups). Trauma itself may inhibit the normal and healing process of mourning, the traumatic images recurring whenever the child tries to summon up an image of the dead parent or sibling, in order to say farewell, a prerequisite of normal mourning.

A child's concept of death develops gradually. It is not until the age of about eight years that most children have a concept of death as something universal, irreversible and permanent, having a cause, and that dead people differ from the living in a number of respects – they cannot move, feel, speak, eat, and so on.[38] Young children may continue to search for their dead parent or sibling or hope for their return, as they find it difficult to understand why they have disappeared, or realise their absence is permanent. Such losses in young children may also lead to disorders of attachment as they cannot transfer their attachment to new caretakers. Separation anxiety expresses itself as school refusal and somatisation disorders in later childhood.

In our first series of 95 children where one parent had killed the other, 40 per cent were suffering from mood disorders, anxiety and depression when first seen. Girls were more vulnerable than boys, especially if they were living with the perpetrator's family and they were given no opportunity to talk about their dead parent.[39]

Children separated from their parents in situations of war are more vulnerable to physical and sexual abuse, leading to further traumatization and resulting in disorders of personality.[40]

Chronic lack of parenting, such as may result from major disaster and war, leaves children and adolescents bereft of guidance, discipline and control as well as education and occupation. Such conditions are a breeding ground for delinquency, conduct disorders and criminality.

Children of parents who suffer PTSD, for example, returning Vietnam veterans, are more likely to suffer from a wide range of psychiatric symptoms than those whose father did not have PTSD.[41] Similarly, children of parents who were tortured or severely maltreated before they were born are much more likely to develop psychiatric disorders (see below). This is confirmed by numerous studies of children born to Holocaust survivors.[42]

Child Witnesses

The individual who witnesses violence being meted out to another may perceive events from the point of view of victim, assailant, or someone else who is present, as well as from the perspective of helpless onlooker. Later, that witness may imagine himself or herself as, or identify with, any of these roles. The witness has less powerful distracters than the victim and hence PTSD may be more intense and more immediate and there may be high levels of guilt and shame at not having intervened more effectively. Children may be especially vulnerable to feelings of guilt. If the victim is a parent, child witnesses older than four to five years may be so preoccupied with the welfare of their loved one and with the urgent need for intervention that they may disregard threats to their own safety, and this tendency may persist and generalize to other situations.[43]

When considering the impact of witnessing violence, torture or other potentially traumatizing experiences on children and adolescents, it is necessary to consider such factors as age, developmental stage, cultural aspects and religious beliefs. As already mentioned, the subjective experiences and the meanings of that trauma for the individual are important to establish.

We have been discussing the effects on children and young people of witnessing violence but it is important to recognize that many of the phenomena we have described are common to some adults too. For example, young children may be described as 'egocentric' – that is, they view the world from their point of view only, without an awareness that it is only their point of view. Hence, a young child may be unable to understand the feelings of others, believe that everything is orientated towards himself or herself, and that everything that happens is because of him or her. A young child may feel irrationally responsible and guilty if something bad happens.[44] However, adults may also regress to egocentric thinking under stress even if they do not usually use this particular mental mechanism.

War and Conflict

The majority of conflicts since the Second World War have been in developing countries, where children form between 40–50 per cent of the population.[45]

The effect of combat on military personnel has been extensively studied,[46] but less attention has been paid to the effect of conflict on civilian populations, particularly children. Factors which influence the ability of a child to deal with the trauma of war may include the child's own resources and developmental characteristics, the 'microsystem' of the family, the 'exosystem' of the community and the 'macrosystem' of the culture, and the level of intensity, duration and suddenness of the conflict.[47] Other studies have suggested that the psychological health of children is protected, at least in part, from the trauma of war by the presence of parents and loving caretakers[48] and by the adults' reaction to the trauma. This needs to be both courageous and open to discussion and explanation, in order to give the children the best chance of coping.[49] High levels of psychiatric and physical morbidity have been found in children of conflict. Children may be induced into bearing arms and becoming boy soldiers themselves. Child combatants may show violent, aggressive behaviour patterns, and guilt and depression when active involvement ceases. Variables which affect their later function[50] may depend more on the ideology and morality of their group and on their experiences rather than the age at which they were conscripted. Children inducted into fighting and trained to commit atrocities by initial brutalization may be at higher risk of later dysfunction than others who voluntarily joined guerilla armies. While not systematically brutalized to the same extent, these children nevertheless have few experiences to help them adapt to normal life and peacetime activities.[51]

Wars are usually protracted, and may result in conditions which, although stressful, may seem normal to children at the time. Moderate degrees of exposure to the stresses of war may result in adaptive, self-protective cognitive styles which allow effective functioning.[52]

Torture

Torture is widespread and is routine in over 90 countries.[53] The effects of torture on adults have been described by several authors[54] but there is little written about the torture of children. The children of torture victims, even those born after the parents have been freed, have themselves been found to suffer from increased levels of psychiatric disorder. As Timerman[55] has written: 'Of all the dramatic situations I witnessed in clandestine prisons, nothing can compare to those family groups who were tortured often together, sometimes separately but in view of one another, or in different cells, while one was aware of the other being tortured. The entire affective world, constructed over the years with utmost difficulty, collapses with a kick in the father's genitals, a smack on the mother's face, an obscene insult to the sister, or the sexual violation of a daughter. Suddenly an entire culture based on familial love, devotion, the capacity for mutual sacrifice collapses. Nothing is possible in such a universe, and that is precisely what the torturers know.'

One small scale study in Denmark of children of refugees from Chile, Uruguay, Turkey, Afghanistan and Iraq, all of whose parents had been arrested, tortured and persecuted, but later released, found that even two to ten years later all the children showed signs of emotional unbalance manifesting itself as anxiety and generalized fear, sleeping problems, including nightmares, depression, regressive features such as bedwetting and temper tantrums, somatic symptoms (headache, pains, eating problems) and behavioural problems. Many of them had learning problems. Examining their coping strategies the researchers found four main ones, withdrawal, mental flight, eagerness to acclimatize, and fighting. The two active strategies were associated with fewer psychological symptoms. When the parents were able to talk to the children about their experiences the children had fewer symptoms.[56] Since most of these children had been born after the parents had escaped, the conclusion is that the children are affected by the effect of the torture on the parents, affecting their parenting.

Children and Political Violence

Children living under regimes which do not obey the rule of law experience direct and indirect fear from the unpredictability of their lives and those of their parents as well as bereavement from the imprisonment, disappearance and possibly death of one or both parents. One study of 68 Guatemalan Mayan Indian children who, between the ages of two years and ten years, had experienced government-sponsored terrorism, which involved the indiscriminate torture and physical elimination of individuals, families, and of entire communities, and forced relocation of many, found that many of these children remained fearful, even five to seven years after the end of terrorism. Those children who had parents and close relatives to support them appeared to find this helpful for recovery, especially if the environment permitted discussion and explanation of the traumatic events.[57] Other studies of political refugees bear out these findings and emphasize the close relationship between the mental health of the children and that of their parents, especially the mother.[58]

Memory

Over recent years, there has been increasing interest in studying the processes of memory in children who have experienced or witnessed traumatic events. The evidence suggests that what children remember is similar to what adults remember but that how much they remember depends on age, personal significance, language, conceptual levels of development, and on the context and style of questioning adopted.[59] Children aged between three and five years are able to provide more reliable accounts of past events when asked direct probing questions than when asked to provide an account of what happened. For example: 'was the man who hurt mummy taller than me, shorter or the same?', rather than 'can you describe the man to me?'. Young children are unlikely to be able to recall information such as times, dates, and locations by themselves, and will benefit from skilled guidance from an interviewer. However, it is essential that the direct questions used are not leading questions, as this may bias the child's memory through the influence of suggestion.

Children are particularly susceptible to suggestion when they are questioned after a long delay, when they feel overwhelmed by an interviewer, when the interviewer's suggestive questions are strongly stated and frequently repeated, or when more than one interviewer makes the same strong suggestions.[60] Adults, too, may be influenced in their responses by such factors. A child is only able to give an account of events within his verbal repertoire, and of significance to him or her.[61] It is difficult for children under five to give a coherent narrative but they can convey what happened through play or drawing. Emotional experiences can often be conveyed by facial expressions, postures, gestures and behaviours.[62]

What is memory?

Memory refers to the processes by which the mind/brain perceives a stimulus, encodes elements of it, and stores them for later retrieval. It may be influenced by active mental models or schemata which link together perceptual biases, associated memories, emotions and prior learning.[63]

At least two forms of memory have been described - *implicit* memory and *explicit* memory. Explicit memory is what people generally think of as 'memory', in which events are recalled from the past and are communicated to others. Implicit memory includes information that is acquired during skill learning, habit formation, and knowledge that is expressed through performance rather than recollection.[64]

In children, it seems that there are very good encoding and retrieval capacities for implicit memory but, whilst explicit memory encoding may be good, retrieval strategies in young children are immature.[65] This may lead to limitations and inconsistencies in recalling personally experienced events, which may be more susceptible to suggestion and influence.[66] Additionally, emotional states may bias the interpretation of stimuli, and affect encoding and the retrieval of memories. This is known as state-dependent learning.[67]

Traumatic memory

Traumatic experiences become encoded differently from non-traumatic events,[68] since only part of the traumatic experience can be processed with the 'conscious' focal attention required for explicit memory processing. Hence much of the traumatic experience may be processed without focal attention. Thus perceptual and emotional flooding, extreme stress and divided attention during trauma may cause impaired explicit processing but leave implicit processing intact. It has also been suggested that the function of the hippocampus, that part of the brain important in the processing of explicit memory, is impaired by excessive stress.[69] The knowledge that human memory is open to suggestion[70] is important. When an account of events is given, gaps may be filled in. The interviewer or therapist may influence the account by asking leading questions, using emphasis in the tone of the voice, giving subtle non-verbal cues, or repeatedly questioning around a topic.

Trauma can affect many memory functions. Four types of functional disturbances have been described:[71]

i.   *Traumatic amnesia,* either complete or partial, may occur in children witnessing intrafamilial suicide or homicide and experiencing sexual abuse as well as in adults who murder, are tortured or take part in war and so on. Amnesia may last for a short time or many years. Recall is triggered by traumatic reminders, including emotional reexperiencing.

ii. *Global memory impairment.* This occurs particularly in young children who are not yet capable of coherent narrative (telling a story) and leaves them especially vulnerable to suggestion.

iii. *Dissociation.* This phenomenon refers to a splitting or compartmentalization of experience so that the separate components of the traumatic experience are stored separately as isolated fragments, including emotional states such as fear. This can range from minor splitting off of experiences, through a feeling of depersonalization at the time of the trauma, to ongoing feelings of depersonalization and rarely to a full blown dissociative disorder, formerly called multiple personality disorder. An excellent account of the way that an individual can be precipitated into such a state by extremely traumatic combat experiences is described by the novelist Pat Barker, in *The Eye in the Door.*[72] The soldier she describes learned to dissociate as a child when he sat helplessly at the head of the stairs listening to his mother's cries as she was beaten by his drunken father. Such dissociation protected him from his feelings of helplessness and became a defensive technique which came automatically into play as an adult after he was shelled and injured on the battlefield in the First World War.

iv. *The sensori-motor organization of traumatic experience.* Unlike non-traumatic sensations and perceptions, traumatic experiences are initially remembered without words, but as feelings, and images and smells. This is particularly so for children who can draw upon fewer experiences and less knowledge to make sense of their perceptions and attach associations to them. For example, one of our patients, a four-year-old boy who had witnessed his father strangle his mother, incessantly and compulsively complained that everything smelled of faeces ('poo'). He appeared to be remembering the smell of his mother who had voided in her agonal fear.

Interventions and Therapy

Understanding the way in which traumatic memories are processed helps clinicians to understand the phenomena of PTSD, especially nightmares and flashbacks, and opens the way to a rational approach to helping the victims of trauma. Increasing evidence is gathering that it may be possible, if we intervene early enough, to inoculate against the development of PTSD by helping the individual to process the images and to attach semantic associations. In the case of the child with the smell of 'poo', it was explained that mummy and daddy had a fight, that his daddy hurt his mummy very much and she was very frightened. He was reminded of something that was within his own experience; that when you are frightened you might do a 'poo' in your pants. Light shone in his eyes as he made the connections which enabled this image to be processed. Although he needed much further counselling to mourn his mother, he ceased to be troubled by the olfactory flashbacks.

In our work with children who have witnessed the homicide of one parent by the other, we have found it helpful if children, recently bereaved and traumatized, are given opportunities to talk about what has happened. We may ask them to draw a picture and discuss it with them. Their experiences and perceptions are explored with close attention being paid to what he or she saw, heard, smelled and felt. We find that adults may not be prepared to bring children for rapid help because they fear that the children may be disturbed by such ventilation whilst the children fear upsetting their caretakers and collude in avoiding the subject. We have found that children who have experienced horrific events need an opportunity to communicate about their experiences and help in understanding them, access to psychiatric services, advocacy, legal protection, and clear long-term plans about where they should live and go to school, to whom they should have access and what treatment, if any, they need. They may be entitled to compensation for psychological injuries.

In developing countries there may be few psychiatrists and even fewer child psychiatrists or psychologists. Tackling the enormous task of reducing the existing suffering and distress involves the 'cascade' method of treatment in which a few highly trained and experienced professionals, often from abroad, train local professionals who in turn train volunteers and lay workers. A project in which UNICEF and the University of London are collaborating in Mostar, Bosnia, involves a clinical psychology team from the Institute of Psychiatry being based in the town and training and supervising teachers and health professionals to support and help traumatized children.[73] A similar model was used by Richman to train teachers to work with children caught up in Mozambique's civil war.[74]

Summary and Conclusions

Children are the innocent victims of adult violence and man-made and natural disasters and appear to be at the same or higher risk of PTSD and other psychiatric disorders compared with adults. More research is needed to determine the effects of age, development, family and community factors and longitudinal follow-up studies will help to assess whether early intervention has adverse or beneficial long-term consequences. Care needs to be taken in interpreting studies from different populations and conflicts, and conclusions drawn from observations made on clinical populations cannot be transferred to non-clinical ones.[75] Protective factors appear to include being shielded from witnessing horrific sights and sounds, not being separated from familiar caretakers, resilience and courage in their parents and an open communication between the adults and children. Early intervention post-trauma may prevent or limit psychological distress, and attention to the provision of substitute parenting where necessary, medical care and education, housing and nutrition are essential to minimizing the secondary effects of traumatic events. Severe trauma may have a lasting effect on the ability of children to develop and learn and can affect their mental health, perhaps permanently.

When considering the subject of the protection of children against torture, cruel and inhuman and degrading treatment, it is impossible for those of us who work in this area to remain completely neutral. Each of us can also play a part in opposing, whenever possible, offensive aggression, ethnic cleansing, the entrapment of children, adolescents and adults in enclaves or detention camps where they are subject to violation of their human rights and dignity, genocide and torture.[76]

Notes

1   Van der Kolk, B. and Fisler, R. (1995), 'Dissociation and the fragmentary nature of traumatic memories: overview and exploratory study', *Journal of Traumatic Stress*, **8**:4, 505–25.
2   Harris-Hendriks, J., Black, D. and Kaplan, T. (1993), *When Father Kills Mother*, London: Routledge.
3   UNICEF (1995), *Children of Rwanda*, Kigali, UNICEF.
4   Parry Jones, W., Barton, J. and van Beinum, M. (1995), *Psychosocial support programmes and mental health services for vulnerable children and young people in FYR Macedonia*, Dept. of Child and Adolescent Psychiatry, University of Glasgow, UK.
5   UNICEF (1995), *Exposure to war trauma among Rwandese children: a brief report of the pilot study*, Kigali, UNICEF, The Trauma Recovery Programme.
6   Black, D., Young, B. and Pynoos, R.S. (1995), *The Children in Need Project in Igalo, Montenegro, A report to UNICEF*. Obtainable from Dr. Black.

7   Udwin, O. (1993), 'Children's reactions to traumatic events', *Journal of Child Psychology and Psychiatry*, **34**:2, 115–27.

8   Harris-Hendriks, J. and Newman, M. (1995), 'Psychological trauma in children and adolescents', *Advances in Psychiatric Treatment*, **1**, 170–5.

9   *Op. cit.*, note 7.

10 American Psychiatric Association (1994), *Diagnostic and Statistical Manual of Mental Disorders (4th. edition)*, Washington, DC: American Psychiatric Association.

11 World Health Organization (1992), *The ICD-10 Classification of Mental and Behavioural Disorders*, Geneva: World Health Organization.

12 Montgomery, E., Krogh, Y., Jacobsen, A. and Lukman, B. (1992), 'Children of torture victims: Reaction and coping', *Child Abuse and Neglect*, **16**, 797–805.

13 Jackson, G. and Rosser, R. (1993), 'Responses to traumatic events', in K. Granville-Grossman (ed.), *Recent Advances in Clinical Psychiatry*, Number 8 (165–82). Edinburgh: Churchill Livingstone.

14 Summerfield, D. (1997), 'The impact of war and atrocity on civilian populations', in D. Black, M. Newman, J. Harris-Harris-Hendricks and G. Mezey (eds), *Psychological Trauma: A Developmental Approach*, (148–55, 172–5), London: Gaskell.

15 Harris-Hendriks, J., Black, D., Newman, M. and Mezey, G. (1997), Overview and comment, in D. Black, M. Newman, J. Harris-Hendriks and G. Mezey (eds), *Psychological Trauma: A Developmental Approach*, (392–401), London: Gaskell.

16. *Op. cit.*, note 10.

17 Scheeringa, M., Zeanah, C., Drell, M. and Larrieu, J. (1995), 'Two approaches to the diagnosis of post-traumatic stress disorder in infancy and early childhood', *Journal of the American Academy of Child and Adolescent Psychiatry*, **34**:2, 191–200 and Correction, same journal, **34**:5, 694.

18 Morris Smith, J. and Doney, A. (1995), 'Working with PTSD in children under 7', paper presented at the European Society for Child and Adolescent Psychiatry Meeting, Utrecht. September.

19 Peterson, K.C., Prout, M.F. and Schwarz, R.A. (1991), 'PTSD in children', Chapter 5 in *Post-Traumatic Stress Disorder: A Clinician's Guide*, New York: Plenum Press.

20 *Op cit.*, note 2.

21 Newman, M. and Lee, D. (1997), 'Diagnosis', in D. Black, M. Newman, J. Harris-Hendriks and G. Mezey (eds), *Psychological Trauma: A Developmental Approach*, (219–29, 235–37), London: Gaskell.

22 *Op. cit.*, note 14.

23 *Op. cit.*, note 7.

24 McFarlane, A.C. (1987), 'Post-traumatic phenomena in a longitudinal study of children following a natural disaster', *Journal of the American Academy of Child and Adolescent Psychiatry*, **26**, 764–69. McFarlane, A.C. (1987), 'Family functioning and overprotection following a natural disaster: the longitudinal effects of post-traumatic morbidity', *Australian and New Zealand Journal of Psychiatry*, **21**, 210–18. Pynoos, R.S., Goenjian, A., Tashjian, M., Karakashian, M., Manjikian, R., Manoukian, G. Steinberg, A.M. and Fairbanks, L.A. (1993), 'Post-traumatic stress reactions in children after the 1988 Armenian earthquake', *British Journal of Psychiatry*, 163, 239–47.

25 Terr, L.C. (1979), 'Children of Chowchilla: Study of psychic trauma', *Psychoanalytic Study of the Child*, **34**, 547–623. Terr, L.C. (1983), 'Chowchilla revisited: The effects of psychic trauma four years after a school-bus kidnapping', *American Journal of Psychiatry*, **140**, 1543–50.

26 Pynoos, R.S., Nader, K., Frederick, C., Gonda, L. and Stuber, M. (1987), 'Grief

reactions in school age children following a sniper attack at school', Special Issue: Grief and bereavement, *Israel Journal of Psychiatry and Related Sciences*, **24**, 53–63.

27   Black, D. and Kaplan, T. (1988), 'Father kills mother: Issues and problems encountered by a child psychiatric team', *British Journal of Psychiatry*, **153**, 624–30. Black, D., Harris-Hendriks, J. and Kaplan, T. (1992), 'Father kills mother: Post-traumatic stress disorder in the children', *Psychotherapy and Psychosomatics*, **57**, 152–57. *Op. cit.*, note 2.

28   Pynoos, R.S. and Nader, K. (1988), 'Children who witness the sexual assaults of their mothers', *Journal of the American Academy of Child and Adolescent Psychiatry*, **27**, 567–72.

29   Magwaza, A.S., Killian, B.J. Petersen, I. and Pillay, Y. (1993), 'The effects of chronic violence on preschool children living in South African townships', *Child Abuse and Neglect*, **17**, 795–803. Osofsky, J.D. (1995), 'The effects of exposure to violence on young children', *American Psychologist*, **50**:9, 782–88.

30   Dunsdon, M.I. (1941), 'A psychologist's contribution to air raid problems', *Mental Health*, **2**, 37–41. Milgram, R.M. and Milgram, N.A. (1976), 'The effect of the Yom Kippur War on anxiety level in Israeli children', *Journal of Psychology*, **94**, 107–13. Nader, K.O., Pynoos, R.S., Fairbanks, L.A., Al-Ajeel, M. and Al-Asfour, A. (1993), 'A preliminary study of PTSD and grief among the children of Kuwait following the Gulf crisis', *British Journal of Clinical Psychology*, **32**:4, 407–16. Ziv, A. and Israeli, R. (1973), 'Effects of bombardment on the manifest anxiety level of children living in kibbutzim', *Journal of Consulting and Clinical Psychology*, **40**, 287–91.

31   Jensen, P.S. and Shaw, J. (1993), 'Children as victims of war: Current knowledge and future research needs', *Journal of the American Academy of Child and Adolescent Psychiatry*, **32**:4, 697–708.

32   Ayalon, O. (1982), 'Children as hostages', *The Practitioner*, **226**, 1773–81.

33   Najarian, L.M., Goenjian, A.K., Pelcovitz, D., Mandel, F. and Najarian, B. (1996), 'Relocation after a disaster: Posttraumatic stress disorder in Armenia after the earthquake', *Journal of the American Academy of Child and Adolescent Psychiatry*, **35**:3, 374–83.

34   *Op. cit.*, note 11.

35   Black, D. (1996), Childhood bereavement. *British Medical Journal*, **312**, 1496. Garmezy, N. and Masten, A.S. (1994), 'Chronic Adversities', in M. Rutter, E. Taylor and L. Hersov (eds), *Child and Adolescent Psychiatry: Modern Approaches* (Chapter 12), Oxford: Blackwell Scientific Publications.

36   Applebaum, D.R. and Burns, G.L. (1991), 'Unexpected childhood death: Post-traumatic stress disorder in surviving siblings and parents', *Journal of Clinical Child Psychology*, **20**:2, 114–20.

37   American Psychiatric Association (1987), *Diagnostic and Statistical Manual of Mental Disorders (3rd. edition, revised)*, Washington, DC.: American Psychiatric Association.

38   Lansdown, R. and Benjamin, G. (1985), 'The development of the concept of death in children aged 5–9 years', *Child: Care, Health and Development*, **11**, 13–20. Speece, M.W. and Brent, S.B. (1984), 'Children's understanding of death: A review of three components of a death concept', *Child Development*, **55**, 1671–86.

39   *Op. cit.*, note 2.

40   Ressler, E., Boothby, N. and Steinbock, D. (1988), *Unaccompanied Children: Care and Protection in Wars, Natural Disasters and Refugee Movements*, New York, Oxford University Press.

41   Jordan, B.K., Marmar, C.R., Fairbanks, J.A., Schlenger, W.E., Kulka, R.A., Hough,

R.L. and Weiss, D.S. (1992), 'Problems in families of male Vietnam veterans with PTSD', *Journal of Consulting and Clinical Psychology*, **60**:6, 916–26.

42   Danieli, Y. (1981), 'Differing adaptational styles in families of survivors of the Nazi holocaust', *Children Today*, 11–12. Krell, R. (1979), 'Holocaust families: the survivors and their children', *Comprehensive Psychiatry*, **20**, 560–68. Sigal, J.J., Silver, D., Rakoff, V. and Ellin, B. (1973), 'Some second-generation effects of survival of the Nazi persecution', *American Journal of Orthopsychiatry*, **43**, 320–27.

43   Kaplan, T. (1996), 'Psychological responses to interpersonal violence: Children', in D. Black, M. Newman, J. Harris-Hendricks and G. Mezey (eds), *Psychological Trauma: A Developmental Approach*, (184–8), London: Gaskell.

44   Mowbray, C.T. (1988), 'Post-traumatic therapy for children who are victims of violence', Chapter 9 in F.M. Ochberg (ed.), *Post-Traumatic Therapy and Victims of Violence*, New York: Brunner/Mazel.

45   Nikapota, A. (1997), The effect of conflict on civilian populations: Children and conflict', in D. Black, M. Newman, J. Harris-Hendriks and G. Mezey (eds), *Psychological Trauma: A Developmental Approach* (161–64, 172–75), London: Gaskell.

46   Deahl, M. (1997), 'The effect of conflict on combatants', in D. Black, M. Newman, J. Harris-Hendriks and G. Mezey (eds), *Psychological Trauma: A Developmental Approach* (134–47), London: Gaskell.

47   Elbedour, S., ten Bensel, R. and Bastien, D.T. (1993), 'Ecological integrated model of children of war: Individual and social psychology', *Child Abuse and Neglect*, **17**, 805–19.

48   Melville, M.B. and Lykes, M.B. (1992), 'Guatemalan Indian children and the sociocultural effects of government-sponsored terrorism', *Social Science and Medicine*, **34**:5, 533–48.

49   Baider, L. and Rosenfeld, E. (1974), 'Effect of parental fears on children in wartime', *Social Casework*, 497–503.

50   Richman, N. (1993), 'Children in situations of political violence', *Journal of Child Psychology and Psychiatry*, **34**:8, 1286–1302.

51   *Op. cit.*, note 45.

52   *Op. cit.*, note 31.

53   *Op. cit.*, note 14.

54   Başoğlu, M., Paker, M., Paker, O., Ozmen, E., Marks, I., Incesu, C., Sahin, D. and Sarimurat, N. (1994), 'Psychological effects of torture: A comparison of tortured with nontortured political activists in Turkey', *American Journal of Psychiatry*, **151**:1, 76–81. Gorst-Unsworth, C., Van Velsen, C. and Turner, S. (1993), 'Prospective pilot study of survivors of torture and organized violence: Examining the existential dilemma', *The Journal of Nervous and Mental Disease*, **181**:4, 263–64. McIvor, R.J. and Turner, S.W. (1995), 'Assessment and treatment approaches for survivors of torture', *British Journal of Psychiatry*, **166**:6, 705–11. Ramsay, R., Gorst-Unsworth, C. and Turner, S. (1993), 'Psychiatric morbidity in survivors of organized state violence including torture: A retrospective series', *British Journal of Psychiatry*, **162**, 55–9.

55   Timerman, J. (1981), *Prisoner Without a Name, Cell Without A Number*, (148), London: Weidenfeld & Nicolson. Translated from the Spanish by Talbot, T.

56   Montgomery, E., Krogh, Y., Jacobsen, A. and Lukman, B. (1992), 'Children of torture victims: Reaction and coping', *Child Abuse and Neglect*, **16**, 797–805.

57   *Op. cit.*, note 48.

58   McCloskey, L.A., Southwick, K., Fernandez-Esquer, M.E. and Locke, C. (1995), 'The psychological effects of political and domestic violence on central American and Mexican immigrant mothers and children', *Journal of Community Psychology*, **23**, 95–

116. *Op. cit.*, note 19. Quirk, G.J. and Casco, L. (1994), 'Stress disorders of families of the disappeared: a controlled study in Honduras', *Social Science and Medicine*, **39**:12, 1675–79.

59   Fundudis, T. (1994), *Children's memory: How good is it? How much do we know about it?* Festschrift in honour of Professor I. Kolvin, London, Tavistock & Portman NHS Trust, September 1994.

60   Goodman, G.S. and Clarke-Stewart, A. (1991), 'Suggestibility in children's testimony: Implications for sexual abuse investigations', in J. Doris (ed.), *The Suggestibility of Children's Recollections*,Washington, DC, American Psychological Association.

61   Sugar, M. (1992), 'Toddlers' traumatic memories', *Infant Mental Health Journal*, **13**:3, 245–51.

62   Garbarino, J. (1993), 'Challenges we face in understanding children and war: A personal essay', *Child Abuse and Neglect*, **17**, 787–93.

63   Siegel, D.J. (1996), 'Memory and trauma', in D. Black, M. Newman, J. Harris-Hendriks and G. Mezey (eds), *Psychological Trauma: A Developmental Approach* (44–53), London: Gaskell.

64   Squire, L.R. (1992), 'Declarative and non-declarative memory: Multiple brain systems supporting learning and memory', *Journal of Cognitive Neuroscience*, **4**:3, 232–43.

65   Fivush, R. and Hudson, J.A. (eds) (1990), *Knowing and Remembering in Young Children,* New York, Cambridge University Press.

66   Ceci, S. and Bruck, M. (1993), 'Suggestibility of the child witness: A historical review and synthesis', *Psychological Bulletin*, **113**: 3, 403–39.

67   Bower, R.A. (1987), 'Commentary on mood and memory', *Behaviour Research and Therapy*, **25**, 443–56. Eich, E. and Metcalfe, J. (1989), 'Mood dependant memory for internal vs. external events', *Journal of Experimental Psychology: Learning, Memory and Cognition*, **15**, 443–55. MacLeod, C. (1990), Mood disorders and Cognition. In M.W. Eysenck (ed.) *Cognitive Psychology – An International Review*. West Sussex, John Wiley and Sons.

68   *Op. cit.*, note 63.

69   Sapolsky, R.M., Uno, H., Rebert, C.S. and Finch, C.E. (1990), 'Hippocampal damage associated with prolonged glucocorticoid exposure in primates', *Journal of Neuroscience*, **10**, 2897–2902.

70   Pettinati, H.M. (ed.) (1988), *Hypnosis and Memory*, New York, Guilford Press. Schumacher, J.F. (ed.) (1991), *Human Suggestibility: Advances in Theory, Research and Applications*, New York, Routledge.

71   *Op. cit.*, note 1.

72   Barker, P. (1994), *The Eye in the Door*, London, Penguin Books

73   Smith, P. and Yule, W. (1996), Paper presented at the European Conference on Stress in Peace Keeping and Humanitarian Forces, Sheffield, UK.

74   Richman, N. (1993), *Communicating with Children. Helping Children in Distress*, London: Save The Children. (Also available in Serbo-Croat).

75   *Op. cit.*, note 31.

76   American College of Physicians (1995), 'The role of the physician and the medical profession in the prevention of international torture and in the treatment of its survivors', *Annals of Internal Medicine*, **122**:8, 607–13.

14 The Torture of Children: Assessing Torture and Devising Methods to Prevent It

Lois Whitman

Introduction

The Children's Rights Project of Human Rights Watch[1] came into being through the issue of the torture of children. In 1992, Human Rights Watch/ Helsinki (then known as Helsinki Watch) released a report, *'Nothing Unusual': The Torture of Children in Turkey*, which documented the torture of children by police during interrogations. Later that year, we released *Children in Northern Ireland: Abused by Security Forces and Paramilitaries*. Both reports were effective. The Turkey report was used, along with other Helsinki Watch reports, to pressure both the United Nations and the European Torture Committees to investigate the systematic use of torture in Turkey. Both committees subsequently issued public condemnations of the systemic, routine use of torture by security forces in Turkey; in each case it was the first time that such a committee statement had been released to the public.

The Northern Ireland report, combined with reports by Amnesty International and the Belfast-based Committee on the Administration of Justice, led to an almost complete end to physical abuse in the holding (detention) centres in Northern Ireland. As a result of these experiences, Human Rights Watch concluded that a Children's Rights Project could play a constructive role in exposing human rights abuses against children and in working to end them. The project began operating in April 1994.

Definition of Torture

International law unequivocally forbids torture. Article 7 of the International Covenant on Civil and Political Rights (ICCPR) states: 'No one shall be subjected to torture or to cruel, inhuman or degrading treatment of punishment.' Both the ICCPR, in Article 4, and the European Convention on Human Rights in Article 15, contain provisions forbidding a country from derogating from anti-torture provisions even in a time of public emergency that threatens the life of the nation. The United Nations Convention on the Rights of the Child in Article 37(a), similarly states that 'No child shall be subjected to torture or other cruel, degrading, or inhuman treatment or punishment ...'

The United Nations Convention Against Torture in Article 1 defines torture as:

> any act by which severe pain or suffering, whether physical or mental, is intentionally inflicted on a person for such purposes as obtaining from him or a third person information or a confession, punishing him for an act he or a third person has committed or is suspected of having committed, or intimidating or coercing him or a third person, or for any reason based on discrimination of any kind, when such pain or suffering is inflicted by or at the instigation of or with the consent or acquiescence of a public official or other person acting in an official capacity ...

The Convention does not define 'cruel, inhuman or degrading treatment'. Instead, it provides that '[E]ach State Party shall undertake to prevent in any territory under its jurisdiction other acts of cruel, inhuman or degrading treatment or punishment which do not amount to torture'. The predominant view among international experts and authorities is that there is no clear border separating torture from cruel, inhuman or degrading treatment or punishment. Decisions of the UN Human Rights Committee, for example, almost always speak of violations of Article 7 of the International Covenant on Civil and Political Rights without specifying whether a given practice constitutes torture, on the one hand, or cruel, inhuman and degrading treatment on the other.[2]

Human Rights Watch has held internal discussions on whether we can distinguish between torture and cruel, inhuman or degrading treatment. Thus far we have not been able to draw a clear line; we believe that each case must be decided on its own facts. One example is the use of isolation; some have described isolation *per se* as torture. Yet the term 'isolation' is used to describe a range of punishments, from being locked in a cell in a corridor in which it may be possible to hear and sometimes see or communicate in some fashion with other people, to a totally closed, dark cell in which it is impossible to see or hear anyone or anything. Isolation is, of course, intentionally inflicted on an inmate; the question is whether the suffering experienced by the inmate was severe. We have concluded that such determinations must be made on a case by case basis.

Cases involving allegations of torture under Article 3 of the European Convention for Human Rights have been brought before the European Court of Human Rights. At least two cases have concerned children. In a 1978 corporal punishment case, *Tyler v. UK,*[3] a 15-year-old boy had been sentenced by a local juvenile court on the Isle of Man to three strokes of the rod as punishment for having hurt another youth in an unprovoked argument. The boy was forced to lower his pants and underwear and bend over. The punishment was carried out in the presence of his father and a doctor. The court held that corporal punishment of a 15-year-old boy did not constitute torture or inhuman treatment under Article 3 of the ECHR. It did find, however, that the punishment was degrading and thus in violation of Article 3. It emphasized that the punishment was a form of institutionalized violence, carried out by people who were strangers to the boy, and that it injured his dignity and physical integrity.

A second case, *Costello-Roberts* v. *United Kingdom,*[4] was decided in 1993. The case involved Jeremy Costello-Roberts, who was seven years old in 1985 and enrolled in a private primary school in England. The director of the school hit Jeremy three times on his shorts with a rubber-soled gym shoe. The Court ruled that the punishment inflicted was not serious enough to violate Article 3.[5]

Children Are, Indeed, Subjected to Torture

There is an understandable reluctance on the part of the public to believe that children are tortured. In many countries, children are described as the hope of the future; many societies think of themselves as child-centred. And yet children are the victims of almost unspeakable acts of torture. Reports issued by the Children's Rights Project have documented many varieties of torture used against children. In Turkey, for example, we talked with children between the ages of 13 and 17 who reported various kinds of treatment during interrogations by police: some had been slapped, punched, hit with truncheons, beaten with wire strips covered with rubber; some were beaten on the palms and on the soles of the feet (falaka); and some had truncheons thrust into the anus. Others had been subjected to a technique called the Palestine hanger, in which a child (or adult) is suspended by the wrists or arms, blindfolded and naked, and then subjected to electric shocks to the genitals and other sensitive parts of the body. In some of the cases we looked into, the children had secured medical reports indicating that their physical condition was consistent with torture.[6]

In Northern Ireland we interviewed at length a 17-year-old boy who reported that he had been punched, choked, kicked and thrown against a wall during interrogation at a police holding centre (detention facility). In addition, the boy reported that police had pulled on his ear so that stitches from an earlier injury were pulled out, causing bleeding. His testicles were repeatedly squeezed, causing bleeding from the penis. He also alleged that police had pulled down his underpants and held a lighted cigarette lighter under his testicles. A doctor who examined the boy later stated in an affidavit that he had found 'severe assaults to his body,' that the boy 'appeared dazed and apprehensive,' and that he could confirm that the boy had been 'subjected to severe ill-treatment'.[7]

In the state of Louisiana in the United States, we found pervasive brutality by guards against children confined in 'training schools' (correctional institutions); children reported being routinely hit and punched. In some cases, guards reportedly separated two children who were fighting, handcuffed them, and then beat them while they were handcuffed. In addition, children were placed in isolation cells for long periods of time.[8] In the state of Georgia in the United States, we found that guards in children's correctional institutions dealt with children who were thought to be suicidal by stripping them to their underwear and using 'four-point restraints' that is, tying them by wrists and ankles to their beds. This technique was also used as punishment for other children.[9] In four major cities in India, we found so-called street children illegally detained by police and severely beaten, most often released without charges after paying bribes to police.[10] In state orphanages in China, we found children tied to their cribs or beds and deliberately deprived of food and water, actually chosen to be starved to death.[11] In other words, we found that these children were first tortured and then deprived of the most basic right – the right to life.[12] This depressing parade of atrocities could, unfortunately, go on and on. We believe that no one would challenge the use of the phrase 'torture, cruel, inhuman and degrading treatment' in describing what police and other government agents did to these children. Addressing these gross abuses within the definition of torture found in the United Nations Committee Against Torture is straightforward and presents no conceptual difficulty.

Other Situations Involving Cruel Treatment of Children

We have investigated other situations that involve appalling treatment of children.

Child Soldiers

We have reported on the use of children, for example, sometimes as young as eight or nine, as soldiers in several countries, most recently in Liberia and Sudan.[13] In Liberia we talked with children between the ages of ten and 16 who had fought, sometimes as long as four years, with one of the warring factions. Some had been forcibly conscripted. Some had been forced by circumstance to join up in order to be fed, or to be taken care of when their families had been killed or had fled. Others had joined from peer pressure and a desire for the power that comes with a loaded rifle. Most had been armed with fully automatic assault weapons, AK 47s or the equivalent. Most had been through experiences that make one wonder how they survived: seeing their parents beheaded; witnessing dreadful atrocities and sometimes being forced to take part in them.

In reporting on these child soldiers and the dreadful experiences they have had, we have sometimes used the language of 'torture, cruel, inhuman and degrading treatment', as for example in describing the cruelties sometimes inflicted on children by the warring factions for which they were fighting (beatings, sexual abuse, elbows tied behind back until rib cage separates (tabay)). But primarily we have looked to the language of humanitarian law, the laws of war, and to Article 39 of the United Nations Convention on the Rights of the Child (CRC) that deals with children in armed conflict.[14] The torture of children within the child soldier context is, in most cases, a secondary consideration.

Bonded Child Labour

In our fact-finding missions to Pakistan and India to look into bonded child labour[15] we have found children as young, unbelievably, as four years old, who had been chained to carpet looms to prevent them from running away. Most children do not start working as bonded labourers at four, however – six or eight are more common ages. Depending on the industry, children can work between 12 and 16 hours a day, six and sometimes seven days a week. Many work in appalling conditions: inhaling chemical fumes or wool fibres that destroy their lungs; carrying molten glass or metal while walking barefoot on shards of broken glass. Some are beaten and cruelly treated. In India we found children who were punished by being hung upside down; those who try to run away are often brought back forcibly by police, in spite of the fact that bonded child labour has been outlawed for many years in both Pakistan and India.

These children, for the most part, are working because their parents have taken an advance payment, sometimes as little as US$17. The children must then work off the advance, but the workplace procedures are set up in such a way that the children can never work off the debt 'interest'; 'expenses' and fines prevent it. In some cases, parents themselves must provide the $17, a virtual impossibility for most. In other cases, children are in 'generational bondage': generations ago a family member was promised to an employer; the understanding is that each generation will provide a new worker to take the older one's place.

Where we find physical abuse, as described above, we use the language and concepts of the United Nations Convention Against Torture. Primarily, however, we look at the International Labour Organization (ILO) Conventions[16] and Article 32 of the Convention on the Rights of the Child for guidance.[17] In general, national laws also forbid the practice of bonded labour. Thus, we examine the ways in which governments fail to comply with their own laws as well as with international treaties and standards. In these cases, we are looking not at abuses directly carried out by governments, but rather at abuses in the private sphere that are tolerated by governments. The failure to protect children is one of omission rather than commission.

Conditions in Detention Facilities and Correctional Institutions in which Children are Confined

We have looked at the conditions in which children are confined in the United States (Louisiana and Georgia, referred to earlier), Jamaica, and Northern Ireland. In Louisiana's secure correctional facilities for children we found pervasive brutality by guards, excessive use of restraints (handcuffs and, on occasion, shackles), excessive use of isolation, inadequate programming and insufficient food. In secure correctional institutions for children in Georgia we found severe overcrowding, poor sanitation, insect infestation, inadequate protection of children from assaults by other children, inadequate programming, and inadequate mental health care. In Jamaica, we found children illegally detained with adults in lockups (jails) in sickening conditions: raw sewage on the floors, insect infestation, overcrowding, excessive heat, poor food.[18] In Northern Ireland we found the Castlereagh Holding Centre (a detention centre) to be dirt-encrusted, smelly and, on occasion, overcrowded. Conditions in the Belfast Remand Centre were unsanitary, crowded. Prisoners, including 17-year-olds, were locked in their cells for as long as 23 hours a day.

In analysing conditions in which children are confined, we have used the term 'torture' only to describe severe physical ill-treatment of children by guards. Nigel Rodley, the UN Special Rapporteur on Torture and other Cruel, Inhuman or Degrading Treatment or Punishment, used the term 'torturous' in describing the 'infernal' conditions he encountered in Moscow's Butyrskaya and Matrosskaya Tishina No 1 remand centres.[19] We have not, however, used this language. Instead, we have focused on the specific ways in which conditions violate specific international standards, chiefly the UN Convention on the Rights of the Child,[20] the UN Rules for the Protection of Juveniles Deprived of their Liberty,[21] the UN Standard Minimum Rules for the Administration of Juvenile Justice (the Beijing Rules),[22] the UN Guidelines for the Prevention of Juvenile Delinquency (Riyadh Guidelines),[23] the Standard Minimum Rules for the Treatment of Prisoners,[24] and the Body of Principles for the Protection of All Persons Under any Form of Detention or Imprisonment.[25] In general, we prefer to refer to specific standards and guidelines.

Methods Used by the Children's Rights Project to Effect Change

The Children's Rights Project uses a number of tools to try to end the abuses that we uncover.

The Use of Documentation

All of our work is dependent on extensive, impartial documentation of abuses. To do this, we research a country's practices here in the United States, using sources from the country concerned and from outside sources. We then send a fact-finding team to the country; the team conducts interviews with victims, families, lawyers, social workers, human rights and religious activists, humanitarian groups, government officials and others. Following the investigation, the team writes a detailed report including its findings and recommendations. It also draws up an advocacy plan for follow-up work.

Working with Local Non-governmental Organizations

Local children's and human rights groups are in a position to know what is actually happening to children. We work closely with local human rights and children's groups, taking our research and advocacy cues from them and working with them to create more community-sensitive, relevant and effective public policies on human rights.

Use of the Media

Publicizing findings on abuses against children, especially in the international press, is extremely important. The media play a crucial role in raising public awareness on human rights abuses. Our work with the media is demonstrated in the release of the recent Human Rights Watch report, *Death by Default: A Policy of Fatal Neglect in China's State Orphanages*. The very wide coverage given to that report around the world by press and television, including a segment on *60 Minutes*, served to bring to light the horrifying plight of orphans who were intentionally left to die. Our report, *The Small Hands of Slavery: Bonded Child Labor in India*, received similar wide coverage.

Embarrassing Offending Governments

Campaigns to end human rights abuses rely, in part, on the ability to hold governments up to public opprobrium, making it more difficult for them to maintain abusive practices than to end them. Sometimes this strategy works; sometimes it doesn't. For it to work, the offending government must be sensitive to international criticism. We employed the strategy of stigmatizing government successfully in Northern Ireland, where we exposed the brutal physical treatment by police during the interrogation of 17-year-olds. The British government, facing broad press coverage and an angry public, ordered the abuses ended. This strategy was also used successfully in Jamaica, where widespread press interest in our findings moved the government to consider our recommendations and take steps to release children from lock-ups in which they had been illegally detained with adults in truly horrifying conditions.

Enlisting the Help of Outside Governments

Other governments can press offending states to change their human rights practices by withholding financial assistance or by isolating them diplomatically. Our China orphanages campaign brought pressure by a number of governments to bear on continuing abusive conditions. Several countries, including Norway, Germany, and Spain, called in their Chinese ambassadors and expressed deep concern about reports of deaths and other neglect in the orphanages.

Pressing International Organizations to Take Action Against Offending Governments

Many international mechanisms exist to promote and protect children's interests, and they can be used to end abuses.[26] Through our advocacy offices in Brussels and Washington, we work to develop campaigns to bring information about the abuse of children to the attention of the European

Union, the Council of Europe, the Organization for Security and Cooperation in Europe, the Organization of American States, and the Organization
for African Unity. Relevant UN agencies include UNICEF, the World Health
Organization, the UN Human Rights Committee, the UN Human Rights
Commission, the International Labour Organization, the Working Group on
Arbitrary Detention, and the Special Rapporteur on Torture. On behalf of
children, the United Nations Committee on the Rights of the Child, the
treaty body that monitors compliance with the UN Convention on the Rights
of the Child, is a particularly useful setting for the dissemination of information about human rights abuses. All of these agencies and instrumentalities
have the capacity to exert diplomatic and/or economic pressure on governments that practice or permit abuse against street children.

The Children's Rights Project has worked closely and with some success
with international organizations. For instance, our report, *United States: A
World Leader in Executing Juveniles*, was used by the United Nations
Committee on Human Rights in March 1995 in strongly criticizing the
United States for its death penalty laws and practices. In addition, our
reports to the UN Committee on the Rights of the Child in Jamaica, Northern Ireland, China, Burma and Bulgaria have been used extensively by that
committee in pressing for change in those countries.

*Establishing and Working with International Coalitions of Children's and
Human Rights Groups for Joint Action*

Many children's organizations that work primarily on child survival and
development are eager to help in the fight to protect children's rights. In this
light, we have co-operated with other children's and human rights organizations on the issues of child soldiers and bonded child labour. We have also
taken part in a UN Study on the Impact of Armed Conflict on Children (the
Machel study), the final report of which was presented to the UN General
Assembly in November 1996.

The strategies enumerated above can bring about significant change; of
course, they don't always work.

The Usefulness of a Multidisciplinary Approach

International law and standards dealing with children frequently refer to
their special vulnerability, and state that children need special care because
they are not as physically and mentally mature as adults. The Children's
Rights Project cites these broad statements, but often cannot give specifics
as to the ways in which, for example, working as a bonded labourer at the
age of six, or serving as a child soldier at eight, can damage children. It

would be useful to be able to give specific citations of the work of psychiatric, psychological and medical authorities who are competent to explain the harm that can result to children in these situations. Professionals with experience and expertise in working with children can explain to governments, intergovernmental groups and private citizens why these abuses can be more damaging to children than to adults. For that reason, we believe that a multidisciplinary approach can be extremely helpful in seeking to end human rights abuses of children around the world.

Notes

1   Human Rights Watch is a nongovernmental monitoring and advocacy organization that investigates human rights abuses in more than 70 countries around the world and works to end them. Its Children's Rights Project was created in 1994 to uncover abuses that uniquely affect children, abuses carried out by governments or by armed rebel groups. Lois Whitman is its director, Jane Schaller is its chair and Geraldine Van Bueren is a member of its Advisory Committee.

2   See General Comment 7(16), para. 2. Report of the Human Rights Committee (1982):

'It may not be necessary to draw sharp distinctions between the various prohibited forms of treatment or punishment.' Cf. above Van Bueren, Opening Pandora's Box: Protecting Children Against Torture or Cruel, Inhuman and Degrading Treatment or Punishment for the potential of such differentiation for children. See also Nikken, *Action contra la torture*, in *The International Fight Against Torture* (Cassese (1991) (ed.)) (concluding that the Inter-American system's conceptual nondifferentiation between torture and cruel, inhuman or degrading treatment has 'enlarged the notion of torture in the context of protecting human rights.')

3   Judgement of the European Court of Human Rights, Series A, No. 26.

4   Judgement of the European Court of Human Rights, Series A, No. 247-C.

5   See the discussion of *Costello-Roberts* in Van Bueren *op. cit.*

6   *'Nothing Unusual': The Torture of Children in Turkey*. Helsinki Watch, New York, 1992.

7   *Children in Northern Ireland: Abused by Security Forces and Paramilitaries*, Helsinki Watch, New York, 1992.

8   *United States: Children in Confinement in Louisiana*, Human Rights Watch Children's Rights Project, New York, 1995.

9   *United States: Modern Capital of Human Rights? Abuses in the State of Georgia*, Human Rights Watch, New York, 1996.

10   *Police Abuse and Killings of Street Children in India*, Human Rights Watch, New York, 1996.

11   *Death by Default: A Policy of Fatal Neglect in China's Orphanages*, Human Rights Watch/Asia, New York, 1996.

12   In other countries we have found children deprived of the most basic right – the right to life. In both Brazil and Colombia we found that thousands of 'street children' had been killed, sometimes by police, and that these extrajudicial executions of children remained almost completely unpunished. *Final Justice: Police and Death Squad Homicides of Adolescents in Brazil*, Human Rights Watch/Americas, New York, 1994.

Generation Under Fire: Children and Violence in Colombia, Human Rights Watch Children's Rights Project, Human Rights Watch/Americas, New York, 1994.

In 1995 we reported that the United States is one of only nine countries in the world that continue to execute people for acts committed before they were 18 years old. The other eight countries were Iraq, Iran, Bangladesh, Pakistan, Saudi Arabia, Yemen, Nigeria and Barbados (Barbadian law since repealed). *United States: A World Leader in Executing Juveniles*. Human Rights Watch Children's Rights Project, New York, 1995.

13   *Easy Prey: Child Soldiers in Liberia*, Human Rights Watch Children's Rights Project, New York, 1994. *Children in Sudan: Slaves, Street Children, and Child Soldiers*, Human Rights Watch/Africa, Human Rights Watch Children's Rights Project, New York, 1995.

14   The Geneva Conventions of 1949 and Protocols I and II (1977) thereto. See further Van Bueren (1995), *The International Law on the Rights of the Child*, Kluwer, at 328–56.

15   *Contemporary Forms of Slavery in Pakistan*. Human Rights Watch/Asia. New York, 1995. *The Small Hands of Slavery: Bonded Child Labour in India*, Human Rights Watch/Children's Rights Project, Human Rights Watch/Asia, New York, 1996.

16   Slavery Convention (1926); Supplementary Convention on the Abolition of Slavery, the Slave Trade, and Institutions and Practices Similar to Slavery (1957); Forced Labour Convention (1930); Abolition of Forced Labour Convention – Convention (105) concerning the Abolition of Forced Labour (1957); and the Convention for the Suppression of the Traffic in Persons and of the Exploitation of the Prostitution of Others (G.A. Resolution 317 (IV) of 2 December 1949.

17   Article 32(1): States Parties recognize the right of the child to be protected from economic exploitation and from performing any work that is likely to be hazardous or to interfere with the child's education, or to be harmful to the child's health or physical, mental, spiritual, moral or social development. See further Van Bueren *The International Law of the Rights of the Child, op. cit.* at 262–75.

18   *Jamaica: Children Improperly Detained in Lockups*, Human Rights Watch Children's Rights Project, New York, 1994.

19   In an oral presentation to the International Symposium on the Protection of Children Against Torture at the Programme on the International Rights of the Child, Queen Mary and Westfield College, University of London; see also UN Economic and Social Council, E/CN.4/1995/34/Add.1. 16 November 1994, 19.

20   G.A. Res. 44/25, 20 November 1989; entered into force 2 September 1990.

21   G.A. Res. 45/13, 2 April 1991.

22   G.A. Res. 40/33, 29 November 1985.

23   G.A. Res. 45/112, 28 March 1991.

24   ECOSOC Res. 663C (XXIV), 31 July 1957 and 2076 (LXII), 13 May 1977.

25   G.A. Res. 43/173, 9 December 1988.

26   See above Sottas, 'A Non-Governmental Organization Perspective of the United Nations' Approach to Children and Torture'.

APPENDICES

Appendix I

United Nations Declaration on the Protection of all Persons from Being Subjected to Torture and Other Cruel, Inhuman or Degrading Treatment or Punishment 1975

Article 1

1. For the purpose of this Declaration, torture means any act by which severe pain or suffering, whether physical or mental, is intentionally inflicted by or at the instigation of a public official on a person for such purposes as obtaining from him or a third person information or confession, punishing him for an act he has committed or is suspected of having committed, or intimidating him or other persons. It does not include pain or suffering arising only from, inherent in or incidental to, lawful sanctions to the extent consistent with the Standard Minimum Rules for the Treatment of Prisoners.
2. Torture constitutes an aggravated and deliberate form of cruel, inhuman or degrading treatment or punishment.

Article 2

Any act of torture or other cruel, inhuman or degrading treatment or punishment is an offence to human dignity and shall be condemned as a denial of the purposes of the Charter of the United Nations and as a violation of the human rights and fundamental freedoms proclaimed in the Universal Declaration of Human Rights.

Article 3

No State may permit or tolerate torture or other cruel, inhuman or degrading treatment or punishment. Exceptional circumstances such as a state of war or a threat of war, internal political instability or any other public emergency may not be invoked as a justification of torture or other cruel, inhuman or degrading treatment or punishment.

Article 4

Each State shall, in accordance with the provisions of this Declaration, take effective measures to prevent torture and other cruel, inhuman or degrading treatment or punishment from being practiced within its jurisdiction.

Article 5

The training of law enforcement personnel and of other public officials who may be responsible for persons deprived of their liberty shall ensure that full account is taken of the prohibition against torture and other cruel, inhuman or degrading treatment or punishment. This prohibition shall also, where appropriate, be included in such general rules or instructions as are issued in regard to the duties and functions of anyone who may be involved in the custody or treatment of such persons.

Article 6

Each State shall keep under systematic review interrogation methods and practices as well as arrangements for the custody and treatment of persons deprived of their liberty in its territory, with a view to preventing any cases of torture of other cruel, inhuman or degrading treatment or punishment.

Article 7

Each State shall ensure that all acts of torture as defined in Article 1 are offences under its criminal law. The same shall apply in regard to acts which constitute participation in, complicity in, incitement to or an attempt to commit torture.

Article 8

Any person who alleges that he has been subjected to torture or other cruel, inhuman or degrading treatment or punishment by or at the instigation of a public official shall have the right to complain to, and to have his case impartially examined by, the competent authorities of the State concerned.

Article 9

Wherever there is reasonable ground to believe that an act of torture as defined in Article 1 has been committed, the competent authorities of the

State concerned shall promptly proceed to an impartial investigation even if there has been no formal complaint.

Article 10

If an investigation under Article 8 or Article 9 establishes that an act of torture as defined in Article 1 appears to have been committed, criminal proceedings shall be instituted against the alleged offender or offenders in accordance with national law. If an allegation of other forms of cruel, inhuman or degrading treatment or punishment is considered to be well founded, the alleged offender or offenders shall be subject to criminal, disciplinary or other appropriate proceedings.

Article 11

Where it is proved that an act of torture or other cruel, inhuman or degrading treatment or punishment has been committed by or at the instigation of a public official, the victim shall be afforded redress and compensation in accordance with national law.

Article 12

Any statement which is established to have been made as a result of torture or other cruel, inhuman or degrading treatment or punishment may not be invoked as evidence against the person concerned or against any other person in any proceedings.

Appendix II

United Nations Convention Against Torture and Other Cruel, Inhuman or Degrading Treatment or Punishment 1984

The States Parties to this Convention,

Considering that, in accordance with the principles proclaimed in the Charter of the United Nations, recognition of the equal and inalienable rights of all members of the human family is the foundation of freedom, justice and peace in the world.

Recognizing that those rights derive from the inherent dignity of the human person,

Considering the obligation of States under the Charter, in particular Article 55, to promote universal respect for, and observance of, human rights and fundamental freedoms.

Having regard to article 5 of the Universal Declaration of Human Rights and article 7 of the International Covenant on Civil and Political Rights, both of which provide that no one shall be subjected to torture or to cruel, inhuman or degrading treatment or punishment.

Having regard also to the Declaration on the Protection of All Persons from Being Subjected to Torture and Other Cruel, Inhuman or Degrading Treatment or Punishment, adopted by the General Assembly on 9 December 1975.

Desiring to make more effective the struggle against torture and other cruel, inhuman or degrading treatment or punishment throughout the world,

Have agreed as follows:

PART I

Article 1

1. For the purposes of this Convention, the term 'torture' means any act by which severe pain or suffering, whether physical or mental, is intentionally

inflicted on a person for such purposes as obtaining from him or a third person information or a confession, punishing him for an act he or a third person has committed or is suspected of having committed, or intimidating or coercing him or a third person, or for any reason based on discrimination of any kind, when such pain or suffering is inflicted by or at the instigation of or with the consent or acquiescence of a public official or other person acting in an official capacity. It does not include pain or suffering arising only from, inherent in or incidental to lawful sanctions.

2.   This article is without prejudice to any international instrument or national legislation which does or may contain provisions of wider application.

Article 2

1.   Each State Party shall take effective legislative, administrative, judicial or other measures to prevent acts of torture in any territory under its jurisdiction.

2.   No exceptional circumstances whatsoever, whether a state of war or a threat of war, internal political instability or any other public emergency, may be invoked as a justification of torture.

3.   An order from a superior officer or a public authority may not be invoked as a justification of torture.

Article 3

1.   No State Party shall expel, return (*"refouler"*) or extradite a person to another State where there are substantial grounds for believing that he would be in danger of being subjected to torture.

2.   For the purpose of determining whether there are such grounds, the competent authorities shall take into account all relevant considerations including, where applicable, the existence in the State concerned of a consistent pattern of gross, flagrant or mass violations of human rights.

Article 4

1.   Each State Party shall ensure that all acts of torture are offences under its criminal law. The same shall apply to an attempt to commit torture and to commit an act by any person which constitutes complicity or participation in torture.

2.   Each State Party shall make these offences punishable by appropriate penalties which take into account their grave nature.

Article 5

1.   Each State Party shall take measures as may be necessary to establish its jurisdiction over the offences referred to in article 4 in the following cases:

   (*a*)   When the offences are committed in any territory under its jurisdiction or on board a ship or aircraft registered in that State;
   (*b*)   When the alleged offender is a national of that State;
   (*c*)   When the victim is a national of that State if that State considers it appropriate.

2.   Each State Party shall likewise take such measures as may be necessary to establish its jurisdiction over such offences in cases where the alleged offender is present in any territory under its jurisdiction and it does not extradite him pursuant to article 8 to any of the States mentioned in paragraph 1 of this article.
3.   This convention does not exclude any criminal jurisdiction exercised in accordance with internal law.

Article 6

1.   Upon being satisfied, after an examination of information available to it, that the circumstances so warrant, any State Party in whose territory a person alleged to have committed any offence referred to in article 4 is present shall take him into custody or take other legal measures to ensure his presence. The custody and other legal measures shall be as provided in the law of that State but may be continued only for such time as is necessary to enable any criminal or extradition proceedings to be instituted.
2.   Such State shall immediately make a preliminary inquiry into the facts.
3.   Any person in custody pursuant to paragraph 1 of his article shall be assisted in communicating immediately with the nearest appropriate representative of the State of which he is a national, or, if he is a stateless person, with the representative of the State where he usually resides.
4.   When a State, pursuant to this article, has taken a person into custody, it shall immediately notify the States referred to in article 5, paragraph 1, of the fact that such person is in custody and of the circumstances which warrant his detention. The State which makes the preliminary inquiry contemplated in paragraph 2 of this article shall promptly report its findings to the said States and shall indicate whether it intends to exercise jurisdiction.

Article 7

1.   The State Party in the territory under whose jurisdiction a person alleged to have committed any offence referred to in article 4 is found shall in the cases contemplated in article 5, if it does not extradite him, submit the case to its competent authorities for the purpose of prosecution.

2.   These authorities shall take their decision in the same manner as in the case of any ordinary offence of a serious nature under the law of that State. In the cases referred to in article 5, paragraph 2, the standards of evidence required for prosecution and conviction shall in no way be less stringent than those which apply in the cases referred to in article 5, paragraph 1.

3.   Any person regarding whom proceedings are brought in connection with any of the offences referred to in article 4 shall be guaranteed fair treatment at all stages of the proceedings.

Article 8

1.   The offences referred to in article 4 shall be deemed to be included as extraditable offences in any extradition treaty existing between States Parties. Parties undertake to include such offences as extraditable offences in every extradition treaty to be concluded between them.

2.   If a State Party which makes extradition conditional on the existence of a treaty receives a request for extradition from another State Party with which it has no extradition treaty, it may consider this Convention as the legal basis for extradition in respect of such offences. Extradition shall be subject to the other conditions provided by the law of the requested State.

3.   States Parties which do not make extradition conditional on the existence of a treaty shall recognize such offences as extraditable offences between themselves subject to the conditions provided by the law of the requested State.

4.   Such offences shall be treated, for the purpose of extradition between State Parties, as if they had been committed not only in the place in which they occurred but also in the territories of the States required to establish their jurisdiction in accordance with article 5, paragraph 1.

Article 9

1.   States Parties shall afford one another the greatest measure of assistance in connection with criminal proceedings brought in respect of any of the offences referred to in article 4, including the supply of all evidence at their disposal necessary for the proceedings.

2.   States Parties shall carry out their obligations under paragraph 1 of this

article in conformity with any treaties on mutual judicial assistance that may exist between them.

Article 10

1.   Each State Party shall ensure that education and information regarding the prohibition against torture are fully included in the training of law enforcement personnel, civil or military, medical personnel, public officials and other persons who may be involved in the custody, interrogation or treatment of any individual subjected to any form of arrest, detention or imprisonment.
2.   Each State Party shall include this prohibition in the rules or instructions issued in regard to the duties and functions of any such persons.

Article 11

Each State Party shall keep under systematic review interrogation rules, instructions, methods and practices as well as arrangements for the custody and treatment of persons subjected to any form of arrest, detention or imprisonment in any territory under its jurisdiction, with a view to preventing any cases of torture.

Article 12

Each State Party shall ensure that its competent authorities proceed to a prompt and impartial investigation, wherever there is reasonable ground to believe that an act of torture has been committed in any territory under its jurisdiction.

Article 13

Each State Party shall ensure that any individual who alleges he has been subjected to torture in any territory under its jurisdiction has the right to complain to, and to have his case promptly and impartially examined by, its competent authorities. Steps shall be taken to ensure that the complainant and witnesses are protected against all ill-treatment or intimidation as a consequence of his complaint or any evidence given.

Article 14

1.   Each State Party shall ensure in its legal system that the victim of an act of torture obtains redress and has an enforceable right to fair and adequate compensation, including the means for as full rehabilitation as possible. In

the event of the death of the victim as a result of an act of torture, his dependants shall be entitled to compensation.

2.　Nothing in this article shall affect any right of the victim or other persons to compensation which may exist under national law.

Article 15

Each State Party shall ensure that any statement which is established to have been made as a result of torture shall not be invoked as evidence in any proceedings, except against a person accused of torture as evidence that the statement was made.

Article 16

1.　Each State Party shall undertake to prevent in any territory under its jurisdiction other acts of cruel, inhuman or degrading treatment or punishment which do not amount to torture as defined in article 1, when such acts are committed by or at the instigation of or with the consent or acquiescence of a public official or other person acting in an official capacity. In particular, the obligations contained in articles 10, 11, 12 and 13 shall apply with the substitution for references to torture or references to other forms of cruel, inhuman or degrading treatment or punishment.

2.　The provisions of this Convention are without prejudice to the provisions of any other international instrument or national law which prohibits cruel, inhuman or degrading treatment or punishment or which relates to extradition or expulsion.

PART II

Article 17

1.　There shall be established a Committee against Torture (hereinafter referred to as the Committee) which shall carry out the functions hereinafter provided. The Committee shall consist of ten experts of high moral standing and recognized competence in the field of human rights, who shall serve in their personal capacity. The experts shall be elected by the States Parties, consideration being given to equitable geographical distribution and to the usefulness of the participation of some persons having legal experience.

2.　The members of the Committee shall be elected by secret ballot from a list of persons nominated by States Parties. Each State Party may nominate one person from among its own nationals. States Parties shall bear in mind the usefulness of nominating persons who are also members of the Human Rights Committee established under the International Covenant on Civil and Political Rights and who are willing to serve on the Committee against Torture.

3. Elections of the members of the Committee shall be held at biennial meetings of States Parties convened by the Secretary-General of the United Nations. At those meetings, for which two thirds of the States Parties shall constitute a quorum, the persons elected to the Committee shall be those who obtain the largest number of votes and an absolute majority of the votes of the representatives of States Parties present and voting.

4. The initial election shall be held no later than six months after the date of the entry into force of this Convention. At least four months before the date of each election, the Secretary-General of the United Nations shall address a letter to the States Parties inviting them to submit their nominations within three months. The Secretary-General shall prepare a list in alphabetical order of all persons thus nominated, indicating the States Parties which have nominated them, and shall submit it to the States Parties.

5. The members of the Committee shall be elected for a term of four years. They shall be eligible for re-election if renominated. However, the term of five of the members elected at the first election shall expire at the end of two years; immediately after the first election the names of these five members shall be chosen by lot by the chairman of the meeting referred to in paragraph 3 of this article.

6. If a member of the Committee dies or resigns or for any other cause can no longer perform his Committee duties, the State Party which nominated him shall appoint another expert from among its nationals to serve for the remainder of his term, subject to the approval of the majority of the States Parties. The approval shall be considered given unless half or more of the States Parties respond negatively within six weeks after having been informed by the Secretary-General of the United Nations of the proposed appointment.

7. States Parties shall be responsible for the expenses of the members of the Committee while they are in performance of Committee duties.

Article 18

1. The Committee shall elect its officers for a term of two years. They may be re-elected.

2. The Committee shall establish its own rules of procedure, but these rules shall provide, *inter alia*, that:

    (*a*) Six members shall constitute a quorum;

(*b*)   Decisions of the Committee shall be made by a majority vote of the members present.

3.   The Secretary-General of the United Nations shall provide the necessary staff and facilities for the effective performance of the functions of the Committee under this Convention.

4.   The Secretary-General of the United Nations shall convene the initial meeting of the Committee. After its initial meeting, the Committee shall meet at such times as shall be provided in its rules of procedure.

5.   The States Parties shall be responsible for expenses incurred in connection with the holding of meetings of the States Parties and of the Committee, including reimbursement to the United Nations for any expenses, such as the cost of staff and facilities, incurred by the United Nations pursuant to paragraph 3 of this article.

Article 19

1.   The States Parties shall submit to the Committee, through the Secretary-General of the United Nations, reports on the measures they have taken to give effect to their undertakings under this Convention, within one year after the entry into force of the Convention for the State Party concerned. Thereafter the States Parties shall submit supplementary reports every four years on any new measures taken and such other reports as the Committee may request.

2.   The Secretary-General of the United Nations shall transmit the reports to all States Parties.

3.   Each report shall be considered by the Committee which may make such general comments on the report as it may consider appropriate and shall forward these to the State Party concerned. That State Party may respond with any observations it chooses to the Committee.

4.   The Committee may, at its discretion, decide to include any comments made by it in accordance with paragraph 3 of this article, together with the observations thereon received from the State Party concerned, in its annual report made in accordance with article 24. If so requested by the State Party concerned, the Committee may also include a copy of the report submitted under paragraph 1 of this article.

Article 20

1.   If the Committee receives reliable information which appears to it to contain well-founded indications that torture is being systematically practiced in the territory of a State Party, the Committee shall invite that State Party to

co-operate in the examination of the information and to this end to submit observations with regard to the information concerned.

2.   Taking into account any observations which may have been submitted by the State Party concerned, as well as any other relevant information available to it, the Committee may, if it decides that this is warranted, designate one or more of its members to make a confidential inquiry and to report to the Committee urgently.

3.   If an inquiry is made in accordance with paragraph 2 of this article, the Committee shall seek the co-operation of the State Party concerned. In agreement with that State Party, such an inquiry may include a visit to its territory.

4.   After examining the findings of its member or members submitted in accordance with paragraph 2 of this article, the Committee shall transmit these findings to the State Party concerned together with any comments or suggestions which seem appropriate in view of the situation.

5.   All the proceedings of the Committee referred to in paragraphs 1 to 4 of this article shall be confidential, and at all stages of the proceedings the co-operation of the State Party shall be sought. After such proceedings have been completed with regard to an inquiry made in accordance with paragraph 2, the Committee may, after consultations with the State Party concerned, decide to include a summary account of the results of the proceedings in its annual report in accordance with article 24.

Article 21

1.   A State Party to this Convention may at any time declare under this article that it recognizes the competence of the Committee to receive and consider communications to the effect that a State Party claims that another State Party is not fulfilling its obligations under this Convention. Such communications may be received and considered according to the procedures laid down in this article only if submitted by a State Party which has made a declaration recognizing in regard to itself the competence of the Committee. No communications shall be dealt with by the Committee under this article if it concerns a State Party which has not made such a declaration. Communications received under this article shall be dealt with in accordance with the following procedure:

(*a*)   If a State Party considers that another State Party is not giving effect to the provisions of this Convention, it may, by written communication, bring the matter to the attention of that State Party. Within three months after the receipt of the communication the receiving State shall afford the State which sent the communication an explanation or any other statement in writing clarifying the matter, which should include, to the extent possible and pertinent, reference to domestic procedures and remedies taken, pending or available in the matter;

(*b*)   If the matter is not adjusted to the satisfaction of both States Parties concerned within six months after the receipt by the receiving State of the initial communications, either State shall have the right to refer the matter to the Committee, by notice given to the Committee and to the other State;

(*c*)   The Committee shall deal with a matter referred to it under this article only after it has ascertained that all domestic remedies have been invoked and exhausted in the matter, in conformity with the generally recognized principles of international law. This shall not be the rule where the application of the remedies is unreasonably prolonged or is unlikely to bring effective relief to the person who is the victim of the violation of this Convention;

(*d*)   The Committee shall hold closed meetings when examining communications under this article;

(*e*)   Subject to the provisions of subparagraph (*c*), the Committee shall make available its good offices to the States Parties concerned with a view to a friendly solution of the matter on the basis of respect for the obligations provided for in this Convention. For this purpose, the Committee may, when appropriate, set up an *ad hoc* conciliation commission;

(*f*)   In any matter referred to it under this article, the Committee may call upon the States Parties concerned, referred to in subparagraph (*b*), to supply any relevant information;

(*g*)   The States Parties concerned, referred to in subparagraph (*b*), shall have the right to be represented when the matter is being considered by the Committee and to make submissions orally and/or in writing;

(*h*)   The Committee shall, within twelve months after the date of receipt of notice under subparagraph (*b*), submit a report:

   (i)   If a solution within the terms of subparagraph (*e*) is reached, the Committee shall confine its report to a brief statement of the facts and of the solution reached;

   (ii)   If a solution within the terms of subparagraph (*e*) is not reached, the Committee shall confine its report to a brief statement of the facts; the written submissions and record of the oral submissions made by the States Parties concerned shall be attached to the report.

In every matter, the report shall be communicated to the States Parties concerned.

2. The provisions of this article shall come into force when five States Parties of this Convention have made declarations under paragraph 1 of this article. Such declarations shall be deposited by the States Parties with the Secretary-General of the United Nations, who shall transmit copies thereof to the other States Parties. A declaration may be withdrawn at any time by notification to the Secretary-General. Such a withdrawal shall not prejudice the consideration of any matter which is the subject of a communication already transmitted under this article; no further communication by any State Party shall be received under this article after the notification of withdrawal of the declaration has been received by the Secretary-General, unless the State Party concerned has made a new declaration.

Article 22

1. A State Party to this Convention may at any time declare under this article that it recognizes the competence of the Committee to receive and consider communications from or on behalf of individuals subject to its jurisdiction who claim to be victims of a violation by a State Party of the provisions of the Convention. No communication shall be received by the Committee if it concerns a State Party which has not made such a declaration.
2. The Committee shall consider inadmissible any communication under this article which is anonymous or which it considers to be an abuse of the right of submission of such communications or to be incompatible with the provisions of this Convention.
3. Subject to the provisions of paragraph 2, the Committee shall bring any communications submitted to it under this article to the attention of the State Party to this Convention which has made a declaration under paragraph 1 and is alleged to be violating any provisions of the Convention. Within six months, the receiving State shall submit to the Committee written explanations or statements clarifying the matter and the remedy, if any, that may have been taken by that State.
4. The Committee shall consider communications received under this article in the light of all information made available to it by or on behalf of the individual and by the State Party concerned.
5. The Committee shall not consider any communications from an individual under this article unless it has ascertained that:

(*a*) The same matter has not been, and is not being, examined under another procedure of international investigation or settlement;
(*b*) The individual has exhausted all available domestic remedies; this shall not be the rule where the application of the remedies is unreas-

onably prolonged or is unlikely to bring effective relief to the person who is the victim of the violation of this Convention.

6.   The Committee shall hold closed meetings when examining communications under this article.

7.   The Committee shall forward its views to the State Party concerned and to the individual.

8.   The provisions of this article shall come into force when five States Parties to this Convention have made declarations under paragraph 1 of this article. Such declarations shall be deposited by the States Parties with the Secretary-General of the United Nations, who shall transmit copies thereof to the other States Parties. A declaration may be withdrawn at any time by notification to the Secretary-General. Such a withdrawal shall not prejudice the consideration of any matter which is the subject of a communication already transmitted under this article; no further communication by or on behalf of an individual shall be received under this article after the notification of withdrawal of the declaration has been received by the Secretary-General, unless the State Party has made a new declaration.

Article 23

The members of the Committee and of the *ad hoc* conciliation commissions which may be appointed under article 21, paragraph 1 (*e*), shall be entitled to the facilities, privileges and immunities of experts on mission for the United Nations as laid down in the relevant sections of the Convention on the Privileges and Immunities of the United Nations.

Article 24

The Committee shall submit an annual report on its activities under this Convention to the States Parties and to the General Assembly of the United Nations.

PART III

Article 25

1.   This Convention is open for signature by all States.

2.   This Convention is subject to ratification. Instruments of ratification shall be deposited with the Secretary-General of the United Nations.

Article 26

This Convention is open to accession by all States. Accession shall be effected by the deposit of an instrument of accession with the Secretary-General of the United Nations.

Article 27

1.   This Convention shall enter into force on the thirtieth day after the date of the deposit with the Secretary-General of the United Nations of the twentieth instrument of ratification or accession.
2.   For each State ratifying this Convention or acceding to it after the deposit of the twentieth instrument of ratification or accession, the Convention shall enter into force on the thirtieth day after the date of the deposit of its own instrument of ratification or accession.

Article 28

1.   Each State may, at the time of signature or ratification of this Convention or accession thereto, declare that it does not recognize the competence of the Committee provided for in article 20.
2.   Any State Party having made a reservation in accordance with paragraph 1 of this article may, at any time, withdraw this reservation by notification to the Secretary-General of the United Nations.

Article 29

1.   Any State Party to this Convention may propose an amendment and file it with the Secretary-General of the United Nations. The Secretary-General shall thereupon communicate the proposed amendment to the States Parties with a request that they notify him whether they favour a conference of States Parties for the purpose of considering and voting upon the proposal. In the event that within four months from the date of such communication at least one third of the State Parties favours such a conference, the Secretary-General shall convene the conference under the auspices of the United Nations. Any amendment adopted by a majority of the States Parties present and voting at the conference shall be submitted by the Secretary-General to all the States Parties for acceptance.
2.   An amendment adopted in accordance with paragraph 1 of this article shall enter into force when two thirds of the States Parties to this Convention have notified the Secretary-General of the United Nations that they have accepted it in accordance with their respective constitutional processes.

3.   When amendments enter into force, they shall be binding on those States Parties which have accepted them, other States Parties still being bound by the provisions of this Convention and any earlier amendments which they have accepted.

Article 30

1.   Any dispute between two or more States Parties concerning the interpretation or application of this Convention which cannot be settled through negotiation shall, at the request of one of them, be submitted to arbitration. If within six months from the date of the request for arbitration the Parties are unable to agree on the organization of the arbitration, any one of those Parties may refer the dispute to the International Court of Justice by request in conformity with the Statute of the Court.

2.   Each State may, at the time of signature or ratification of this Convention or accession thereto, declare that it does not consider itself bound by paragraph 1 of this article. The other States Parties shall not be bound by paragraph 1 of this article with respect to any State Party having made such a reservation.

3.   Any State Party having made a reservation in accordance with paragraph 2 of this article may at any time withdraw this reservation by notification to the Secretary-General of the United Nations.

Article 31

1.   A State Party may denounce this Convention by written notification to the Secretary-General of the United Nations. Denunciation becomes effective one year after the date of receipt of the notification by the Secretary-General.

2.   Such a denunciation shall not have the effect of releasing the State Party from its obligations under this Convention in regard to any act or omission which occurs prior to the date at which the denunciation becomes effective, nor shall denunciation prejudice in any way the continued consideration of any matter which is already under consideration by the Committee prior to the date at which the denunciation becomes effective.

3.   Following the date at which the denunciation of a State Party becomes effective, the Committee shall not commence consideration of any new matter regarding that State.

Article 32

The Secretary-General of the United Nations shall inform all States Members of the United Nations and all States which have signed this Convention or acceded to it of the following:

(*a*) Signatures, ratifications and accessions under articles 25 and 26;
(*b*) The date of entry into force of this Convention under article 27 and the date of the entry into force of any amendments under article 29;
(*c*) Denunciations under article 31.

Article 33

1. This Convention, of which the Arabic, Chinese, English, French, Russian and Spanish texts are equally authentic, shall be deposited with the Secretary-General of the United Nations.
2. The Secretary-General of the United Nations shall transmit certified copies of this Convention to all States.

Appendix III

Inter-American Convention to Prevent and Punish Torture 1985

The American States signatory to the present Convention,

Aware of the provision of the American Convention on Human Rights that no one shall be subjected to torture or to cruel, inhuman, or degrading punishment or treatment;

Reaffirming that all acts of torture or any other cruel, inhuman, or degrading treatment or punishment constitute an offense against human dignity and a denial of the principles set forth in the Charter of the Organization of American States and in the Charter of the United Nations and are violations of the fundamental human rights and freedoms proclaimed in the American Declaration of the Rights and Duties of Man and the Universal Declaration of Human Rights;

Noting that, in order for the pertinent rules contained in the aforementioned global and regional instruments to take effect, it is necessary to draft an Inter-American Convention that prevents and punishes torture;

Reaffirming their purpose of consolidating in this hemisphere the conditions that allow for recognition of and respect for the inherent dignity of man, and ensure the full exercise of his fundamental rights and freedoms,

Have agreed upon the following:

Article 1

The States Parties shall prevent and punish torture in accordance with the terms of this Convention.

Article 2

For the purposes of this Convention, torture shall be understood to be any act intentionally performed whereby physical or mental pain or suffering is inflicted on a person for purposes of criminal investigation, as a means of intimidation, as personal punishment, as a preventive measure, as a penalty, or for any other purpose. Torture shall also be understood to be the use of methods upon a person intended to obliterate the personality of the victim or to diminish his physical or mental capacities, even if they do not cause physical pain or mental anguish.

The concept of torture shall not include physical or mental pain or suffering that is inherent in or solely the consequence of lawful measures, provided that they do not include the performance of the acts or use of the methods referred to in this article.

Article 3

The following shall be held guilty of the crime of torture:

(a) A public servant or employee who acting in that capacity orders, instigates or induces the use of torture, or who directly commits it or who, being able to prevent it, fails to do so.

(b) A person who at the instigation of a public servant or employee mentioned in subparagraph (a) orders, instigates or induces the use of torture, directly commits it or is an accomplice thereto.

Article 4

The fact of having acted under orders of a superior shall not provide exemption from the corresponding criminal liability.

Article 5

The existence of circumstances such as a state of war, threat of war, state of siege or of emergency, domestic disturbance or strife, suspension of constitutional guarantees, domestic political instability, or other public emergencies or disasters shall not be invoked or admitted as justification for the crime of torture.

Neither the dangerous character of the detainee or prisoner, nor the lack of security of the prison establishment or penitentiary shall justify torture.

Article 6

In accordance with the terms of Article 1, the States Parties shall take effective measures to prevent and punish torture within their jurisdiction.

The States Parties shall ensure that all acts of torture and attempts to commit torture are offenses under their criminal law and shall make such acts punishable by severe penalties that take into account their serious nature.

The States Parties likewise shall take effective measures to prevent and punish other cruel, inhuman, or degrading treatment or punishment within their jurisdiction.

Article 7

The States Parties shall take measures so that, in the training of police officers and other public officials responsible for the custody of persons temporarily or definitively deprived of their freedom, special emphasis shall be put on the prohibition of the use of torture in interrogation, detention, or arrest.

The States Parties likewise shall take similar measures to prevent other cruel, inhuman, or degrading treatment or punishment.

Article 8

The States Parties shall guarantee that any person making an accusation of having been subjected to torture within their jurisdiction shall have the right to an impartial examination of his case.

Likewise, if there is an accusation or well-grounded reason to believe that an act of torture has been committed within their jurisdiction, the States Parties shall guarantee that their respective authorities will proceed ex officio and immediately to conduct an investigation into the case and to initiate, whenever appropriate, the corresponding criminal process.

After all the domestic legal procedures of the respective State and the corresponding appeals have been exhausted, the case may be submitted to the international fora whose competence have been recognized by that state.

Article 9

The States Parties undertake to incorporate into their national laws regulations guaranteeing adequate compensation for victims of torture.

None of the provisions of this article shall affect the right to receive compensation that the victim or other persons may have by virtue of existing national legislation.

Article 10

No statement that is verified as having been obtained through torture shall be admissible as evidence in a legal proceeding, except in a legal action taken against a person or persons accused of having elicited it through acts of torture, and only as evidence that the accused obtained such statement by such means.

Article 11

The States Parties shall take the necessary steps to extradite anyone accused of having committed the crime of torture or sentenced for commission of that crime, in accordance with their respective national laws on extradition and their international commitments on this matter.

Article 12

Every State Party shall take the necessary measures to establish its jurisdiction over the crime described in this Convention in the following cases:

(*a*) When torture has been committed within its jurisdiction;
(*b*) When the alleged criminal is a national of that State; or
(*c*) When the victim is a national of that State and it so deems appropriate.

Every State Party shall also take the necessary measures to establish its jurisdiction over the crime described in this Convention when the alleged criminal is within the area under its jurisdiction and it does not proceed to extradite him in accordance with Article 11.

This Convention does not exclude criminal jurisdiction exercised in accordance with domestic law.

Article 13

The crime referred to in Article 2 shall be deemed to be included among the extraditable crimes in every extradition treaty entered into between States Parties. The States Parties undertake to include the crime of torture as an extraditable offence in every extradition treaty to be concluded between them.

Every State Party that makes extradition conditional on the existence of a treaty may, if it receives a request for extradition from another State Party with which it has no extradition treaty, consider this Convention as the legal basis for extradition in respect of the crime of torture. Extradition shall be subject to the other conditions that may be required by the law of the requested State.

States Parties which do not make extradition conditional on the existence of a treaty shall recognize such crimes as extraditable offences between themselves, subject to the conditions required by the laws of the requested State.

Extradition shall not be granted nor shall the person sought be returned when there are grounds to believe that his life is in danger, that he will be subjected to torture or to cruel, inhuman or degrading treatment, or that he will be tried by special or ad hoc courts in the requesting State.

Article 14

When a State Party does not grant the extradition, the case shall be submitted to its competent authorities as if the crime had been committed within its jurisdiction, for the purposes of investigation, and when appropriate, for criminal action, in accordance with its national law. Any decision adopted by these authorities shall be communicated to the State that has requested the extradition.

Article 15

No provision of this Convention may be interpreted as limiting the right of asylum, when appropriate, nor as altering the obligations of the States Parties in the matter of extradition.

Article 16

This Convention shall not affect the provisions of the American Convention on Human Rights, other conventions on the subject, or the Statutes of the Inter-American Commission on Human Rights, with respect to the crime of torture.

Article 17

The States Parties shall inform the Inter-American Commission on Human Rights of any legislative, judicial, administrative, or other measures they adopt in application of his Convention.

In keeping with its duties and responsibilities, the Inter-American Commission on Human Rights will endeavour in its annual report to analyze the existing situation in the member states of the Organization of American States in regard to the prevention and elimination of torture.

Article 18

This Convention is open to signature by the member states of the Organization of American States.

Article 19

This Convention is subject to ratification. The instruments of ratification shall be deposited with the General Secretariat of the Organization of American States.

Article 20

This Convention is open to accession by any other American state. The instruments of accession shall be deposited with the General Secretariat of the Organization of American States.

Article 21

The States Parties may, at the time of approval, signature, ratification, or accession, make reservations to this Convention, provided that such reservations are not incompatible with the object and purpose of the Convention and concern one or more specific provisions.

Article 22

This Convention shall enter into force on the thirtieth day following the date on which the second instrument of ratification is deposited. For each State ratifying or acceding to the Convention after the second instrument of ratification has been deposited, the Convention shall enter into force on the thirtieth day following the date on which that State deposits its instrument of ratification or accession.

Article 23

This Convention shall remain in force indefinitely, but may be denounced by any State Party. The instrument of denunciation shall be deposited with the General Secretariat of the Organization of American States. After one year from the date of deposit of the instrument of denunciation, this Convention shall cease to be in effect for the denouncing State but shall remain in force for the remaining State Parties.

Article 24

The original instrument of this Convention, the English, French, Portuguese, and Spanish texts of which are equally authentic, shall be deposited with the General Secretariat of the Organization of American States, which shall send a certified copy to the Secretariat of the United Nations for registration and publication, in accordance with the provisions of Article 102 of the United Nations Charter. The General Secretariat of the Organization of American States shall notify the member states of the Organization and the states that have acceded to the Convention of signatures and of deposits of instruments of ratification, accession, and denunciations, as well as reservations, if any.

2.   To remind the member states that, under the terms of Article 18 of the above Convention, it is open to signature by the member states of the Organization of American States.

3.   To invite the governments of the member states to sign the Inter-American Convention to Prevent and Punish Torture during the fifteenth regular sessions of the General Assembly.

Appendix IV

The European Convention for the Prevention of Torture and Inhuman or Degrading Treatment or Punishment 1987

The member States of the Council of Europe, signatory hereto,

Having regard to the provisions of the Convention for the Protection of Human Rights and Fundamental Freedoms;

Recalling that, under Article 3 of the same Convention, 'no one shall be subjected to torture or to inhuman or degrading treatment or punishment';

Noting that the machinery provided for in that Convention operates in relation to persons who allege that they are victims of violations of Article 3;

Convinced that the protection of persons deprived of their liberty against torture and inhuman or degrading treatment or punishment could be strengthened by non-judicial means of a preventive character based on visits,

Have agreed as follows:

CHAPTER 1

Article 1

There shall be established a European Committee for the Prevention of Torture and Inhuman or Degrading Treatment or Punishment (hereinafter referred to as 'the Committee'). The Committee shall, by means of visits, examine the treatment of persons deprived of their liberty with a view to strengthening, if necessary, the protection of such persons from torture and from inhuman or degrading treatment or punishment.

Article 2

Each party shall permit visits, in accordance with this Convention, to any place within its jurisdiction where persons are deprived of their liberty by a public authority.

Article 3

In the application of this Convention, the Committee and the competent national authorities of the Party concerned shall co-operate with each other.

CHAPTER II

Article 4

1. The Committee shall consist of a number of members equal to that of the Parties.
2. The members of the Committee shall be chosen from among persons of high moral character, known for their competence in the field of human rights or having professional experience in the areas covered by this Convention.
3. No two members of the Committee may be nationals of the same State.
4. The members shall serve in their individual capacity, shall be independent and impartial, and shall be available to serve the Committee effectively.

Article 5

1. The Members of the Committee shall be elected by the Committee of Ministers of the Council of Europe by an absolute majority of votes, from a list of names drawn up by the Bureau of the Consultative Assembly of the Council of Europe; each national delegation of the Parties in the Consultative Assembly shall put forward three candidates, of whom two at least shall be its nationals.
2. The same procedure shall be followed in filling casual vacancies.
3. The members of the Committee shall be elected for a period of four years. They may only be re-elected once. However, among the members elected at the first election, the terms of three members shall expire at the end of two years. The members whose terms are to expire at the end of the initial period of two years shall be chosen by lot by the Secretary General of the Council of Europe immediately after the first election has been completed.

Article 6

1. The Committee shall meet in camera. A quorum shall be equal to the majority of its members. The decisions of the Committee shall be taken by a majority of the members present, subject to the provisions of Article 10, paragraph 2.
2. The Committee shall draw up its own rules of procedure.
3. The Secretariat of the Committee shall be provided by the Secretary General of the Council of Europe.

CHAPTER III

Article 7

1. The Committee shall organize visits to places referred to in Article 2. Apart from periodic visits, the Committee may organize such other visits as appear to it to be required in the circumstances.
2. As a general rule, the visits shall be carried out by at least two members of the Committee. The Committee may, if it considers it necessary, be assisted by experts and interpreters.

Article 8

1. The Committee shall notify the Government of the Party concerned of its intention to carry out a visit. After such notification, it may at any time visit any place referred to in Article 2.
2. A Party shall provide the Committee with the following facilities to carry out its task:

(*a*) access to its territory and the right to travel without restriction;
(*b*) full information on the places where persons deprived of their liberty are being held;
(*c*) unlimited access to any place where persons are deprived of their liberty, including the right to move inside such places without restriction;
(*d*) other information available to the Party which is necessary for the Committee to carry out its task. In seeking such information, the Committee shall have regard to applicable rules of national law and professional ethics.

3.   The Committee may interview in private persons deprived of their liberty.

4.   The Committee may communicate freely with any person whom it believes can supply relevant information.

5.   If necessary, the Committee may immediately communicate observations to the competent authorities of the Party concerned.

Article 9

1.   In exceptional circumstances, the competent authorities of the Party concerned may make representatives to the Committee against a visit at the time or to the particular place proposed by the Committee. Such representations may only be made on grounds of national defence, public safety, serious disorder in places where persons are deprived of their liberty, the medical condition of a person or that an urgent interrogation relating to a serious crime is in progress.

2.   Following such representations, the Committee and the Party shall immediately enter into consultations in order to clarify the situation and seek agreement on arrangements to enable the Committee to exercise its functions expeditiously. Such arrangements may include the transfer to another place of any person whom the Committee proposed to visit. Until the visit takes place, the Party shall provide information to the Committee about any person concerned.

Article 10

1.   After each visit, the Committee shall draw up a report on the facts found during the visit, taking account of any observations which may have been submitted by the Party concerned. It shall transmit to the latter its report containing any recommendations it considers necessary. The Committee may consult with the Party with a view to suggesting, if necessary, improvements in the protection of persons deprived of their liberty.

2.   If the Party fails to co-operate or refuses to improve the situation in the light of the Committee's recommendations, the Committee may decide, after the Party has had an opportunity to make known its views, by a majority of two-thirds of its members to make a public statement on the matter.

Article 11

1.   The information gathered by the Committee in relation to a visit, its report and its consultations with the Party concerned shall be confidential.

2. The Committee shall publish its report, together with any comments of the Party concerned, whenever requested to do so by that Party.
3. However, no personal data shall be published without the express consent of the person concerned.

Article 12

Subject to the rules of confidentiality in Article 11, the Committee shall every year submit to the Committee of Ministers a general report on its activities which shall be transmitted to the Consultative Assembly and made public.

Article 13

The members of the Committee, experts and other persons assisting the Committee are required, during and after their terms of office, to maintain the confidentiality of the facts or information of which they have become aware during the discharge of their functions.

Article 14

1. The names of persons assisting the Committee shall be specified in the notification under Article 8, paragraph 1.
2. Experts shall act on the instructions and under the authority of the Committee. They shall have particular knowledge and experience in the areas covered by this Convention and shall be bound by the same duties of independence, impartiality and availability as the members of the Committee.
3. A Party may exceptionally declare that an expert or other person assisting the Committee may not be allowed to take part in a visit to a place within its jurisdiction.

CHAPTER IV

Article 15

Each Party shall inform the Committee of the name and address of the authority competent to receive notifications to its Government, and of any liaison officer it may appoint.

Article 16

The Committee, its members and experts referred to in Article 7, paragraph 2, shall enjoy the privileges and immunities set out in the annex to this Convention.

Article 17

1.   This Convention shall not prejudice the provisions of domestic law or any international agreement which provide greater protection for persons deprived of their liberty.
2.   Nothing in this Convention shall be construed as limiting or derogating from the competence of the organs of the European Convention on Human Rights or from the obligations assumed by the Parties under that Convention.
3.   The Committee shall not visit places which representatives or delegates of protecting powers or the International Committee of the Red Cross effectively visit on a regular basis by virtue of the Geneva Conventions of 12 August 1949 and the Additional Protocols of 18 June 1977 thereto.

CHAPTER V

Article 18

This Convention shall be open for signature by the member States of the Council of Europe. It is subject to ratification, acceptance or approval. Instruments of ratification, acceptance or approval shall be deposited with the Secretary General of the Council of Europe.

Article 19

1.   This Convention shall enter into force on the first day of the month following the expiration of a period of three months after the date on which seven member States of the Council of Europe have expressed their consent to be bound by the Convention in accordance with the provisions of Article 18.
2.   In respect of any member State which subsequently expresses its consent to be bound by it, the Convention shall enter into force on the first day of the month following the expiration of a period of three months after the date of the deposit of the instrument of ratification, acceptance or approval.

Article 20

1. Any State may at the time of signature or when depositing its instrument of ratification, acceptance or approval, specify the territory or territories to which this Convention shall apply.
2. Any State may at any later date, by a declaration addressed to the Secretary General of the Council of Europe, extend the application of this Convention to any other territory specified in the declaration. In respect of such territory the Convention shall enter into force on the first day of the month following the expiration of a period of three months after the date of receipt of such declaration by the Secretary General.
3. Any declaration made under the two preceding paragraphs may, in respect of any territory specified in such declaration, be withdrawn by a notification addressed to the Secretary General. The withdrawal shall become effective on the first day of the month following the expiration of a period of three months after the date of receipt of such notification by the Secretary General.

Article 21

No reservation may be made in respect of the provisions of this Convention.

Article 22

1. Any Party may, at any time, denounce this Convention by means of a notification addressed to the Secretary General of the Council of Europe.
2. Such denunciation shall become effective on the first day of the month following the expiration of a period of twelve months after the date of receipt of the notification by the Secretary General.

Article 23

The Secretary General of the Council of Europe shall notify the member States of the Council of Europe of:

(*a*)   any signature;
(*b*)   the deposit of any instrument of ratification, acceptance or approval;
(*c*)   any date of entry into force of this Convention in accordance with Articles 19 and 20;
(*d*)   any other act, notification or communication relating to this Convention, except for action taken in pursuance of Articles 8 and 10.

In witness whereof, the undersigned, being duly authorized thereto, have signed this Convention.

Done at Strasbourg, this 26th day of November 1987, in English and French, both texts being equally authentic, in a single copy which shall be deposited in the archives of the Council of Europe. The Secretary General of the Council of Europe shall transmit certified copies to each member State of the Council of Europe.

ANNEX
Privileges and Immunities

(Article 16)

1.   For the purpose of this annex, references to members of the Committee shall be deemed to include references to experts mentioned in Article 7, paragraph 2.

2.   The members of the Committee shall, while exercising their functions and during journeys made in the exercise of their functions, enjoy the following privileges and immunities:

   (*a*)   immunity from personal arrest or detention and from seizure of their personal baggage and, in respect of words spoken or written and all acts done by them in their official capacity, immunity from legal process of every kind;

   (*b*)   exemption from any restrictions on their freedom of movement: on exit from and return to their country of residence, and entry into and exit from the country in which they exercise their functions, and from alien registration in the country which they are visiting or through which they are passing in the exercise of their functions.

3.   In the course of journeys undertaken in the exercise of their functions, the members of the Committee shall, in the matter of customs and exchange control, be accorded:

   (*a*)   by their own government, the same facilities as those accorded to senior officials travelling abroad on temporary official duty;

   (*b*)   by the governments of other Parties, the same facilities as those accorded to representatives of foreign governments on temporary official duty.

4.   Documents and papers of the Committee, insofar as they relate to the business of the Committee, shall be inviolable.

The official correspondence and other official communications of the Committee may not be held up or subjected to censorship.

5.   In order to secure for the members of the Committee complete freedom of speech and complete independence in the discharge of their duties, the immunity from legal process in respect of words spoken or written and all acts done by them in discharging their duties shall continue to be accorded, notwithstanding that the persons concerned are no longer engaged in the discharge of such duties.

6.   Privileges and immunities are accorded to the members of the Committee, not for the personal benefit of the individuals themselves but in order to safeguard the independent exercise of their functions. The Committee alone shall be competent to waive the immunity of its members; it has not only the right, but is under a duty, to waive the immunity of one of its members in any case where, in its opinion, the immunity would impede the course of justice, and where it can be waived without prejudice to the purpose for which the immunity is accorded.

Appendix V

United Nations Convention on the Rights of the Child 1989

Article 1

For the purposes of the present Convention, a child means every human being below the age of eighteen years unless, under the law applicable to the child, majority is attained earlier.

Article 2

1.   States Parties shall respect and ensure the rights set forth in the present Convention to each child within their jurisdiction without discrimination of any kind, irrespective of the child's or his or her parent's or legal guardian's race, colour, sex, language, religion, political or other opinion; national, ethnic or social origin, property, disability, birth or other status.
2.   States Parties shall take all appropriate measures to ensure that the child is protected against all forms of discrimination or punishment on the basis of the status, activities, expressed opinions, or beliefs of the child's parents, legal guardians, or family members.

Article 3

1.   In all actions concerning children, whether undertaken by public or private social welfare institutions, courts of law, administrative authorities or legislative bodies, the best interests of the child shall be a primary consideration.
2.   States Parties undertake to ensure the child such protection and care as is necessary for his or her well-being, taking into account the rights and duties of his or her parents, legal guardians, or other individuals legally responsible for him or her, and, to this end, shall take all appropriate legislative and administrative measures.

3.   States Parties shall ensure that the institutions, services and facilities responsible for the care or protection of children shall conform with the standards established by competent authorities, particularly in the areas of safety, health, in the number and suitability of their staff, as well as competent supervision.

Article 4

States Parties shall undertake all appropriate legislative, administrative, and other measures for the implementation of the rights recognized in the present Convention. With regard to economic, social and cultural rights, States Parties shall undertake such measures to the maximum extent of their available resources and, where needed, within the framework of international cooperation.

Article 5

States Parties shall respect the responsibilities, rights and duties of parents or, where applicable, the members of the extended family or community as provided for by local custom, legal guardians or other persons legally responsible for the child, to provide, in a manner consistent with the evolving capacities of the child, appropriate direction and guidance in the exercise by the child of the rights recognized in the present Convention.

Article 6

1.   States Parties recognize that every child has the inherent right to life.
2.   States Parties shall ensure to the maximum extent possible the survival and development of the child.

Article 7

1.   The child shall be registered immediately after birth and shall have the right from birth to a name, the right to acquire a nationality and, as far as possible, the right to know and be cared for by his or her parents.
2.   States Parties shall ensure the implementation of these rights in accordance with their national law and their obligations under the relevant international instruments in this field, in particular where the child would otherwise be stateless.

Article 8

1.   States Parties undertake to respect the right of the child to preserve his or her identity, including nationality, name and family relations as recognized by law without unlawful interference.

2.   Where a child is legally deprived of some or all of the elements of his or her identity, States Parties shall provide appropriate assistance and protection, with a view to speedily re-establishing his or her identity.

Article 9

1.   States Parties shall ensure that a child shall not be separated from his or her parents against their will, except when competent authorities subject to judicial review determine, in accordance with applicable law and procedures, that such separation is necessary for the best interests of the child. Such determination may be necessary in a particular case such as one involving abuse or neglect of the child by the parents, or one where the parents are living separately and a decision must be made as to the child's place of residence.

2.   In any proceedings pursuant to paragraph 1 of the present Article, all interested parties shall be given an opportunity to participate in the proceedings and make their views known.

3.   States Parties shall respect the right of the child who is separated from one or both parents to maintain personal relations and direct contact with both parents on a regular basis, except if it is contrary to the child's best interests.

4.   Where such separation results from any action initiated by a State Party, such as the detention, imprisonment, exile, deportation or death (including death arising from any cause while the person is in the custody of the State) of one or both parents or of the child, that State Party shall, upon request, provide the parents, the child or, if appropriate, another member of the family with the essential information concerning the whereabouts of the absent member(s) of the family unless the provision of the information would be detrimental to the well-being of the child. States Parties shall further ensure that the submission of such a request shall of itself entail no adverse consequences for the person(s) concerned.

Article 10

1.   In accordance with the obligation of States Parties under Article 9, paragraph 1, applications by a child or his or her parents to enter or leave a State Party for the purpose of family reunification shall be dealt with by

States Parties in a positive, humane and expeditious manner. States Parties shall further ensure that the submission of such a report shall entail no adverse consequences for the applicants and for the members of their family.

2.   A child whose parents reside in different States shall have the right to maintain on a regular basis, save in exceptional circumstances personal relations and direct contacts with both parents. Towards that end and in accordance with the obligation of States Parties under Article 9, paragraph 2, States Parties shall respect the right of the child and his or her parents to leave any country, including their own, and to enter their own country. The right to leave any country shall be subject only to such restrictions as are prescribed by law and which are necessary to protect the national security, public order (*ordre public*), public health or morals or the rights and freedoms of others and are consistent with the other rights recognized in the present Convention.

Article 11

1.   States Parties shall take measures to combat the illicit transfer and non-return of children abroad.

2.   To this end, States Parties shall promote the conclusion of bilateral or multilateral agreements or accession to existing agreements.

Article 12

1.   States Parties shall assure to the child who is capable of forming his or her own views the right to express those views freely in all matters affecting the child, the views of the child being given due weight in accordance with the age and maturity of the child.

2.   For this purpose, the child shall in particular be provided the opportunity to be heard in any judicial and administrative proceedings affecting the child, either directly, or through a representative or an appropriate body, in a manner consistent with the procedural rules of national law.

Article 13

1.   The child shall have the right to freedom of expression; this right shall include freedom to seek, receive and impart information and ideas of all kinds, regardless of frontiers, either orally, in writing or in print, in the form of art, or through any other media of the child's choice.

2.   The exercise of this right may be subject to certain restrictions, but these shall only be such as are provided by law and are necessary:

(*a*) For respect of the rights or reputations of others; or

(*b*) For the protection of national security or of public order (*ordre public*), or of public health or morals.

Article 14

1. States Parties shall respect the right of the child to freedom of thought, conscience and religion.

2. States Parties shall respect the rights and duties of the parents and, when applicable, legal guardians, to provide direction to the child in the exercise of his or her right in a manner consistent with the evolving capacities of the child.

3. Freedom to manifest one's religion or beliefs may be subject only to such limitations as are prescribed by law and are necessary to protect public safety, order, health or morals, or the fundamental rights and freedoms of others.

Article 15

1. States Parties recognize the rights of the child to freedom of association and to freedom of peaceful assembly.

2. No restrictions may be placed on the exercise of these rights other than those imposed in conformity with the law and which are necessary in a democratic society in the interests of national security or public safety, public order (*ordre public*), the protection of public health or morals or the protection of the rights and freedoms of others.

Article 16

1. No child shall be subjected to arbitrary or unlawful interference with his or her privacy, family, home or correspondence, nor to unlawful attacks on his or her honour and reputation.

2. The child has the right to the protection of the law against such interference or attacks.

Article 17

States Parties recognize the important function performed by the mass media and shall ensure that the child has access to information and material from a diversity of national and international sources, especially those aimed at the promotion of his or her social, spiritual and moral well-being and physical and mental health. To this end, States Parties shall:

(*a*)   Encourage the mass media to disseminate information and material of social and cultural benefit to the child and in accordance with the spirit of Article 29;

(*b*)   Encourage international co-operation in the production, exchange and dissemination of such information and material from a diversity of cultural, national and international sources;

(*c*)   Encourage the production and dissemination of children's books;

(*d*)   Encourage the mass media to have particular regard to the linguistic needs of the child who belongs to a minority group or who is indigenous;

(*e*)   Encourage the development of appropriate guidelines for the protection of the child from information and material injurious to his or her well-being, bearing in mind the provisions of Articles 13 and 18.

Article 18

1.   States Parties shall use their best efforts to ensure recognition of the principle that both parents have common responsibilities for the upbringing and development of the child. Parents or, as the case may be, legal guardians, have the primary responsibility for the upbringing and development of the child. The best interests of the child will be their basic concern.

2.   For the purpose of guaranteeing and promoting the rights set forth in the present Convention, States Parties shall render appropriate assistance to parents and legal guardians in the performance of their child-rearing responsibilities and shall ensure the development of institutions, facilities and services for the care of children.

3.   States Parties shall take all appropriate measures to ensure that children of working parents have the right to benefit from child-care services and facilities for which they are eligible.

Article 19

1.   States Parties shall take all appropriate legislative, administrative, social and educational measures to protect the child from all forms of physical or mental violence, injury or abuse, neglect or negligent treatment, maltreatment or exploitation, including sexual abuse, while in the care of parent(s), legal guardian(s) or any other person who has the care of the child.

2.   Such protective measures should, as appropriate, include effective procedures for the establishment of social programmes to provide necessary support for the child and for those who have the care of the child, as well as for other forms of prevention and for identification, reporting, referral,

investigation, treatment and follow-up of instances of child maltreatment described heretofore, and, as appropriate, for judicial involvement.

Article 20

1.   A child temporarily or permanently deprived of his or her family environment, or in whose own best interests cannot be allowed to remain in that environment, shall be entitled to special protection and assistance provided by the State.
2.   States Parties shall in accordance with their national laws ensure alternative care for such a child.
3.   Such care could include, *inter alia*, foster placement, *kafalah* of Islamic law, adoption or if necessary placement in suitable institutions for the care of children. When considering solutions, due regard shall be paid to the desirability of continuity in a child's upbringing and to the child's ethnic, religious, cultural and linguistic background.

Article 21

States Parties that recognize and/or permit the system of adoption shall ensure that the best interests of the child shall be the paramount consideration and they shall:

(*a*)   Ensure that the adoption of a child is authorized only by competent authorities who determine, in accordance with applicable law and procedures and on the basis of all pertinent and reliable information, that the adoption is permissible in view of the child's status concerning parents, relatives and legal guardians and that, if required, the persons concerned have given their informed consent to the adoption on the basis of such counselling as may be necessary;

(*b*)   Recognize that inter-country adoption may be considered as an alternative means of child's care, if the child cannot be placed in a foster or an adoptive family or cannot in any suitable manner be cared for in the child's country of origin;

(*c*)   Ensure that the child concerned by inter-country adoption enjoys safeguards and standards equivalent to those existing in the case of national adoption;

(*d*)   Take all appropriate measures to ensure that, in inter-country adoption, the placement does not result in improper financial gain for those involved in it;

(*e*)   Promote, where appropriate, the objectives of the present article by concluding bilateral or multilateral arrangements or agreements, and endeavour, within this framework, to ensure that the placement of the child in another country is carried out by competent authorities or organs.

Article 22

1.   States Parties shall take appropriate measures to ensure that a child who is seeking refugee status or who is considered a refugee in accordance with applicable international or domestic law and procedures shall, whether unaccompanied or accompanied by his or her parents or by any other person, receive appropriate protection and humanitarian assistance in the enjoyment of applicable rights set forth in the present Convention and in other international human rights or humanitarian instruments to which the said States are Parties.

2.   For this purpose, States Parties shall provide, as they consider appropriate, co-operation in any efforts by the United Nations and other competent inter-governmental organizations or non-governmental organizations co-operating with the United Nations to protect and assist such a child and to trace the parents or other members of the family or any refugee child in order to obtain information necessary for reunification with his or her family. In cases where no parents or other members of the family can be found the child shall be accorded the same protection as any other child permanently or temporarily deprived of his or her family environment for any reason, as set forth in the present Convention.

Article 23

1.   States Parties recognize that a mentally or physically disabled child should enjoy a full and decent life, in conditions which ensure dignity, promote self-reliance and facilitate the child's active participation in the community.

2.   States Parties recognize the right of the disabled child to special care and shall encourage and ensure the extension, subject to available resources, to the eligible child and those responsible for his or her care, of assistance for which application is made and which is appropriate to the child's condition and to the circumstances of the parents or others caring for the child.

3.   Recognizing the special needs of a disabled child, assistance extended in accordance with paragraph 2 of the present article shall be provided free of charge, whenever possible, taking into account the financial resources of the parents or others caring for the child, and shall be designed to ensure that the disabled child has effective access to and receives education, training, health care services, rehabilitation services, preparation for employ-

ment and recreation opportunities in a manner conducive to the child's achieving the fullest possible social integration and individual development, including his or her cultural spiritual development.

4. States Parties shall promote, in the spirit of international co-operation, the exchange of appropriate information in the field of preventive health care and of medical, psychological and functional treatment of disabled children, including dissemination of and access to information concerning methods of rehabilitation, education and vocational services, with the aim of enabling States Parties to improve their capabilities and skills and to widen their experience in these areas. In this regard, particular account shall be taken of the needs of developing countries.

Article 24

1. States Parties recognize the right of the child to the enjoyment of the highest attainable standard of health and to facilities for the treatment of illness and rehabilitation of health. States Parties shall strive to ensure that no child is deprived of his or her right of access to such health care services.

2. States Parties shall pursue full implementation of this right and, in particular, shall take appropriate measures:

(*a*) To diminish infant and child mortality;
(*b*) To ensure the provision of necessary medical assistance and health care to all children with emphasis on the development of primary health care;
(*c*) To combat disease and malnutrition, including within the framework of primary health care, through, *inter alia*, the application of readily available technology and through the provision of adequate nutritious foods and clean drinking-water, taking into consideration the dangers and risks of environmental pollution;
(*d*) To ensure appropriate pre-natal and post-natal health care for mothers;
(*e*) To ensure that all segments of society, in particular parents and children, are informed, have access to education and are supported in the use of basic knowledge of child health and nutrition, the advantages of breast-feeding, hygiene and environmental sanitation and the prevention of accidents;
(*f*) To develop preventive health care, guidance for parents and family planning education and services.

3. States Parties shall take all effective and appropriate measures with a view to abolishing traditional practices prejudicial to the health of children.

4.   States Parties undertake to promote and encourage international co-operation with a view to achieving progressively the full realization of the right recognized in the present article. In this regard, particular account shall be taken of the needs of developing countries.

Article 25

States Parties recognize the right of a child who has been placed by the competent authorities for the purposes of care, protection or treatment of his or her physical or mental health, to a periodic review of the treatment provided to the child and all other circumstances relevant to his or her placement.

Article 26

1.   States Parties shall recognize for every child the right to benefit from social security, including social insurance, and shall take the necessary measures to achieve the full realization of this right in accordance with their national law.
2.   The benefits should, where appropriate, be granted, taking into account the resources and the circumstances of the child and persons having responsibility for the maintenance of the child, as well as any other consideration relevant to an application for benefits made by or on behalf of the child.

Article 27

1.   States Parties recognize the right of every child to a standard of living adequate for the child's physical, mental, spiritual, moral and social development.
2.   The parent(s) or others responsible for the child have the primary responsibility to secure, within their abilities and financial capacities, the conditions of living necessary for the child's development.
3.   States Parties, in accordance with national conditions and within their means, shall take appropriate measures to assist parents and others responsible for the child to implement this right and shall in case of need provide material assistance and support programmes, particularly with regard to nutrition, clothing and housing.
4.   States Parties shall take all appropriate measures to secure the recovery of maintenance for the child from the parents or other persons having financial responsibility for the child, both within the State Party and from abroad. In particular, where the person having financial responsibility for the child lives in a State different from that of the child, State Parties shall

promote the accession to international agreements or the conclusion of such agreements, as well as the making of other appropriate arrangements.

Article 28

1.   States Parties recognize the right of the child to education, and with a view to achieving this right progressively and on the basis of equal opportunity, they shall, in particular:

(a)   Make primary education compulsory and available free to all;
(b)   Encourage the development of different forms of secondary education, including general and vocational education, make them available and accessible to every child, and take appropriate measures such as the introduction of free education and offering financial assistance in case of need;
(c)   Make higher education accessible to all on the basis of capacity by every appropriate means;
(d)   Make educational and vocational information and guidance available and accessible to all children;
(e)   Take measures to encourage regular attendance at schools and the reduction of drop-out rates.

2.   States Parties shall take all appropriate measures to ensure that school discipline is administered in a manner consistent with the child's human dignity and in conformity with the present Convention.
3.   States Parties shall promote and encourage international co-operation in matters relating to education, in particular with a view to contributing to the elimination of ignorance and illiteracy throughout the world and facilitating access to scientific and technical knowledge and modern teaching methods. In this regard, particular account shall be taken of the needs of developing countries.

Article 29

1.   States Parties agree that the education of the child shall be directed to:

(a)   The development of the child's personality, talents and mental and physical abilities to their fullest potential;
(b)   The development of respect for human rights and fundamental freedoms, and for the principles enshrined in the Charter of the United Nations;
(c)   The development of respect for the child's parents, his or her own

cultural identity, language and values, for the national values of the country in which the child is living, the country from which he or she may originate, and for civilizations different from his or her own;

(*d*)　The preparation of the child for responsible life in a free society, in the spirit of understanding, peace, tolerance, equality of sexes, and friendship among all people, ethnic, national and religious groups and persons of indigenous origin;

(*e*)　The development of respect for the natural environment.

2.　No part of the present Article or Article 28 shall be construed so as to interfere with the liberty of individuals and bodies to establish and direct educational institutions, subject always to the observance of the principles set forth in paragraph 1 of the present Article and to the requirements that the education given in such institutions shall conform to such minimum standards as may be laid down by the State.

Article 30

In those States in which ethnic, religious or linguistic minorities or persons of indigenous origin exist, a child belonging to such a minority or who is indigenous shall not be denied the right, in community with other members of his or her group, to enjoy his or her own culture, to profess and practice his or her own religion, or to use his or her own language.

Article 31

1.　States Parties recognize the right of the child to rest and leisure, to engage in play and recreational activities appropriate to the age of the child and to participate freely in cultural life and the arts.

2.　States Parties shall respect and promote the life of the child to participate fully in cultural and artistic life and shall encourage the provision of appropriate and equal opportunities for cultural, artistic, recreational and leisure activity.

Article 32

1.　States Parties recognize the right of the child to be protected from economic exploitation and from performing any work that is likely to be hazardous or to interfere with the child's education, or to be harmful to the child's health or physical, mental, spiritual, moral or social development.

2.　States Parties shall take legislative, administrative, social and educational measures to ensure the implementation of the present article. To this end, and having regard to the relevant provisions of other international instruments, States Parties shall in particular:

(*a*) Provide for a minimum age or minimum ages for admission to employment;
(*b*) Provide for appropriate regulation of the hours and conditions of employment;
(*c*) Provide for appropriate penalties or other sanctions to ensure the effective enforcement of the present article.

Article 33

States Parties shall take all appropriate measures, including legislative, administrative, social and educational measures, to protect children from the illicit use of narcotic drugs and psychotropic substances as defined in the relevant international treaties, and to prevent the use of children in the illicit production and trafficking of such substances.

Article 34

States Parties undertake to protect the child from all forms of sexual exploitation and sexual abuse. For these purposes, States Parties shall in particular take all appropriate national, bilateral and multilateral measures to prevent:

(*a*) The inducement or coercion of a child to engage in any unlawful sexual activity;
(*b*) The exploitative use of children in prostitution or other unlawful sexual practices;
(*c*) The exploitative use of children in pornographic performances and materials.

Article 35

States Parties shall take all appropriate national, bilateral and multilateral measures to prevent the abduction of, the sale of or traffic in children for any purpose or in any form.

Article 36

States Parties shall protect the child against all other forms of exploitation prejudicial to any aspects of the child's welfare.

Article 37

States Parties shall ensure that:

(*a*) No child shall be subjected to torture or other cruel, inhuman or degrading treatment or punishment. Neither capital punishment nor life imprisonment without possibility of release shall be imposed for offences committed by persons below eighteen years of age;

(*b*) No child shall be deprived of his or her liberty unlawfully or arbitrarily. The arrest, detention or imprisonment of a child shall be in conformity with the law and shall be used only as a measure of last resort and for the shortest appropriate period of time;

(*c*) Every child deprived of liberty shall be treated with humanity and respect for the inherent dignity of the human person, and in a manner which takes into account the needs of persons of his or her age. In particular, every child deprived of liberty shall be separated from adults unless it is considered in the child's best interest not to do so and shall have the right to maintain contact with his or her family through correspondence and visits, save in exceptional circumstances;

(*d*) Every child deprived of his or her liberty shall have the right to prompt access to legal and other appropriate assistance, as well as the right to challenge the legality of the deprivation of his or her liberty before a court or other competent, independent and impartial authority, and to a prompt decision on any such action.

Article 38

1.   States Parties undertake to respect and to ensure respect for rules of international humanitarian law applicable to them in armed conflicts which are relevant to the child.

2.   States Parties shall take all feasible measures to ensure that persons who have not attained the age of fifteen years do not take a direct part in hostilities.

3.   States Parties shall refrain from recruiting any person who has not attained the age of fifteen years into their armed forces. In recruiting among those person who have attained the age of fifteen years but who have not attained the age of eighteen years, States Parties shall endeavour to give priority to those who are oldest.

4.   In accordance with their obligations under international humanitarian law to protect the civilian population in armed conflicts, States Parties shall take all feasible measures to ensure protection and care of children who are affected by an armed conflict.

Article 39

States Parties shall take all appropriate measures to promote physical and psychological recovery and social reintegration of a child of: any form of neglect, exploitation, or abuse; torture or any other form of cruel, inhuman or degrading treatment or punishment; or armed conflicts. Such recovery and reintegration shall take place in an environment which fosters the health, self-respect and dignity of the child.

Article 40

1. States Parties recognize the right of every child alleged as, accused of, or recognized as having infringed the penal law to be treated in a manner consistent with the promotion of the child's sense of dignity and worth, which reinforces the child's respect for the human rights and fundamental freedoms of others and which takes into account the child's age and the desirability of promoting the child's reintegration and the child's assuming a constructive role in society.

2. To this end, and having regard to the relevant provisions of international instruments, States Parties shall, in particular, ensure that:

(*a*) No child shall be alleged as, be accused of, or recognized as having infringed the penal law by reason of acts or omissions that were not prohibited by national or international law at the time they were committed;

(*b*) Every child alleged as or accused of having infringed the penal law has at least the following guarantees:

(i) To be presumed innocent until proven guilty according to law;

(ii) To be informed promptly and directly of the charges against him or her, and, if appropriate, through his or her parents or legal guardians, and to have legal or other appropriate assistance in the preparation and presentation of his or her defence;

(iii) To have the matter determined without delay by a competent, independent and impartial authority or judicial body in a fair hearing according to law, in the presence of legal or other appropriate assistance and, unless it is considered not to be in the best interests of the child, in particular, taking into account his or her age or situation, his or her parents or legal guardians;

(iv) Not to be compelled to give testimony or to confess guilt; to examine or have examined adverse witnesses and to obtain the participation and examination of witnesses on his or her behalf under conditions of equality;

(v)   If considered to have infringed the penal law, to have this decision and any measures imposed in consequence thereof reviewed by a higher competent, independent and impartial authority or judicial body according to law;

(vi)   To have the free assistance of an interpreter if the child cannot understand or speak the language used;

(vii)   To have his or her privacy fully respected at all stages of the proceedings.

3.   States Parties shall seek to promote the establishment of laws, procedures, authorities and institutions specifically applicable to children alleged as, accused of, or recognized as having infringed the penal law, and, in particular:

(*a*)   The establishment of a minimum age below which children shall be presumed not to have the capacity to infringe the penal law;

(*b*)   Whenever appropriate and desirable, measures for dealing with such children without resorting to judicial proceedings, providing that human rights and legal safeguards are fully respected.

4.   A variety of dispositions, such as care, guidance and supervision orders; counselling; probation; foster care; education and vocational training programmes and other alternatives to institutional care shall be available to ensure that children are dealt with in a manner appropriate to their well-being and proportionate both to their circumstances and the offence.

Article 41

Nothing in the present Convention shall affect any provisions which are more conducive to the realization of the rights of the child and which may be contained in:

(*a*)   The law of a State Party; or
(*b*)   International law in force for that State.

PART II

Article 42

States Parties undertake to make the principles and provisions of the Convention widely known, by appropriate and active means, to adults and children alike.

Article 43

1. For the purpose of examining the progress made by States Parties in achieving the realization of the obligations undertaken in the present Convention, there shall be established a Committee on the Rights of the Child, which shall carry out the functions hereinafter provided.
2. The Committee shall consist of ten experts of high moral standing and recognized competence in the field covered by this Convention. The members of the Committee shall be elected by States Parties from among their nationals and shall serve in their personal capacity, consideration being given to equitable geographical distribution, as well as to the principal legal systems.
3. The members of the Committee shall be elected by secret ballot from a list of persons nominated by States Parties. Each State Party may nominate one person from among its own nationals.
4. The initial election to the Committee shall be held no later than six months after the date of the entry into force of the present Convention and thereafter every second year. At least four months before the date of each election, the Secretary-General of the United Nations shall address a letter to States Parties inviting them to submit their nominations within two months. The Secretary-General shall subsequently prepare a list in alphabetical order of all persons thus nominated, indicating States Parties which have nominated them, and shall submit it to the States Parties to the present Convention.
5. The elections shall be held at meetings of States Parties convened by the Secretary-General at United Nations Headquarters. At those meetings, for which two thirds of States Parties shall constitute a quorum, the persons elected to the Committee shall be those who obtain the largest number of votes and an absolute majority of the votes of the representatives of States Parties present and voting.
6. The members of the Committee shall be elected for a term of four years. They shall be eligible for re-election if renominated. The term of five of the members elected at the first election shall expire at the end of two years; immediately after the first election, the names of these five members shall be chosen by lot by the Chairman of the meeting.

7.   If a member of the Committee dies or resigns or declares that for any other cause he or she can no longer perform the duties of the Committee, the State Party which nominated the member shall appoint another expert from among its nationals to serve for the remainder of the term, subject to the approval of the Committee.

8.   The Committee shall establish its own rules of procedure.

9.   The Committee shall elect its officers for a period of two years.

10.   The meetings of the Committee shall normally be held at United Nations Headquarters or at any other convenient place as determined by the Committee. The Committee shall normally meet annually. The duration of the meetings of the Committee shall be determined, and reviewed, if necessary, by a meeting of the States Parties to the present Convention, subject to the approval of the General Assembly.

11.   The Secretary-General of the United Nations shall provide the necessary staff and facilities for the effective performance of the functions of the Committee under the present Convention.

12.   With the approval of the General Assembly, the members of the Committee established under the present Convention shall receive emoluments from United Nations resources on such terms and conditions as the Assembly may decide.

Article 44

1.   States Parties undertake to submit to the Committee, through the Secretary-General of the United Nations, reports on the measures they have adopted which give effect to the rights recognized herein and on the progress made on the enjoyment of those rights:

(*a*)   Within two years of the entry into force of the Convention for the State Party concerned;

(*b*)   Thereafter every five years.

2.   Reports made under the present Article shall indicate factors and difficulties, if any, affecting the degree of fulfilment of the obligations under the present Convention. Reports shall also contain sufficient information to provide the Committee with a comprehensive understanding of the implementation of the Convention in the country concerned.

3.   A State Party which has submitted a comprehensive initial report to the Committee need not, in its subsequent reports submitted in accordance with paragraph 1 (*b*) of the present Article, repeat basic information previously provided.

4. The Committee may request from States Parties further information relevant to the implementation of the Convention.

5. The Committee shall submit to the General Assembly, through the Economic and Social Council, every two years, reports on its activities.

6. States Parties shall make their reports widely available to the public in their own countries.

Article 45

In order to foster the effective implementation of the Convention and to encourage international co-operation in the field covered by the Convention:

(*a*) The specialized agencies, the United Nations Children's Fund, and other United Nations organs shall be entitled to be represented at the consideration of the implementation of such provisions of the present Convention as fall within the scope of their mandate. The Committee may invite the specialized agencies, the United Nations Children's Fund and other competent bodies as it may consider appropriate to provide expert advice on the implementation of the Convention in areas falling within the scope of their respective mandates. The Committee may invite the specialized agencies, the United Nations Children's Fund, and other United Nations organs to submit reports on the implementation of the Convention in areas falling within the scope of their activities;

(*b*) The Committee shall transmit, as it may consider appropriate, to the specialized agencies, the United Nations Children's Fund and other competent bodies, any reports from States Parties that contain a request, or indicate a need, for technical advice or assistance, along with the Committee's observations and suggestions, if any, on these requests or indications;

(*c*) The Committee may recommend to the General Assembly to request the Secretary-General to undertake on its behalf studies on specific issues relating to the rights of the child;

(*d*) The Committee may make suggestions and general recommendations based on information received pursuant to Articles 44 and 45 of the present Convention. Such suggestions and general recommendations shall be transmitted to any State Party concerned and reported to the General Assembly, together with comments, if any, from States Parties.

PART III

Article 46

The present Convention shall be open for signature by all States.

Article 47

The present Convention is subject to ratification. Instruments of ratification shall be deposited with the Secretary-General of the United Nations.

Article 48

The present Convention shall remain open for accession by any State. The instruments of accession shall be deposited with the Secretary-General of the United Nations.

Article 49

1.   The present Convention shall enter into force on the thirtieth day following the date of deposit with the Secretary-General of the United Nations of the twentieth instrument of ratification or accession.
2.   For each State ratifying or acceding to the Convention after the deposit of the twentieth instrument of ratification or accession, the Convention shall enter into force on the thirtieth day after the deposit by such State of its instrument of ratification or accession.

Article 50

1.   Any State Party may propose an amendment and file it with the Secretary-General of the United Nations. The Secretary-General shall thereupon communicate the proposed amendment to States Parties, with a request that they indicate whether they favour a conference of States Parties for the purpose of considering and voting upon the proposals. In the event that, within four months from the date of such communications, at least one third of the States Parties favour such a conference, the Secretary-General shall convene the conference under the auspices of the United Nations. Any amendment adopted by a majority of States Parties present and voting at the conference shall be submitted to the General Assembly for approval.
2.   An amendment adopted in accordance with paragraph 1 of the present article shall enter into force when it has been approved by the General

Assembly of the United Nations and accepted by a two-thirds majority of States Parties.

3. When an amendment enters into force, it shall be binding on those States Parties which have accepted it, other States Parties still being bound by the provisions of the present Convention and any earlier amendments which they have accepted.

Article 51

1. The Secretary-General of the United Nations shall receive and circulate to all States the text of reservations made by States at the time of ratification or accession.

2. A reservation incompatible with the object and purpose of the present Convention shall not be permitted.

3. Reservations may be withdrawn at any time by notification to that effect addressed to the Secretary-General of the United Nations, who shall then inform all States. Such notification shall take effect on the date on which it is received by the Secretary-General.

Article 52

A State Party may denounce the present Convention by written notification to the Secretary-General of the United Nations. Denunciation becomes effective one year after the date of receipt of the notification by the Secretary-General.

Article 53

The Secretary-General of the United Nations is designated as the depositary of the present Convention.

Article 54

The original of the present Convention, of which the Arabic, Chinese, English, French, Russian and Spanish texts are equally authentic, shall be deposited with the Secretary-General of the United Nations.

In witness thereof the undersigned plenipotentiaries, being duly authorized thereto by their respective Governments, have signed the present Convention.

Index

dehmitt

St. Louis Community College
at Meramec
Library